'Perhaps the most important story in the education sector over the last two decades. This book should be required reading both for those who seek to develop school systems that achieve similar successes, as well as those who seek to avoid undermining what has been so remarkably accomplished.'

Doug Lemov (author, Teach Like a Champion)

'*Reforming Lessons* tells the story of how England's schools were transformed in a decade of reform. It's essential reading for any education policy maker who is serious about wanting real improvements in children's reading and higher academic standards.'

Governor Jeb Bush

'*Reforming Lessons* compellingly explains how Nick's close study of effective classroom practice from around the world, underpinned with an understanding of the science of knowledge acquisition, ensured we had a programme ready for government.'

Michael Gove, Education Secretary 2010–14

Reforming Lessons

Reforming Lessons provides a first-hand account of the ambitious programme of reform that has led to a transformation in English schools since 2010 and seen pupils rise through the ranks of international comparison tests such as PIRLS and PISA.

Co-authored by former Schools Minister Nick Gibb and Headteacher Robert Peal, the book explores the key principles behind the reforms and reveals the impact they had on school leadership, accountability, teaching methods, curriculum design, and pupil behaviour. Addressing the long legacy of 'progressive' approaches to teaching in English schools, and the development of evidence-led alternatives, the book shows that approaches to education such as 'warm-strict', 'teacher-led instruction', and 'knowledge-rich curriculum' have been simultaneously both controversial and hugely successful. Chapters cover:

- Reforms to the primary curriculum—phonics and mathematical mastery
- The return of rigour in the secondary curriculum
- School structures—academies and free schools
- Academic standards
- Grassroot reforms
- Changes to teacher training and the introduction of the Early Career Framework

Providing a fascinating insight into the major reforms that have shaped England's school system and the drivers behind them, this is essential reading for anyone working in the education sector, policy-makers, and those interested in education reform.

Nick Gibb was the Conservative Member of Parliament for Bognor Regis and Littlehampton from 1997 to 2024. Nick's interest in education policy led to his appointment as Shadow Schools Minister in 2005. He was Schools Minister from 2010 to 2012 and again from 2014 to September 2021. He was reappointed by Rishi Sunak in October 2022 and resigned prior to the cabinet reshuffle in November 2023 to advocate for evidence-led education policy internationally. He received a knighthood in the 2025 New Years Honours List.

Robert Peal is joint Headteacher of the West London Free School, a high-performing state comprehensive school in Hammersmith. He is the author of *Progressively Worse* (2014), a critique of child-centred teaching methods in English schools, *Meet the Georgians* (2021), and the *Knowing History* series of school textbooks. From 2015 to 2016, he worked at the Department for Education as a speechwriter and policy adviser to Nick Gibb. He received an MBE for services to education in the 2024 King's Birthday Honours list.

Reforming Lessons

Why English Schools Have Improved Since 2010 and How This Was Achieved

Nick Gibb and Robert Peal

Routledge
Taylor & Francis Group

LONDON AND NEW YORK

First published 2026
by Routledge
4 Park Square, Milton Park, Abingdon, Oxon OX14 4RN

and by Routledge
605 Third Avenue, New York, NY 10158

Routledge is an imprint of the Taylor & Francis Group, an informa business

British Library Cataloguing-in-Publication Data
A catalogue record for this book is available from the British Library

ISBN: 978-1-032-87595-8 (hbk)
ISBN: 978-1-032-87594-1 (pbk)
ISBN: 978-1-003-53347-4 (ebk)

DOI: 10.4324/9781003533474

Typeset in Melior
by Apex CoVantage, LLC

Printed and bound in Great Britain by Bell & Bain Ltd, Glasgow

RP136190

For Product Safety Concerns and Information please contact our EU representative Taylor & Francis Verlag GmbH, Kaufingerstraße 24, 80331 München, Germany GPSR@taylorandfrancis.com

Contents

Acknowledgements

I am not one of those people who go through life thinking that one day they'll write a book. I found the thought of writing 100,000 words daunting and probably unachievable. Many former colleagues in the House of Commons were inveterate keepers of a diary. I never knew how they found the energy or the time.

And so when it was suggested that I write about England's education reforms, I was less than enthusiastic. But Michael, my husband, kept chipping away at me and as more and more people started to say the same thing – particularly after I stepped down as Schools Minister in November 2023 after more than 10 years on and off in the same role – I was finally convinced.

I knew that I would need help. I had many conversations and even made a start with the help of a talented journalist friend. However, I soon realised that if I were to do justice to the subject, I needed a co-author who was as steeped in the reforms as I was. I am incredibly fortunate that Robert Peal volunteered. Rob is the joint head teacher at the top-rated West London Free School, the author of the seminal book, *Progressively Worse*, and was a brilliant adviser at the Department for Education. He's also a great friend and fellow believer in evidence-led approaches to education. I could not have found a better partner to bring this book to life.

As I hope will be clear to anyone reading *Reforming Lessons*, the education reforms were a joint endeavour between politicians supported by civil servants who mostly saw their job as being to help implement the policies of the elected government, and countless educationalists, heads and teachers. The importance of key individuals will be clear to the reader. I am indebted to them all and I hope they will forgive me for not mentioning them here. I hope they will also excuse me if I mention two people: Ruth Miskin and Tim Oates whose influence across the reforms since their earliest inception in opposition has been critical to their success.

Others – who played an important role – are not mentioned in the text because their expertise was in an area we haven't covered in detail. People such as Diane Rochford, who led a review into SEND assessment and whose expertise I hope will continue to be called upon by the DfE as the government develops its plans for SEND, Christine Ryan, who was Chief Inspector of Independent Schools and was Chair of Ofsted until March 2025, and Amy Leonard a source of wise counsel especially in my dealings with the media.

I am grateful to the hundreds of civil servants who helped shape and deliver the reforms. There are four people I would particularly like to thank – Huw Leslie, Jessie Smith, Yuin Chin and Harriette Cradock – who at different times ran my office, kept me on track, made sure I had the papers needed for policy discussions and helped drive the reform process. Their advice and support were invaluable. And I should mention and thank our policy adviser David Thomas and special adviser Iain Mansfield for their genius in driving policy development.

There are many other people to thank for their help with the book. Kirsty Buchanan, who set the ball rolling, Loic Menzies for his early advice, and Nick Thomas and Gilat Levy for their help with our research. Thank you also to Ian Hunter at the Knowledge Schools Trust for giving Rob leave to help with the book, and to his joint headteacher Ben McLaughlin and the rest of the senior team at the West London Free School for covering in his absence. For reading early drafts of the book and providing feedback, thank you to Jonathan Simons, Tom Bennett and Daisy Christodoulou.

Finally, I'd like to thank Michael, my husband of nearly 10 years, partner for nearly 40 and best friend throughout for making me work harder than I otherwise would if left to my own devices and for his sage and loving advice whenever I asked for it which was often.

Nick Gibb

Foreword

I remember in my first year of teaching, back in 2007, being given a photocopied pile of A3 'Assessing Pupil Progress' forms. Each piece of paper had a grid on it with levels 1–8 down the side and a list of different skills along the top. Every student had a piece of paper, and their job was to progress from level 1, at the bottom, to level 8, at the top. A level 1 student would only be able to make 'reasonable inferences at a basic level', whereas a level 7 student could 'begin to develop an interpretation of the text(s), making connections between insights, teasing out meanings or weighing up evidence.'

These eight levels were a statutory part of the national curriculum, and they were, by design, devoid of content. No allowance was made for the fact that making a basic inference about a lengthy nineteenth-century novel was much more challenging than teasing out the meaning of a TV advert. The assumption of the APP grids, and much of the curriculum design thinking of that era, was that skills were easily transferable from one domain to another and that you could practice skills like inference, creativity, problem-solving, and collaboration in the way that you might exercise a muscle, and that if you did need any content knowledge you could simply look it up on the internet.

All these assumptions were wrong, and all of them ignored the science of how the human mind works. Our working memories are highly limited, and we rely on facts stored in long-term memory to be able to think. Problem-solving and creativity are not generic skills that can be applied to any old content; they are learned and applied within specific contexts. It's possible for an eminent physicist to think critically and creatively when it comes to solving a physics problem—but not when it comes to solving a marital problem. As a result, committing facts to memory is a vital part of education. In the words of one famous research paper, if nothing has changed in long-term memory, nothing has been learned.

Fortunately, a teacher starting out today is in a much better situation than I was in 2007. Since 2010, English education has undergone a series of far-reaching reforms which have replaced misguided ideas about transferable skills with a more accurate and evidence-based concept of how learning works. Over the same time,

England's performance on international league tables of educational attainment has steadily increased, meaning there is growing global interest in what England has done differently.

This book tells the story of these reforms by the politician who made many of them happen. Its author, Nick Gibb, was a shadow schools minister for the Conservative Party in opposition and then Minister of State in the education department for over ten years. Content knowledge is at the heart of the story in more ways than one. One of the fundamental tensions of education reform is whether structures or content are more important. Do you focus on the way schools are organised and governed or on what is being taught and how well students are doing?

As Nick shows in Chapter 3, before 2005, the Conservative Party's two preferred education reform policies were both structural. Social conservatives wanted a return to academic selection and grammar schools, while the libertarian wing of the party wanted a privatised voucher system that would have opened up education to free market competition.

On the left, the mirror image policy positions were to eliminate selection completely and/ or to strengthen the role of local educational authorities. The debates between left and right were bitter, but they shared an underlying assumption: get the structures right, and great schools would automatically follow.

From my perspective, as a new teacher struggling under the weight of the APP grids, this felt like a particularly heroic assumption. I began my teaching career in a local authority which was home to selective grammar schools, non-selective comprehensives, and the new style of academy schools, which had more freedom from the local authority. All the different types of schools had far more in common than they had apart. They all used the content-free national curriculum levels. They all prepared their students for qualifications that had increasingly greater proportions of coursework which was increasingly open to being gamed. They all followed Ofsted guidance which recommended limiting the amount of teacher direction. On its own, converting a local authority school to an academy made very little difference to any of this.

Together with the Secretary of State for Education Michael Gove, Nick moved Conservative policy away from grammars and vouchers and, more generally, moved it away from a narrow focus on structures and towards a series of policies designed to address the problems with the curriculum and qualifications. After the Conservatives came into power in 2010, these policies were implemented. I would highlight five in particular that have had a concrete, tangible impact on the education of millions of students.

● Systematic synthetic phonics: Teaching students to read is the most fundamental job schools do. Chapters 1 and 5 tell the story of the creation of the phonics check, which is now taken by every student at the end of year 1, and the phonics matched resources programme.

- Qualifications reform: GCSEs are taken by every student in England at the end of Year 11, and Chapter 6 explains how they were reformed. The removal of modules and the reduction of non-examined assessments have made it harder for students to cram and forget.

- League table reform: Chapter 6 also provides the detail on the new metric used for secondary accountability, Progress 8. It's designed to measure the value a school adds to students, not their final attainment, and to reduce some of the obvious gaming that was taking place with the old measure, which recorded the number of students getting five Cs or above. Previously, schools would run intensive intervention classes for students at that C/D threshold, but now they are rewarded for the progress made by all students.

- Ofsted reform: Alongside league table data, the other major element of school accountability is inspection. Ofsted has enormous power, to the extent that even a false rumour about 'what Ofsted wants' can make a difference. Before 2010, Ofsted had lost sight of the evidence about how students learn and was actively encouraging poor practice. Chapters 7 and 11 show how it was overhauled.

- Curriculum reform: Chapter 5 shows how the national curriculum was rewritten to be more specific and content-rich. This was an important move, but perhaps not as important as qualification reform, as the majority of the curriculum is not examined, and exam syllabuses often—for good or for bad—take precedence when schools decide what to teach. As part of the curriculum rewrite, national curriculum levels were abolished, which freed schools from generic and bureaucratic internal assessments.

Of course, structural reform was not ignored. The changes mentioned in this list ran alongside a major expansion of academy schools and a free schools programme, which allowed for innovative new schools to be set up. The direct impact of the free schools programme was smaller than the policies outlined previously: most teachers don't teach in a free school, and most students don't attend one. However, the indirect impact has been enormous: as Chapter 10 shows, a handful of free schools have been incredibly successful, and their influence is felt throughout the English system and abroad.

Underpinning all these reforms was Nick's willingness to debate new ideas about education and to make a compelling case for the value of teaching knowledge. If these debates had taken place without any policies attached, it would have been mere window-dressing. But, the combination of specific reforms together with frequent public explanations of the evidence base behind them was extraordinarily powerful. It brought the work of thinkers like Daniel Willingham and E.D. Hirsch to big new audiences, ensured that content knowledge was harder to caricature as right-wing nostalgia, and established a new norm that evidence mattered.

At a time when many democratic countries are struggling to improve public services, there are lessons here that go beyond education—and again, the lesson is that content is important. As Chapter 3 shows, Nick and his advisers spent significant time studying education whilst in opposition. They weren't attempting to graft generic structural solutions onto whatever policy area they could get their hands on. They visited schools, spoke to teachers and head teachers, and read the relevant research. They were also intensely interested in understanding what levers of power existed within government, what impact those levers had on schools, and what the potential unintended consequences might be. They did not assume that announcing something meant it had happened or that providing a pot of money for something meant it would succeed.

All this is rare in politics. It is partly a function of knowledge, which in itself is partly a function of time. Nick Gibb was the Schools Minister for more than ten years. Over the last 50 years, the average tenure of a Cabinet minister in the UK was just two years. Between 2019 and 2024, it was just eight months. When ministers are constantly being rotated, it's almost impossible for them to build up the domain-specific knowledge they need to understand their brief and make effective decisions. If there is a general principle to be drawn from this book, it's that generalists have their limitations. Content knowledge is king, whether that's in the classroom or in ministerial office.

Daisy Christodoulou

Introduction

In July 2023, *The Economist* published a piece entitled 'The strange success of the Tories' Schools policy.' The opening paragraph concluded, 'After 13 years of Conservative government, the country's public services are not in fine fettle. There is an exception. Under the Conservatives, England's schools have improved.'[1]

I read that piece as my ten-year career as Schools Minster in England was coming to an end, and I did so with some satisfaction. There was a time when educational underachievement was seen as one of the insoluble problems in English public life. Many seemed simply to accept that state-funded schools in England were not very good, and try as you might, this was unlikely ever to change. Different theories were proffered for why this was the case. Those on the left would point to inequality, the class system, or the popularity in England of private schools as the intractable root cause, whilst those on the right were more likely to cite the end of selective 'grammar school' education during the 1960s and 1970s, or a generalised critique of public sector provision.

I became Schools Minster in a coalition government of the Conservatives and Liberal Democrat parties in 2010. At the time, there were some early signs of improvement from the previous government but a sense of malaise still hung over English schools. During the preceding decades, stories of failing schools, poor pupil behaviour, and low literacy and numeracy had become fixtures in the national conversation. Of course, across the more than 24,000 primary and secondary schools in England, the picture was mixed. Throughout those years, there were model schools providing an excellent education for their pupils. But in aggregate, the national view was one of entrenched mediocrity and a general hopelessness about the potential for change.

How different the picture is today. On a number of separate measures, English schools have made significant improvements over the past 15 years. In November 2023, I stood down as Schools Minister and announced that I would not run in the 2024 General Election. A Labour victory in the coming election already looked very likely, and newspaper coverage of the past 14 years of Conservative government took on a valedictory tone. Whilst many commentators listed opportunities

DOI: 10.4324/9781003533474-1

missed and promises unfulfilled, the success of English schools was frequently singled out for praise. As *The Economist* wrote in July 2023,

> Compared with the rest of the government's record, England's schools are a relative success. The Conservatives decided what was wrong and how they wanted to fix it. . . . It was a simple formula that the Conservatives could have replicated. Britain would be much better off if they had.[2]

In December 2024, a commentator at *The Times* wrote a piece entitled 'On schools, the Tories were a class act', in which she argued that the 'main' achievement of the coalition and Conservative governments from 2010 to 2024 was schools.[3]

The most commonly cited evidence for such a verdict are the international education league tables. Since the late 1990s, the Paris-based Organisation for Economic Co-operation and Development (OECD) has carried out studies at three-year intervals, comparing the attainment of 15-year-olds in mathematics, reading, and science. Most recently, in 2021, this involved 80 different nations and jurisdictions. Known as the Programme for International Student Assessment (PISA), these studies had become firmly established as a crucial mainstay of education debates by the time we entered office in 2010. Not only did they allow us to compare how our pupils were achieving with their peers abroad, they also provided an external assessment of English pupils' achievement, unprejudiced by domestic political pressures.

In the PISA league tables, England's results are normally included as part of an overall score for the United Kingdom. However, Scotland has always had a separate education system to England, as have Wales and Northern Ireland since they gained devolution in 1998. Since the mid-2000s, and more so since we took office in 2010, English education policy has travelled in a very different direction from our neighbours, particularly in Scotland and Wales. This has made for something of a natural experiment: four nations, with similar histories and populations, and experiencing similar economic conditions, each pursuing different education policies. How would they compare? Thankfully, PISA publish a breakdown of separate results for England, Wales, Northern Ireland and Scotland, so that question can be answered.

Figures 0.1, 0.2, and 0.3 show the ranking of England, Wales, Northern Ireland, and Scotland as separate nations from 2009 to 2022, against only those nations which participated in all five surveys to ensure comparability in the rankings.[4] This allows us to see how British pupils' performance has changed over time compared to their international peers. Back in 2009, the PISA study placed England in the middle of the pack for Maths and Reading, at 27th and 25th, respectively, and slightly higher for Science, where we ranked 14th. In the intervening years, England has climbed the league tables in Maths from 27th in 2009 to 11th in 2022, in Reading from 25th in 2009 to 13th in 2022, and in Science from 14th in 2009 to 13th in 2022. Prior to the new millennium, Scotland prided itself on having a superior education system to their English neighbours, but this national advantage has been well and truly lost over the past two decades. Scotland's PISA ranking in Maths has fallen from 19th in 2009 to 32nd in 2022, and in Science from 15th in 2009 to 32nd in 2022, though their ranking in Reading has risen from 17th to 14th. England's comparison with Wales and Northern Ireland since 2009 is less stark but nonetheless tells a similar story: whilst the level of attainment of 15-years-olds has

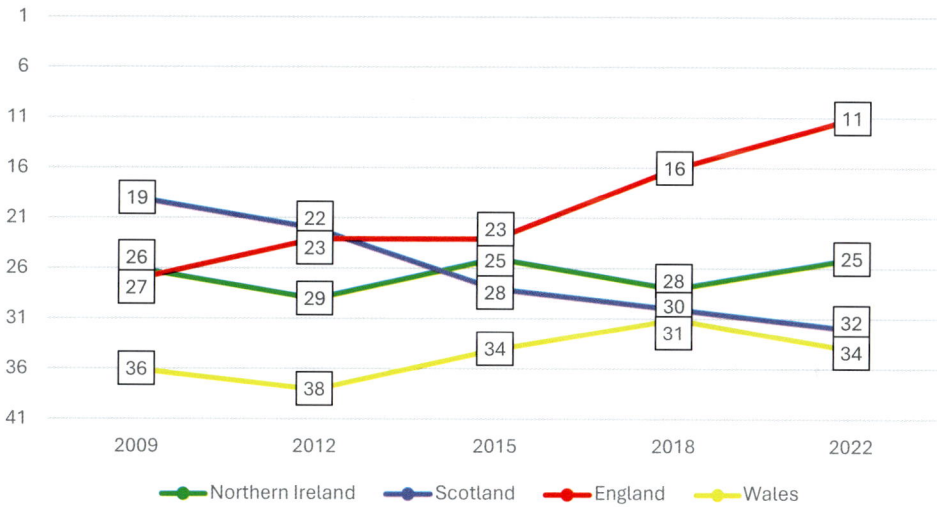

Figure 0.1 PISA ranking of England, Northern Ireland, Scotland, and Wales for the performance of 15-year-olds in Mathematics, amongst nations participating in all five surveys, 2009 to 2022.

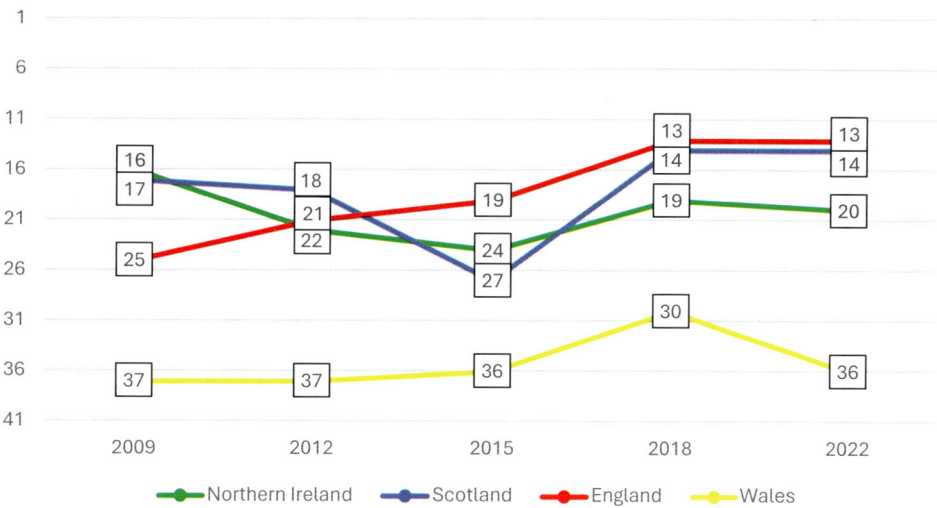

Figure 0.2 PISA ranking of England, Northern Ireland, Scotland, and Wales for the performance of 15-year-olds in Reading, amongst nations participating in all five surveys, 2009 to 2022.

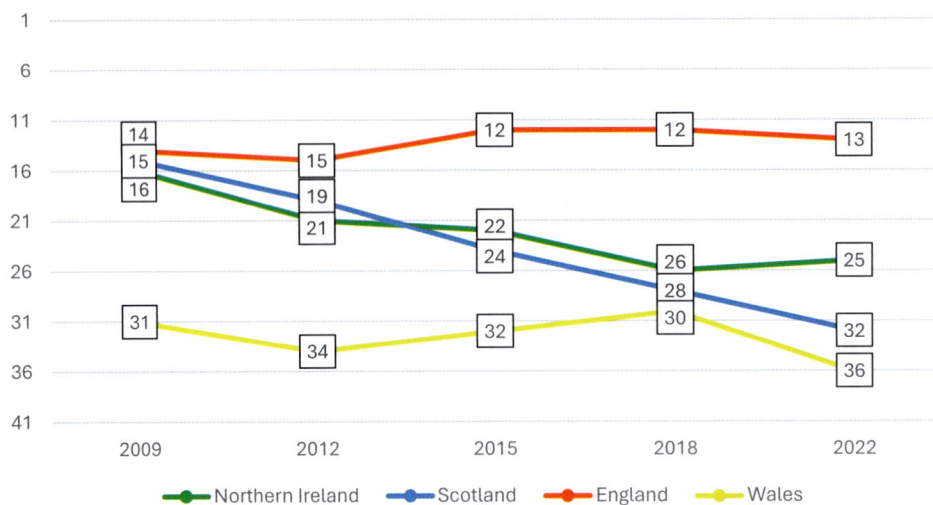

Figure 0.3 PISA ranking of England, Northern Ireland, Scotland, and Wales for the performance of 15-year-olds in Science, amongst nations participating in all five surveys, 2009 to 2022.

either stagnated or fallen in the rest of the United Kingdom, pupils in England have pulled ahead.

The Progress in International Reading Literacy Study (PIRLS) is another well-established international education study carried out by an Amsterdam-based research group, the International Association for the Evaluation of Educational Achievement. It compares the reading achievement of 9 to 10-year-olds and has been carried out on a five-year cycle since 2001. Wales does not take part in the PIRLS study, and Scotland dropped out after 2006, so a direct comparison with those nations is not possible. However, England's ranking in the reading ability of primary-age pupils has risen steadily from 19th in 2006 to 4th in 2021. That year, the literacy of English pupils was beaten only by those in Singapore, Hong Kong, and Russia, leading England to be declared the 'best in the west' when it comes to teaching early reading.[5] Of course, this data does not tell the whole story, but the pattern shown by both studies is undeniable: in England's schools, something seems to be going right.*

In conversations about schools today, I often hear this verdict confirmed anecdotally. Schools in England are far from perfect and have—as with schools around the world—faced significant struggles since the Covid-19 pandemic, and performance in some parts of the country is still letting pupils and parents down. However, it

---

* In the 2021 PIRLS study, Ireland and Northern Ireland did achieve a higher score than England. However, due to the Covid-19 pandemic, they chose to delay the assessment of pupils in their schools by approximately six months. In both of these education systems, the pupils included in the assessment were, therefore, older than the usual samples for those systems in PIRLS, so their results are not included in this analysis.

	2006	2011	2016	2021

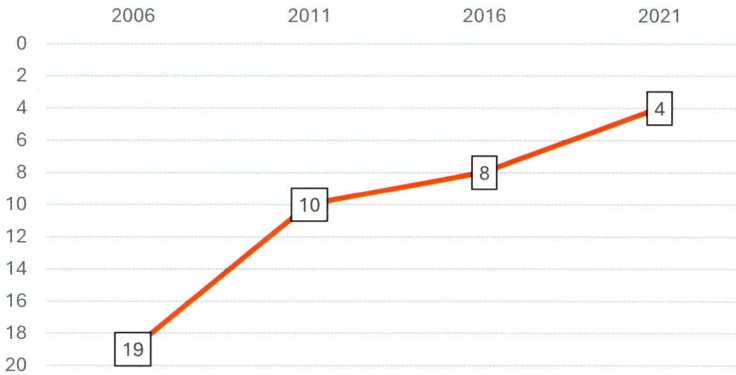

Figure 0.4 PIRLS ranking of the reading ability of 9 to 10-year-olds in England, 2009 to 2022.

is not uncommon to hear today's parents of primary and secondary-aged pupils, most of whom will have been educated during the 1980s and 1990s, commenting on how much better their children's experience of attending a state-funded school is compared to their own. There is data to verify this impression. The British Social Attitudes Survey is carried out every year by the National Centre for Social Research and is Britain's most authoritative measure of national sentiment. At ten-year intervals, they have asked the public how much confidence they have in different areas of public life, including schools. The proportion of the British population with either 'complete confidence' or 'a great deal of confidence' in British schools has risen from 22 percent in 1998 to 27 percent in 2008, to 36 percent in 2018. Ask anyone in England whether their child would receive a better education at a state-funded school today or one 20 years ago, and you are likely to get the same answer. It would be a similar answer, I suspect, were you to ask them whether they think their child would receive a better education at a state-funded school in England or over the border in Scotland or Wales.

Internationally, other countries are taking notice, with delegations from across the globe visiting England's highest-attaining schools. These visitors want to see first-hand the education offered by exceptional schools which owe their existence to our reforms, such as Michaela Community School in Northwest London. Established by its visionary headmistress, Katharine Birbalsingh, Michaela has become internationally famous for the radical approach of its teachers and the staggering achievements of its pupils, many of whom come from deprived backgrounds. Away from the capital, schools such as Trinity Dixons Academy in Bradford and Mercia Academy in Sheffield are becoming similarly well-known, both in England and abroad. All three schools featured in this book. Twenty years ago, English teachers and policy-makers would fly around the world to gain inspiration from American Charter Schools, Singaporean maths lessons, and the so-called 'Finnish miracle'. They no longer need to do so. As the leading American educationist, Doug Lemov observed speaking to teachers at an event at the House of Lords in October 2024, some of the most exciting and innovative schools in the world can currently be found on English soil.

Today, schools are a rare example in English public life of an area where sustained improvement is taking place. What is more, schools are set on a trajectory where further improvements are—I believe—still to come. Although our period of Conservative education reform ended with Labour's victory in the July 2024 election, and the new government is introducing changes which look likely to blunt the effectiveness of our reforms, the education reform movement we helped to create remains strong. When we gained office in 2010, we promised to create a 'self-improving' school system in England. Looking at England's schools today, I remain optimistic that we succeeded.

The Diagnosis

I entered office in May 2010, working alongside Michael Gove as Education Secretary. We were both driven by an anger that the school system was letting too many children down and wanted to build a system that was a driver of social justice. However, we also held an optimistic belief that English schools had the potential to improve and a passionate desire not to let the opportunity we had been served go to waste. Two years previously, the 2008 financial crisis had pushed the United Kingdom's economy into recession, and our government was elected with a mandate to lead an economic recovery. As a consequence, there were no reserves of spending to put behind our reform agenda. Solutions for educational underachievement that are popular during times of plenty—such as smaller class sizes, better-paid teachers, or new buildings—were not available to us. In addition, we resisted calls for reform initiatives which would move resources from one area to another without spurring any system-wide change. Zero-sum policies, such as moving good teachers to underprivileged areas, or overhauling admissions codes so disadvantaged pupils were admitted to better schools, were of little interest.[6] We wanted to unleash thoroughgoing, system-wide change.

At root, we believed the only way to improve schools in England was to improve the quality of teaching in classrooms. From the perspective of government funding, the cost implication of a teacher using effective teaching methods, compared to a teacher using ineffective methods, is zero. In a world of frozen departmental budgets, this was the only change that stood a chance of significantly tackling education underperformance, particularly for disadvantaged pupils. This belief lies behind this book's title, *Reforming Lessons*. Firstly, it is my modest hope that the reforms we made to English schools have lessons for school systems around the world which want to make similar improvements. Secondly, the ultimate aim of any education reform must always remain that somewhere—often down a long and convoluted causal chain—teachers are empowered to deliver better lessons. In my rough estimation, some 1.5 million lessons are taught every day in England, and it is these events that any education reform must ultimately aim to improve.

For a politician hoping to improve the quality of lessons in English schools, the approach that you take might seem straightforward: gather the doyens of the education establishment, define what makes good teaching, and impose those approaches on schools around the country. This, in very crude terms, was the approach taken by our predecessor, the New Labour government, from 1997 to 2010 (see Chapter 1). They almost doubled state expenditure on education from £49.7 billion in 1998 to £88.6 billion in 2010 (based on 2010 prices).[7] Much of this money was spent on centrally directed initiatives designed to make teachers adopt 'best practices' in countless areas of school life, from teaching initial reading to dealing with bullying. Most emblematic of this approach were the literacy and numeracy National Strategies for primary schools, which combined in 2004 to become the National Strategy and had reached an eventual cost of £1.9 billion by 2008.[8] However, as international surveys during the New Labour years showed, this attempt to drive improvements from the centre through enormous, costly initiatives did not result in any significant improvement in pupil outcomes. As Chapter 2 explains, the challenge with politicians attempting to define what makes good practice is that they inevitably do so through figures within the education establishment, and figures within the education establishment inevitably promote the existing orthodoxies. If you want innovation, more of the same is never going to be the catalyst.

Following my appointment to the House of Commons Education Select Committee in December 2003, I began paying close attention to New Labour's programme of education reform. The more I learnt about contemporary teaching methods, the more I came to suspect that an existing orthodoxy on what made good teaching was the single biggest barrier to school improvement. My gateway into these debates was an encounter in January 2004, when I had my first of two revelatory experiences on the path to becoming an education reformer: meeting the primary school headteacher Ruth Miskin. She explained how, for decades, the education establishment in England had proscribed an effective, evidence-based approach to teaching reading called 'phonics', simply because its formal, didactic approach contradicted the 'progressive' orthodoxy supported by the education establishment. Ruth told me how instead of endorsing evidence-based approaches, New Labour's National Literacy Strategy was recycling the same approaches which, for decades, led pupils to underachieve.

I spent the next two years campaigning for phonics teaching to be given more prominence in the National Literacy Strategy. Following the success of this campaign, I was given the job of Shadow Schools Minister in May 2005 and began to widen my interests away from the teaching of initial literacy in primary schools and towards curriculum and teaching methods more generally. This led in the summer of 2006 to the second of my two revelations: discovering the work of the American educational thinker E. D. Hirsch. In his 1996 book, *The Schools We Need,* Hirsch explains how the American education establishment had become dominated by an intellectual thoughtworld. Loosely termed 'progressive' education, these ideas were beguiling in their appeal, idealistic in their intent, but destructive in their implementation. Progressive education had its origins in eighteenth-century romanticism, began being applied in American classrooms during the early twentieth century, achieved mainstream approval during the 1960s, and by the end of the twentieth century, had become an orthodoxy within America's education establishment. On reading Hirsch, I suspected that the story he told of this 'thoughtworld' in America was applicable to what had happened over the Atlantic in British schools, albeit along a slightly delayed timeframe.

The Progressivist Ideology

What is progressive education? As an educational philosophy, it takes principles of political progressivism and applies them to the realm of education. For this reason, it proved highly popular amongst young idealistic teachers during the 1960s and continues to have a strong emotional appeal to modern sympathies. Today, many of the more optimistic nostrums you might hear about children's learning have their origins in this philosophy: 'children learn best when finding things out for themselves'; 'education should start with the interests of the child'; 'real learning happens when children have fun'; 'memorising facts will kill a child's imagination.' Inspired by E. D. Hirsch's work, my co-author Robert Peal wrote a book on the growth of progressive education in England and its subsequent failure to live up to its promise. Entitled *Progressively Worse* and published in 2014, it helped clarify much of my thinking on the nature of these ideas.

Robert summarises progressive education as consisting of four key tenets, the first of which is the idea that teaching should be 'child-centred'. In contrast to the more traditional vision of a teacher standing at the front of the classroom instructing the whole class simultaneously, the progressive classroom recommends a more individualised approach, where pupils pursue their own learning with the help, but not direction, of a teacher. This belief has taken on many guises since it first achieved prominence during the 1960s: constructivism, discovery learning, project work, independent learning, and so on. However, at the core of each of these ideas is the same fundamental principle that the child has agency in the classroom, and the teacher is a facilitator whose job is not to teach from the front but to construct an environment in which their pupils learn for themselves.

The second tenet of progressive education is that a school curriculum should be built around skills or competencies, not knowledge. Progressive and non-progressive teachers tend to agree that the ultimate outcome of education should be complex skills such as creativity, critical thinking, or problem-solving. However, the progressive educator believes that these skills can and should be taught explicitly and made the basis of a school curriculum. The stuff of learning—chemical formulae, historical dates, French irregular verbs, and so on—are not seen as a means to achieving these skills but as potential impediments. Over the past few decades, this belief has taken on a techno-futurist tinge with the idea of 'twenty-first century learning'. In the age of the internet, when all possible human knowledge can be accessed through a handheld device, it is commonly claimed that knowledge and memorisation have become redundant, and school curricula can focus exclusively on skills.

These first two tenets of progressive education attempt to overturn the teacher's authority as a subject expert, directly teaching a body of knowledge to their students. The third tenet of progressive education attempts to overturn the teacher's moral authority as an adult part of whose role it is to uphold common standards of behaviour. Amongst progressive educators, poor behaviour in schools is seen not as the fault of the child but the fault of the teacher or institution. This belief gives progressivists their aversion to rules and sanctions in schools, such as uniform policies, silent corridors, or after-school detentions. Steeped in idealistic notions about the innate goodness of the child, the progressivist assures us that engaging teaching can overcome poor behaviour. It became something of a received wisdom in English schools that if lessons were made sufficiently engaging and relevant to children's interests, poor behaviour would be reduced or even eliminated. For the progressive educator, finding pupils' intrinsic motivation to learn is paramount, and using extrinsic pressures such as rewards or sanctions to motivate pupils to learn is seen as somehow inauthentic or even destructive of a child's potential.

The fourth and final tenet of progressive education is less an approach to teaching like the previous three but instead a sociological attempt to explain away their subsequent failure to improve pupil attainment. It is the idea that socio-economic background dictates success. As progressive education gained popularity, schools began deemphasising knowledge in their curriculum, moving rows of desks into islands to encourage 'group work', and abandoning whole-school behaviour policies based on sanctions and rewards. When these innovations did not bring the breakthrough in pupil attainment they promised, progressive educators looked to social inequality and deprivation to explain away their failure. Like all poorly conceived ideas, there is a kernel of truth at its heart: pupils from less advantaged backgrounds do, all things being equal, achieve less well at school. However, this sociological truth, if seized upon too readily within schools, can become a self-fulfilling prophecy. It is usually expressed in sympathetic tones, as in the notorious question, 'What can you expect of these kids?', but leads to a school culture in which failure is accepted. Or, as President George W Bush famously put it in a speech in 2000, the 'soft bigotry of low expectations.'

Throughout the book, I refer to these ideas collectively as the 'progressivist ideology'. I have tried to avoid using the word 'progressive', as it feels too generous a term for an educational philosophy which has brought no discernible progress for schools or society. Instead, the term 'progressi*vist*' captures the ideological status this thoughtworld achieved within England's education establishment. By 2010, it had become, quite simply, a professional creed to which those working in state education had to subscribe if they wanted any hope of career advancement. In *Progressively Worse*, Robert covers how this happened in far more detail than our book has space for. Suffice it to say that, during my years as a shadow schools minister, I never met a member of the education establishment who did not at least pay lip service to its ideology.

It is vital to stress that when I refer to the 'education establishment', I do not include teachers and school leaders. I have always admired the pragmatism that teachers gain through the frontline demands of working in a school. Amongst the best teachers I met whilst in opposition, references they made to the modish buzzwords of progressivism ('personalisation', 'differentiation', 'independent learning', and so on) were accompanied by an arched eyebrow before quietly confiding the clever ways they had developed to sidestep the expectation that these should be followed within their classrooms. Instead, the true gatekeepers of this ideology were the education establishment. These are figures who may have started their careers in the classroom but had long since moved out to work in local authorities,* government agencies (often known as 'quangos'), or the university education faculties which offer initial teacher training. To my mind, these three domains—local authorities, government quangos, and universities—were the three strongest redoubts of the progressivist ideology prior to 2010.

Ideologies thrive wherever individuals are able to impose their ideas upon the public, with little accountability for their subsequent success or failure. From the offices of a government agency or the comfort of a university seminar room, ideologues can indulge in idealistic notions without having to reckon directly with their impact on the ground. This was also true of local authorities, who in 2010 still held a near monopoly over the management of schools. In theory, they were democratically accountable to their electorate. In reality, council elections were rarely, if ever, decided on the basis of school performance, and councillors delegated the running of schools to Chief Education Officers, who often remained in place regardless of which party was in charge. Similarly, prior to 2010, the majority of new entrants to the profession still trained through a university-based route, to which schools in the surrounding area were captive customers. Knowing that trainee teachers would struggle to hold onto their progressivist ideals the moment they were faced with a class of 30 pupils, university education faculties almost saw it as their professional duty to teach the trainees the most idealistic version possible of child-centred teaching in the hope that some ember of that flame might remain once they landed in the classroom. Lastly, government quangos, whose size and power grew to deliver New Labour's myriad school improvement initiatives, became a thriving ecosystem for the progressive ideologue.

But what of the schools? During the 2000s, a decade which I label 'Peak Progressivism' in Chapter 2, schools had the choice of going—broadly speaking—in one of either two directions. Some school leaders were true believers and worked with

---

* For non-UK readers, local authorities have historically been responsible for education in their local area, normally operating in the same jurisdiction as a county or borough council. There are currently 152 in England.

enormous effort to fulfil the promise of the progressivist ideology. In such schools, learning was personalised, classrooms were replaced with 'social learning environments', and the curriculum was redesigned around twenty-first-century skills. However, despite significant efforts, there was no breakthrough in pupil results: the burden of bad ideas meant teachers were pedalling very hard in a very low gear. In a second type of school, any conviction that these ideas might work was lost, but no alternative philosophy of education could thrive in its place. Instead, lip-service was paid to the progressivist ideology, failure became expected, and cynicism reigned. I came to believe that it was this inability to depart from the progressivist orthodoxy which led to the uniform mediocrity that was so often observed in English schools at the time. The phrase 'bog standard comprehensive', coined by Tony Blair's Director of Communications, Alastair Campbell, caught on for a reason (and much to his chagrin).

There was a third type of school that—in 2010—were still very few in number, but in which we invested our hopes for future reform. This was the school that departed from the progressivist ideology and attempted to put into practice new philosophies of education. Most of these schools owed their existence to the Academies policy, devised by my New Labour predecessor, the visionary Schools Minster Andrew Adonis, and covered in Chapter 3. Much like Charter Schools in the United States, or *friskola* in Sweden, these were state schools that operated outside of local authority control, giving them the autonomy to pioneer new approaches to teaching and school organisation. Two of the most influential academies established during the New Labour years were Mossbourne Academy and King Solomon Academy, which are discussed in Chapters 3 and 8, respectively. These successful early academies were an inspiration to Michael Gove and me, providing an early vision for how system-wide change in English education might look.

High Autonomy

The mantra that came to describe our vision for school reform was 'high autonomy, high accountability'. Firstly, autonomy. Michael and I believed that the only way in which orthodoxies could be overturned was through giving schools the freedom to innovate and devise alternative approaches. To do so, the education establishment's redoubts had to be weakened, and new institutions given permission to build in their place. Chapter 4 explains how the Academies Act passed through Parliament in July 2010 and expanded the option for schools to operate outside of local authority control to every school in the country. In addition, the Act allowed organisations that were not local authorities to set up new schools from scratch, a policy Labour had pioneered, but which we hoped to turbo-charge by giving such schools a new designation: 'Free Schools'. The aim of academies and free schools was simple: we wanted to remove from local authorities their historic monopoly on managing schools and unleash an unprecedented level of innovation. In little over a decade, the Free Schools policy led to the creation of some 650 new schools, which educate more than 350,000 pupils and include some of the highest-performing schools in the country.[9]

As is explained in Chapter 8, schools quickly embraced the freedom of academisation. When we entered office, 203 secondary school academies had been created by New Labour, representing 5 percent of secondary schools in England and no primary schools. At the time of writing, there are 10,640 academies in England, representing 82 percent of secondary schools and 43 percent of primary schools. Recently, we have passed a milestone where over half of all pupils in England—56 percent at the time of writing—now attend an academy.[10] This is, without doubt, the greatest restructuring of schools that has taken place in England since the 1960s. The hold that local authorities once had as the organising principle for English schools has been consigned to history. In their place, Multi-Academy Trusts (MATs), which oversee multiple different academies, have evolved as new organisations for school management. As I explain in Chapter 12, these MATs can grow or shrink according to their success and, as a consequence, are more accountable for their results than local authorities ever were. This gives them a stronger institutional bias towards evidence-led approaches, away from the failed ideologies of the past.

At the time of writing, there are 1,180 MATs in England, up from just 66 in 2011.[11] The best contemporary thinking about school organisation, curriculum design, pastoral care, school leadership, and teaching methods emanates from them, and MATs have become the true power players in England's education system. The reaction in public and in private of MAT leaders to the current government's retrograde plans to remove some important academy freedoms, such as teacher pay and curriculum design, give me some confidence that the fundamental role of MATs in our education system is now both well embedded and a safeguard of the reforms.

School autonomy also meant less central direction from the government, and an end to the education quangocracy. As explained in Chapter 4, during our first three years in government we closed or merged nine different education quangos. This held two clear benefits: firstly, it saved us millions of pounds, which we were able to redirect to schools. Secondly, it dealt a blow to the intellectual hegemony of the progressivist ideology.

Our final challenge to the education establishment was in teacher training. Here, we wanted to break the monopoly held by universities and encourage schools to devise new training routes with more practical, evidence-led approaches. Chapter 11 explains how we took the small but popular 'school-led' training programmes established by previous governments, and gave them more prominence within the system. Consequently, the number of postgraduate trainee teachers entering the classroom through school-led routes almost tripled from 5,371 in 2012 to 14,231 in 2015.[12] That year, school-led trainees overtook those entering the profession through university-led routes for the first time, a situation that has been maintained ever since. This reform has empowered groups of schools across the country to devise teacher training programmes, which are shorn of academic theorising, and are instead based on approaches which give teachers the greatest chance of success early on in their careers.

Academisation, reforms to central government administration, and school-led teacher training all share a common theme. They have allowed teachers to challenge the dominant orthodoxies within English education and created an ecosystem of school autonomy in which new, evidence-led ideas can thrive. In pursuing them, we were often accused of 'marketising' education. As local authorities and universities lost their historic power, it was predicted that this was simply the first step towards the privatisation of state education or the arrival of profit-making state schools. Fifteen years on, none of these predictions have come true. Despite the oft-repeated accusations of our detractors, Michael Gove and I never wanted to introduce a free market for schools. Instead, we wanted to introduce a free market for ideas.

High Accountability

Our education reforms were based on the hope that if schools were given the autonomy to devise new approaches, the best of them would achieve nationally leading results and act as beacons for the rest of the sector to follow. Nothing succeeds like success, and in an education system characterised by autonomy, school-to-school emulation is the greatest driver of improvement. However, identifying schools in England with the 'best' results was a vexed issue in 2010. The Labour government's accountability measures, which should—in theory—allow you to pinpoint successful schools, were fraught with problems such as grade inflation, low-quality qualifications, poorly designed coursework, and the tactical 'gaming' of pupil results. As a consequence, we decided that the whole architecture of school accountability needed to be redesigned.

School accountability already existed in the English system, but it was an unfinished revolution. The 1988 Education Reform Act had, for the first time, introduced a National Curriculum to English schools, and the 1992 Education (Schools) Act made pupil attainment in national exams at both primary and secondary levels public for the first time. This ushered in the era of league tables, where schools could be compared against each other according to the achievement of their pupils. However, insufficient thought was given to how these measures of pupil achievement were designed. At the secondary level, the main measure of school effectiveness was the percentage of pupils who passed a threshold of five GCSEs at a Grade C or above, known as '5 A* to C measure'. However, this measure was easily manipulated by schools in ways unforeseen by its original designers. At primary level, the testing of reading, mathematics, and science was so poorly delivered that in 2010 a nationwide teacher boycott threatened to undermine the entire principle of primary assessment. Chapters 5 and 6 explain how we overhauled the school accountability system so that it could live up to its original promise: to offer teachers, pupils, and their families clear, valid data on the success of their schools.

Underpinning the changes to school accountability was a new National Curriculum, devised during our first four years in government and launched in 2014. Inspired by the curriculum from those nations which regularly top the international league tables, such as Singapore and Japan, as well as the writings of knowledge-advocates such as E. D. Hirsch and his disciples, the 2014 National Curriculum put subject knowledge at the centre of teaching in English schools. We wanted pupils to know more, and we wanted pupils to be able to do more with that knowledge. As such, we countered decades of dumbing down at primary level, GCSE, and A-level by introducing assessments which were more academically challenging. It was our intention to set a new bar for what children at all levels of their education were expected to achieve, in the belief that ambitious, well-run schools would be more than capable of meeting it.

Creating A Movement

How schools reached this new, higher bar was—in line with our belief in school autonomy—left up to them. With the exception of mandating phonics teaching in all primary schools, the aim of our reforms was never to drive improvement from the centre. We wanted schools, and increasingly Multi-Academy-Trusts, to lead a self-improving system. In policy terms, this was a gamble. For our reforms to work, the new freedoms given to schools would have to catalyse a grassroots, teacher-led movement pioneering new approaches to teaching. I spent my early days in office desperately looking for signs that such a movement was materialising, and within a couple of years, it was clear that something was happening. Today, the reform movement that is taking place in English schools has surpassed even my most optimistic hopes.

Sometime around 2012, a counter-movement to the progressivist orthodoxy began to coalesce amongst English teachers. As Chapter 7 explains, we gained office at the same time social media was taking off, and its impact on the education debate was immense. Teacher blogs and online platforms such as Twitter seemed custom-made to unite renegade teachers, allowing them to share research findings and articles like *samizdat* literature in the old Soviet Union and to challenge the power of the education establishment. What started as blogs and tweets during the early 2010s quickly turned into books and events such as researchED during the mid-2010s, and by the end of the decade, had found an institutional home in many of the best academies and free schools. I do believe that our reforms deserve some credit for giving English teachers the freedom to imagine and implement alternative approaches, but the agency and energy for doing so has most certainly come from the ground up. Central to this movement has been a new emphasis on evidence-led teaching, as teachers in England began finding out for themselves what 'the research' really says. Breakthroughs in our understanding of human cognition, first explained by academics such as Daniel Willingham and popularised in England by the likes of Daisy Christodoulou, have reasserted the role of knowledge and memory in learning. Meanwhile, empirical research into effective classroom practices has demonstrated the power of whole-class teaching and laid bare the lack of evidence behind the orthodoxy of child-centred instruction.

Our academies and free school reforms have allowed teachers to put this evidence into practice with a speed and level of innovation that would never have been possible before. Today, the schools that they have created are the most important evidence that exists for the power of new approaches to achieve extraordinary results for pupils in some of the most disadvantaged parts of the country. In Chapter 10, I explain how such exemplary schools have become the centres of the education reform movement in English schools. Most excitingly, this reform movement has moved debates over teaching methods away from the tired dichotomies of progressivism versus traditionalism, or child-centred versus teacher-led, and towards a new understanding of effective practice which defies previous labels. There once was a time when I embraced the term 'traditionalist teaching', but not anymore. What I see today in England's best schools is something new. In some ways, it resembles the best of 'traditional teaching', but in other ways, it is very different and far superior. Perhaps best labelled 'evidence-led' teaching, in Chapter 10, I try to explain four of its main components: knowledge-rich curriculum and resourcing, direct instruction, checking for understanding, and retrieval practice.

The confluence of our reforms to encourage greater school autonomy and a grassroots movement of teachers pioneering new, evidence-led practices has created what one *Guardian* writer approvingly described as a 'Cambrian Explosion' in our schools.[13] The greatest legacy of our reforms has been this effervescence of new thinking on teaching methods and the curriculum. It is no exaggeration to say that today, when visiting one high-performing school, I see more good teaching in a day than I did in a decade of school visits prior to becoming a minister. For anyone open to having their mind changed on education, visiting such schools is the single most powerful course of action they can take. Doug Lemov has called this 'existence proof'. Exemplar schools take conversations away from academic theorising and quibbles over effect sizes and control groups and instead confront visitors with the joyful sight of pupils excelling through methods that had—up until a decade ago—been all but unheard of in mainstream schools. Few who see such ideas in action can fail to be impressed.

The Battle of Ideas

When I began this journey, I would often try to explain to friends and colleagues the power of the progressivist ideology in schools, and they would look at me with suspicion. Rational, liberal-minded policy makers don't like to think that humans can be so susceptible to group think and dogma. The practical men and women of Whitehall believe that public sector reform is all about structures, incentives, and funding streams, and any talk of ideologies seems rather embarrassing—surface froth not to be taken too seriously. I have never been so sure.

My interest in politics came through the world of ideas. As a teenager during the 1970s, I became a devotee of the writings of Milton Friedman and Friedrich von Hayek and a keen advocate of monetarist economic theory. Following her election as leader of the Conservative Party in 1975, I saw in Margaret Thatcher a political leader who took ideas seriously and engaged thoroughly with the substance of her opponents' worldview. During the 1970s, the writings of monetarist economists were a rebuke not only to the United Kingdom's failing postwar economic settlement but also to the Communist empire of the Soviet Union, whose continued existence left me feeling deeply unsettled. So, with all the folly of youth, I decided—on graduating from the University of Durham—to do something about it. I worked with the London branch of the Russian Solidarist Movement (NTS), an organisation formed by Russian emigres to fight communism. One of their chief activities was smuggling free-market propaganda and letters for anti-Communist dissidents into Russia in the hope that by toppling the intellectual edifice of communism, they may ultimately topple the political power of the Soviet Union. The NTS used Westerners posing as tourists to deliver letters to dissidents behind the Iron Curtain, and in 1982, I volunteered my services.

Following a crash course in the Russian alphabet from a man called George at a café near Victoria station, I set off on a £200 Thompsons Package Tour to Leningrad. To this day, one of the most nerve-wracking moments of my life was walking through Russian immigration with 100 letters stuffed into the sides of my boots, over which I had draped a pair of baggy jeans. Thankfully, I was not caught and spent the next week delivering small batches of letters to post boxes around Leningrad. It was exhilarating work, fighting a battle of ideas against communism one letter at a time. However, it was also very boring. Straight out of university, I had little extra money to enjoy my holiday, so I spent hours wandering the city. This was the tail end of the Brezhnev era, a period when deep economic stagnation was causing widespread, but widely supressed, dissatisfaction amongst the Russian people. I could not believe how drab life was for them: people's faces were sullen, shops were empty, and queues seemed to snake around every street corner. Those who were willing to risk arrest found some escape in Western indulgences: I spent an evening listening to the Beatles at a student bar, and—letters delivered—sold my jeans at an exorbitant price, something I later discovered was a capital offence for the purchaser.

However, what shocked me most was the compliance. These small rebellions aside, the entire population was willing to go along with an ideology whose failure to fulfil its promises seemed apparent in every facet of their lives. I returned home with a new appreciation of how an ideology can survive long after it has failed to fulfil its original promise. If those in positions of power owe their authority to that ideology's promise, the vested interests keeping it in place are simply too strong for their self-evident failure alone to herald an alternative.

I do not for a moment draw a parallel of any sort between Russian Communism and the progressivist ideology in English schools. However, I do want to make the argument that ideas matter. The period that I enjoyed, beginning with my appointment to the Education Select Committee in 2003 to becoming Schools Minister in 2010, was crucial to becoming an effective reformer. It allowed me to meet teachers, read widely, and understand—as thoroughly as I could—the ideas that were present within English schools. Michael Gove and I came to a shared diagnosis that the progressivist ideology was holding schools back, and this gave coherence and internal logic to every one of our reforms.

Michael Gove achieved such an astonishing amount as Education Secretary that it is often forgotten that he was in post for only a little over four years, from May 2010 to July 2014. Following his departure, I returned to the post of Schools Minister—with another brief interruption—for eight further years until November 2023. As such, I was often characterised as the man entrusted with guarding the flame of Goveite reform, a characterisation I would proudly embrace. Michael had a thoroughly developed vision for English schools, which set the template for his reforms whilst in office and for many years after. However—as I hope the following pages illustrate—a great deal of evolution also occurred following 2014, as my colleagues at the Department for Education and I turned the changes brought by Michael's reforming energy into a sustainable school system.

In explaining how England's new school system was built, this book should appeal to anyone seeking a greater understanding of education in England, a topic that is—I would argue—particularly worthy of study considering the recent improvement in the international performance of English pupils. This may well be teachers working in English schools who want to understand more about how the system in which they work came to be. However, I also hope that the book will be of interest to reformers from other countries looking for inspiration as to how they might emulate England's success. As I explain further in the conclusion, there is considerable—and growing—international interest in our reforms, and I hope that this book will add to that growth.

Needless to say, I would be delighted if some of those in English education policy who are currently close to the levers of power take an interest in this book. At the time of writing, the Labour Government is still developing its education policy, but the early signs are not encouraging. Our education system is far from perfect, and there remain many aspects that are in need of attention and reform. However, in doing so, I hope that the new government does not change the fundamental architecture of the system we built. This system has already recorded unarguable improvements in pupil outcomes and, if maintained, will—I believe—deliver even greater improvements in the years to come. Whatever direction the Labour government chooses to take its education reforms, it should be wary of knocking down the pillars which have made such gains possible. For any such individuals reading this book, it will—I hope—offer them a greater understanding of what those pillars are, and why they were put in place.

In 2010, the great majority of state-funded schools in England were governed by a series of orthodoxies which made any sustained improvement impossible.

Our reforms gave teachers the power to challenge these orthodoxies and devise new approaches. As a direct consequence, England has become one of the most improved education systems in the world over the past 15 years. This is the story of how that was achieved.

Notes

1 'The strange success of the Tories' schools policy', *The Economist*, 13 July 2023.
2 'The strange success of the Tories' schools policy', 13 July 2023.
3 E. Duncan, 'On schools, the Tories were a class act', *The Times*, 5 December 2024.
4 Thank you to Gabriel Heller Sahlgren, the economist and expert on international education surveys, for compiling this data.
5 Department for Education, 'Press release: England among highest performing western countries in education', 5 December 2023.
6 Though we did tweak the admissions code in 2011 to allow schools to prioritise the admission of disadvantaged pupils.
7 Ruth Lupton and Polina Obolenskaya, 'Labour's record on education: Policy, spending and outcomes 1997–2010', *Social Policy in a Cold Climate Working Paper WP03*, 2013, p. 16.
8 Hansard House of Commons Debate, vol. 480, 14 October 2008.
9 'Free schools—how we are creating 12,000 new school places in disadvantaged areas', *The Education Hub Blog: Department for Education*, 22 August 2023.
10 'Schools, pupils and their characteristics', *Department for Education*, 26 September 2024.
11 'Multi-academy trusts by trust characteristics data', *Department for Education*, 1 February 2024 and M. Lucas et al., 'Transitioning to a multi-academy trust led system: What does the evidence tell us?', *National Foundation for Educational Research*, 2023, p. 5.
12 Figures taken from the Initial Teacher Training Census, published each November or December by the Department for Education.
13 Ian Leslie, 'The revolution that could change the way your child is taught', *The Guardian*, 11 March 2015.

The Inheritance

> What a wise parent would wish for their children, so the state must wish for all its children.
>
> R. H. Tawney, cited in James Callaghan's Ruskin College speech,
> 18 October 1976

In 1976, the Prime Minister, James Callaghan, delivered what became known as the Ruskin College Speech, in which he made the case that politicians should assume a greater role in addressing the mounting public concern over the quality of schools in Britain. It was a daring speech for a Labour Prime Minister to make in 1976 and, prior to delivering it, many had advised him 'to keep off the grass' of the education world. Callaghan observed, 'It is almost as though some people would wish that the subject matter and purpose of education should not have public attention focused on it; nor that profane hands should be allowed to touch it.' Callaghan was taking the first tentative steps into the 'secret garden' of education policy, seen by many at the time as the exclusive preserve of educationalists. To justify his decision to do so, he quoted the previous epigraph from the Christian Socialist R. H. Tawney, offering it as the overriding principle of his government's nascent reform programme. It was also the principle that lay behind every one of our education reforms from 2010 onwards.

Reading the Ruskin speech today, you see outlined many of the weaknesses that still permeated the education system in 2010. 'I am concerned', Callaghan told his audience 'to find complaints from industry that new recruits from school sometimes do not have the basic tools to do the job that is required.' He cited his concern about standards of basic numeracy and literacy amongst school leavers and the teaching methods widely suspected to be responsible for their decline. As he explained,

> On another aspect, there is the unease felt by parents and others about the new informal methods of teaching which seems to produce excellent results when they are in well-qualified hands but are much more dubious when they are not.[1]

DOI: 10.4324/9781003533474-2

Eleven years prior to Callaghan's speech, a previous Labour administration led by Harold Wilson had begun the most far-reaching education reforms in the nation's history. A year after winning the 1964 election, Wilson's government began the long process of comprehensivisation in England and Wales. Previously, the majority of children had attended secondary-modern schools or a small number of technical schools, whilst the high-attaining minority went to academic grammar schools. The decision on which school a child would attend depended upon how they performed in an exam at age 11 (known as the '11-plus'). Following 'Circular 10/65' distributed by Wilson's Education Secretary Anthony Crosland, all local authorities were asked to combine the different elements of this 'tripartite system' into single schools, known as 'comprehensives'. This process of comprehensivisation had the historical misfortune of coinciding with another seismic change: the growing power of the progressivist ideology, which also enjoyed its first flurry of popularity in Britain during the 1960s. Though aimed at primary level education, the government's 1967 'Plowden Report' gave progressivist teaching methods official sanction and became the foundational document for progressive education in Britain, with its now infamous declaration that '"Finding out" has proved to be better for children than "being told".'[2] Comprehensive schooling thus became associated in many people's minds with the 'informal methods of teaching' about which Callaghan warned in 1976.

My school career began the same year that Labour launched its policy of comprehensivisation. In September 1965, I was dragged—crying and screaming—into the first year of Langton's Infant School in Hornchurch, Essex, aged 5-years-old. Thus, my thirteen years of school education overlapped entirely with what was then the most ambitious period of education reform in English history. What is more, due to my father's peripatetic career as a civil engineer, I attended almost every different type of school conceivable during that period.

Following an infant school in Essex, I moved to a state elementary school in Ontario, Canada, then back to England and a junior school in Northamptonshire followed by two years at a grant-aided independent school in Bedford. My first secondary school was a grammar school in Kent. Then after my family moved to Yorkshire, I finished my education at two recently established comprehensive schools: a former grammar school turned comprehensive in Roundhay, Leeds, where standards remained high, and a comprehensive school in Wakefield where standards did not. It was at this school, which was notorious for classroom disruption and pupil violence, that I took my A-levels, and gained the same number of A-grades as the rest of my year group combined. This was not, I hasten to add, due to any genius on my part, but simply because—unlike most of my peers—I had the fortune of having been taught at some excellent schools before attending a failing comprehensive.

My mother was a primary school teacher, a 35-year career she pursued throughout our family's travels. Combined with the panoply of schools attended by my younger brother and me, this meant that conversations around the dinner table often strayed towards the merits and drawbacks of different types of teaching methods and schools. For this reason, I suspect my interest in the politics of education reform was unusually keen compared to most teenagers during the 1970s. When I left school in 1978, my primary political interest was economics and the monetarist revolution soon to be unleashed by Margaret Thatcher. However, education remained a close second. It was one of the main motivations behind my decision, as a young chartered accountant living in London during the 1990s, to embark upon a career in politics.

Education, Education, and Education

I entered Parliament as the Member for Bognor Regis and Littlehampton following the 1997 General Election. It was a strange year to enter Parliament as a Conservative MP, being as it was the largest Labour victory in British history. I was one of just 31 new Conservative MPs, out of only 165 in total, representing a Party shell-shocked by the scale of its defeat. Meanwhile, Tony Blair's 'New Labour' project swept into power with reforming Britain's schools at the forefront of its campaign. When he took to the stage at the Labour Party Conference in Blackpool a year earlier, Blair famously demanded, 'Ask me my three main priorities for Government' and answered, 'Education, education, and education.' Blair and the Labour Party were responding to widespread dismay at the quality of schools in Britain. In their 1997 general election manifesto, they bemoaned the fact that nearly half of 11-year-olds in England and Wales failed to reach expected standards in English and maths. It read, 'Education has been the Tories' biggest failure. It is Labour's number one priority.'[3]

In fairness, the late 1980s and early 1990s had seen a burst of important Conservative education reforms. Following the Education Reform Act of 1988, the government created the first National Curriculum for England and Wales, establishing the fundamental knowledge and skills all children should be taught from the ages of 5 to 16. Shortly afterwards, the 1992 Education (Schools) Act revolutionised school accountability. Pupils taking national exams at ages 16 and 18 had long been a feature of English secondary schools, and National Curriculum Assessments were introduced for primary school pupils in 1991. However, there was no way for parents to know how well pupils were doing in these exams at a school level. From 1992 onwards, the Department for Education made school-level exam data public, allowing parents to make informed choices about which state school they might choose to send their child to. This reform allowed newspapers to publish schools' exam results in 'league tables', a term which became the colloquial term for the policy. The 1992 Act also created Ofsted, a new schools inspectorate which would use publicly available exam data, along with myriad other information, to assess the quality of education offered by schools.

By 1997, the three pillars of school accountability—the National Curriculum, school league tables, and Ofsted—had been built. Despite much internal pressure to dismantle them, Tony Blair's Labour Party pledged to keep them all. However, accountability measures alone do not a good school system make. By 1997, school leaders had been made more accountable than ever for the communities they serve and pupil results, but they had not been given the requisite autonomy to improve them. What is more, funding for state schools was in a parlous state, and the stock of school buildings—many of which had not been updated since the first wave of comprehensivisation during the 1960s—was deteriorating. Mouldy concrete and shattered glass were potent symbols of a system widely perceived to be in decline. By 1997, the quality of Britain's state schools remained a significant national concern and one that I shared.

I visited schools in my constituency as often as possible. Despite being in West Sussex, a relatively prosperous county on England's south coast, my school tours were reliably troubling. Quite aside from the unprepossessing exteriors of many schools, what was happening inside was not much better. Lessons were rarely the scene of clear and purposeful study, often appearing more like social gatherings in which the teacher played a peripheral role. School uniform was a shabby sweatshirt. Even as a visiting local MP, I would witness defiant pupil behaviour, as teachers failed to summon the requisite authority to chivvy pupils to lessons or correct poor behaviour. At one secondary school, I remember being told that 50 percent of children who joined at age 11 had a reading age below their chronological age, 25 percent by two years or more. I was baffled at how, in the fifth-largest economy in the world, schooling could be so poor.

Most depressing was the sense of defeatism whenever I enquired whether things should be better. 'What do you expect?' was the response before pointing to two commonly cited explanations for underperformance: a lack of school funding and pupil poverty, both materially and in terms of aspiration. I remember being told in one school that some of their pupils had never even been to the beach, which was less than a mile away. They neglected to mention that most of the pupils were from comfortable working or middle-class backgrounds and had certainly been to the beach in Bognor Regis and probably Spain as well.

High Energy, Low Impact

However, on school funding, critics of the Conservative government did have a point. Education spending had declined as a proportion of GDP during their final years in power, from 5 percent in 1991–92 to 4.5 percent in 1997–98. On gaining office, the Labour Party made good on its promise to reverse this trend. After the Labour Party came to power, public expenditure on education (based on 2010 prices) almost doubled from £49.7 billion in 1998 to £88.6 billion in 2010.[4] Though I have never believed that more money is a magic bullet that will fix declining standards, watching on from the opposition benches, it was hard not to be impressed by the billions of pounds New Labour committed to state schools.

However, I was less impressed by how indiscriminately this money was spent. Much of it funded a hyperactive flurry of expensive but short-lived initiatives. In 1998, Labour launched the Beacon Schools programme, which gave high-achieving schools 'beacon' status and grants to spread effective practice. They introduced Education Action Zones to improve schools in deprived areas at the ultimate cost of £290 million.[5] There was Fresh Start (not to be confused with Sure Start), where failing schools were closed and reopened with new names and new leadership, often to then fail again, but in a more high-profile fashion. And there were Specialist Schools, where schools were given grants to develop a 'specialism' such as sport, music, languages, or technology (at a cost of £1.5 billion by 2007).[6] The following year, the Excellence in Cities Programme was launched to drive improvement in inner-city schools. It ultimately cost £1.6 billion but, according to a 2005 report from the National Foundation for Educational Research (NFER), did little to improve pupil outcomes.[7] Each of these initiatives seemed to be driven by a belief that more energy and more money were all that were required to improve our schools. Little thought was given to whether they would change what teachers were teaching or how schools were run. Schools were essentially being given more money to carry on pursuing the same unsuccessful approaches.

New Labour's first education secretary, David Blunkett, had at least understood the dangers of the progressivist ideology. A working-class Yorkshireman, he trained as a teacher during the 1970s and had little patience for what he termed 'trendy teaching'. In his 1995 biography, Blunkett wrote of his outlook on education: 'I believe in discipline, solid mental arithmetic, learning to read and write accurately, plenty of homework, increasing expectations and developing potential.'[8] Following the 1997 election, Blunkett declared his admiration for the Chief Inspector of Schools, Chris Woodhead. Despite being a Conservative appointee and an outspoken critic of progressive teaching methods, Woodhead's contract was extended for four more years. During the early New Labour years, I was encouraged by these signals that Blunkett would stand up to the progressivist ideology. However, in 2001, David Blunkett was reshuffled to the Home Office, and his presence was missed. Four Labour Education Secretaries entered and left the Department over the six years that followed: Estelle Morris, Charles Clarke, Ruth Kelly, and Alan Johnson. With such short tenures, none of them were able to get to grips with the education establishment, although the London Challenge initiative, launched in 2002, was a rare example of evidence-based, school-led policy-making.

In contrast, I was enjoying the luxury of time as an opposition MP to pursue my interests and read widely. Having been appointed a shadow Treasury minister in 1998, I became shadow Energy minister in 1999. Following the 2001 general election, I turned down a position on the opposition frontbench and spent two years on the Public Accounts Committee. However, I became more and more interested in Labour's education reforms and concerned that they were not living up to their early promise. I asked the party whips for a place on the Education Select Committee, and my wish was granted in December 2003.

The Scourge of Illiteracy

Select Committees play a significant role in Westminster politics. They are made up of MPs from across the different parties, who collectively scrutinise the work of government departments. Sitting on the Education Select Committee, I took a particular interest in what was being done to combat childhood illiteracy in Britain. It is often said that literacy is not a part of a child's education, but a precondition. If a child does not master the ability to read and write early on at school, all other aspects of the curriculum remain out of reach. Literacy is the *sine qua non* of educational success and was quite rightly central to Labour's drive on education standards. In 1999, the Moser Report found that 6 percent of Britain's adult population had a 'very low' literacy level, and a further 13 percent had a 'low' literacy level, defined as below that expected of an 11-year-old child. In practical terms, this meant that one in five British adults could not—for example—use a telephone directory to locate the details of a plumber.[9]

It was during the 1990s that organisations began conducting international surveys of education attainment, which now play such a significant role in today's education debates. In 1997, the OECD conducted a small-scale survey of literacy levels in 12 different countries. A forerunner of the PISA reports, it placed 23 percent of British adults in their lowest category for literacy. This was ahead of only Poland and Ireland and well behind the likes of Australia, Canada, Germany, and the Netherlands.[10] Education reformers who focus on basic skills such as literacy are often accused of being reductionist. Once I became Schools Minster, I was frequently told that education is about so much more than learning to read. It is, of course. However, one should never forget the pain of being illiterate in the modern world. It is a miserable fate for any individual to suffer, bringing with it embarrassment, low self-esteem, and severely curtailed employment prospects. For a developed nation such as the UK to have millions of functionally illiterate citizens is an unforgivable waste of human potential. During the 1990s, the effect of this failure could be seen across British society, from classrooms to job centres, to jails—where surveys still show that well over half the inmates are functionally illiterate.

On becoming Secretary of State, David Blunkett promised to raise the proportion of eleven-year-olds reaching the 'expected standard' of literacy and numeracy from 63 percent in 1997 to 80 percent by 2002 or else resign as Education Secretary.[11] His means for fulfilling this promise was the much-vaunted National Literacy Strategy, a hugely ambitious programme to provide training and materials for primary teaching across the country, at the eventual cost of £531 million by 2004.[12] Launched in 1998, the National Strategies had been running for five years when I joined the Education Select Committee. David Blunkett's target had not been met, but as he had been promoted to Home Secretary, his promise to resign was quietly forgotten.

Nevertheless, a large improvement had been reported, with 75 percent of 11-year-olds reaching the expected standard in English in the summer of 2003.

However, there was widespread suspicion that this improvement did not reflect genuine change, particularly among secondary school teachers who found pupils arriving in Year 7 having supposedly 'passed' their Year 6 National Curriculum Assessments but still struggling to read. As will be covered in Chapter 3, this suspicion was reinforced by academic research suggesting much of this improvement had been gained due to grade inflation.

Grade inflation or not, there were still over 150,000 children leaving primary school each year unable to read at the expected standard despite five years of energetic and costly reform. As I became more and more preoccupied with discovering the root cause of this failure, the same name kept coming up as someone I needed to meet: a primary school headteacher who was achieving extraordinary things in one of the most deprived areas of London. Her name was Ruth Miskin, and she was using an approach called phonics. I arranged to have tea with Ruth in January 2004, and it would prove to be the most consequential meeting of my career. Looking back, my journey towards being an education reformer began that afternoon.

Ruth Miskin

When I met Ruth in the lobby of St Ermin's Hotel in Westminster, she had recently finished her third headship in a 34-year teaching career. The daughter of two teachers, my first impression was what an exceptional headteacher she must have been. Slight in stature but fizzing with energy, she combined warmth with firmness and—as she explained her approach to teaching reading—would ensure my attention never wandered with a disarming habit of asking questions to check my understanding. Born in Wigan, her mild northern accent would become more pronounced as her moral outrage at childhood illiteracy grew. However, unlike many of the critics of Britain's education system that I had met, Ruth was no defeatist. The only thing stronger than her fury at childhood illiteracy was her conviction that it could be solved.

As a young teacher during the late 1970s, Ruth had followed the prevalent method of the day for teaching reading, known as 'whole-word'. This method involved teaching children to memorise words by sight with little attention to letters. As such, children learnt through 'reading schemes', which were made up of books with a steadily increasing number of words, books such as *Peter and Jane* or *Roger Red Hat.* Having been appointed Deputy Headteacher of a Dorset primary school in 1982, Ruth, along with many others, fell under the influence of the American psycholinguists Frank Smith and Kenneth Goodman, who promoted a 'real books' approach to teaching reading. This approach rejected the whole-word reading schemes as dull and advocated that pupils learn to read through generously illustrated 'real books' instead. In theory, through multiple readings of these stories, children would learn to read words by internalising their meanings, and eventually, their understanding of the role being played by individual letters would emerge. In practice, pupils were memorising the stories but not learning to read the words. Consequently, Ruth saw reading scores for pupils at her Dorset school plummet following the introduction of this approach.

Ruth progressed to headships in Plymouth and Leeds, and at each school she was concerned about the number of pupils who left each year still unable to read. Some of these pupils were being diagnosed with learning difficulties such as having Special Educational Needs (SEN), but Ruth suspected a more accurate diagnosis for many of these children might be ABT—'Ain't Being Taught'. After seven years in primary education, they were being failed in the most basic way possible.

In 1994, Ruth was appointed headteacher of a new primary school in Tower Hamlets, a deprived borough in London's old East End with a predominantly Bangladeshi population. It was named Kobi Nazrul Primary School after the national poet of Bangladesh. At Kobi Nazrul, 95 percent of the pupils spoke a language other than English at home, the majority a Bangladeshi dialect called Sylheti. Ruth knew the sooner she could get her pupils reading with fluency, the sooner they would read independently and gain a thirst for learning. However, for such pupils, learning to read could not be left to trial and error, and their parents would struggle to help at home. If these pupils were going to succeed, they needed to start reading via the surest route possible. Ruth began to supplement the reading schemes used in her previous schools with whole-class teaching of the alphabetic code. She was aware that this approach—known as 'phonics'—was once used in primary schools. However, having trained to teach during the 1970s, she had never actually seen a phonics scheme in practice. So, she began creating her own.

The English language has 26 letters and 44 different sounds. There are over 100 common ways of representing these sounds using different combinations of letters. For example, the sound 'j', can be written with 'j' in *jam*; 'ge' in *george*; 'g' in 'gym'; and 'dge' in 'budge'. This makes English a most difficult alphabetic code to learn, compared to languages such as Spanish, where the correspondence of sounds to letters is straightforward. The entire way in which teachers of Ruth's generation had been trained was based on the belief that pupils' understanding of these letters and sounds would emerge through reading schemes or—latterly—real books. She came to realise that this belief, though well-intentioned, was ill-founded.

Ruth developed a teaching scheme which gave the children at Kobi Nazrul an intensive introduction to the relationship between letters and sounds and how to blend those sounds into words. This introduction was approached in a structured fashion, starting with single letters, then letter pairs such as 'ch', and ending with more complex graphemes, such as 'igh'. Once this was complete, pupils would be ready to move on to read simple, easily decodable books to fit with pupils' level of phonic knowledge. As Ruth developed her approach to teaching reading, her pupils' pass rates in reading assessments and—more importantly—confidence as readers began to turn a corner.

As a new school, Kobi Nazrul grew from the ground up one year at a time, giving Ruth and her team the perfect opportunity to develop a scheme for teaching phonics in a methodical fashion. By the time the first cohort of Kobi Nazrul pupils left the school in 2001, every single one of them had reached the Department for Education's expected standard of reading. This was a significantly higher proportion than at Ruth's previous school, in a middle-class suburb of Leeds, demonstrating one of her key convictions—social deprivation need not be a barrier to becoming a proficient reader. Kobi Nazrul was made one of David Blunkett's 'Beacon Schools', and teachers came in droves to witness the achievement of its pupils and learn how it was being done. Ruth even began running Saturday morning sessions for teachers who, afraid of their school finding out they were interested in teaching phonics, needed to attend covertly.

Speaking to Ruth over tea that afternoon in 2004, I kept on asking her why this patently successful approach was still so rare in our primary schools. Her response was one that I would hear again and again—it was quite simply 'not allowed'. Thus began my education about the 'reading wars', which had been raging through the education sector for over half a century.

Reading Wars

The rival approaches of whole-word versus phonics teaching date right back to the early twentieth century. By the middle of the century, the consensus amongst primary school teachers appears to have been that both approaches had their relative merits, and a mixture of whole-word and phonics teaching was the best means of ensuring all children in a school learnt to read. As the *Plowden Report* observed in 1967:

> Children are helped to read by memorising the look of words and phrases, often with the help of pictures, by guessing from a context which is likely to bring them success, and by phonics, beginning with initial sounds. They are encouraged to try all the methods available to them and not to depend on only one method. Instead of relying on one reading scheme, many teachers use a range of schemes with different characteristics, selecting carefully for each child.[13]

However, as child-centred teaching became an orthodoxy in English schools, the phonics component of teaching children to read was increasingly dismissed. Phonics teaching is unavoidably teacher-led, often involving teachers holding up flashcards and asking a whole class of pupils to repeat them back as sounds. During the 1960s, this led phonics teaching to be criticised as boring, and it was often caricatured as asking rows of children to 'bark at print.' In addition, whole-word advocates argued that the phonetic code in English is so inconsistent that learning to read through phonics can be confusing for children. Words such as 'once' or 'tough' are challenging to decode using phonics, and—it was argued—much better to be learnt as complete words.

The whole-word approach was far better suited to the child-centred temperament of the times. Instead of a classroom of children looking up at a teacher and their flash cards, you could have a classroom scattered with children working out how to read at their own pace from their own picture books. Freed from the central authority of the teacher, children would learn not only how to read but how to love reading. By the time Ruth trained as a primary teacher during the late 1970s, the whole-word approach had become an orthodoxy, and phonics teaching something of a lost art. By the 1980s, it was the more radical successor of 'whole language', which was gaining popularity in the schools where Ruth worked, with its focus on pupils learning to read from real books. As such, Ruth's experience was not exceptional. In 1991, the NFER conducted a survey entitled *What Teachers in Training are Taught about Reading*, where they reviewed the core reading lists of 92 institutions of initial teacher training in Britain. Out of the 30 most popular books, 29 advocated a 'whole-word' approach, or that of its many successors—such as 'whole language', 'look-and-say', 'onset and rime', and 'real books'.[14]

Ruth was not alone in her attempt to develop new reading schemes based on phonics. Others were doing similarly, such as Sue Lloyd, who developed 'Jolly Phonics' at her Suffolk primary during the 1980s, and Irina Tyk, who developed 'Butterfly Phonics' whilst working as Headteacher of Holland House School during the 1990s. These phonics pioneers and their acolytes often had to pursue their work in the face of opposition from local authority advisers, school inspectors, and university education departments. They would joke that it was only when the door was closed, the blinds were down, and the corridors were empty that they felt able to take out their phonics flash cards. To support each other, this dissident group of phonics teachers created a campaign group known as the Reading Reform Foundation (RRF).

One of the key functions of the RRF was to popularise research evidence in favour of phonics which, though overwhelming, had been conspicuously absent from their own training. Much of this originated from the USA, where the Carnegie Corporation funded a systematic review of half a century of research into literacy teaching as far back as 1967. Led by Harvard Professor Dr Jeanne Chall, the final report *Learning to Read* came out in favour of phonics over whole-word approaches. Similarly, in 1990, the US Department of Education commissioned the cognitive psychologist Marlyn Jager Adams to provide a synthesis of all available evidence regarding the competing methods of teaching pupils to read. It also came out in favour of phonics. Regardless, the British education establishment remained wedded to the whole-word approach. As the educational psychologist Martin Turner, whose advocacy for phonics led him to lose his job at the Croydon Education Authority, wrote in 1996, 'Writers and lecturers genuinely seem never to have considered scientific evidence and, given a choice, always to prefer sentimental excitement.'[15]

By the time David Blunkett became Education Secretary in 1997, the RRF had enough clout for its members to advise on his landmark National Literacy Strategy (NLS). They pushed hard for the strategy to stipulate teaching phonics 'first and fast' but were unable to win the argument. The Teaching Framework that was distributed to schools in 1998 was a whole-word approach, with aspects of phonics to be used as a supplement—an approach often termed 'mixed methods', and similar in spirit to the extract of the 1967 *Plowden Report* quoted previously. As the NLS Framework stated:

> All teachers know that pupils become successful readers by learning to use a range of strategies to get at the meaning of a text. This principle is at the heart of the National Curriculum for English and has formed the basis of successful literacy teaching for many years. The range of strategies can be depicted as a series of searchlights, each of which sheds light on the text.[16]

In doing so, the designers of the NLS chose to try to please all the different camps of the reading wars over what was proven to work best. The result was, in the words of the teacher and phonics advocate Tom Burkard, 'a dog's breakfast of competing and often contradictory strategies, which leave many children hopelessly confused.'[17] As Ruth Miskin later explained in her oral evidence to the Education Select Committee in 2005:

> [As a child], if you have to work very hard at reading every single word that you come across, asking yourself 'Shall I use a picture cue? Shall I use a context cue? Shall I use a picture cue with a letter cue? Shall I read on a little bit and try to work out what the word is in the middle?' the child cannot make that decision while they are reading. The children who are at the lower end find that almost impossible to do, so they then get the image of themselves as not very good readers.

In the same evidence session, Ruth set out the approach she believes most effectively teaches children to read.

> We taught children . . . basic letter sounds really, really quickly, so that they could read them effortlessly and then they could read some words effortlessly and the impact that can have, the empowering effect on children who may have been considered in the past not to be able to read, or hard to teach to read, was massive. . . . If a child can decode a text effortlessly, it means all their resources, all their energies go into working out what the book is about.[18]

Following the launch of the NLS, Ruth brimmed with frustration that hundreds of millions of pounds were about to be spent on a government strategy that did not take an evidence-led approach. She told officials that at Kobi Nazrul, she would refuse to adopt the National Literacy Strategy, continue to teach using phonics, outperform the national average for pupil achievement, and tell the press how deficient she believed the NLS to be (all of which she subsequently did).[19] By the time Ruth and I met in 2004, she had left headship and was travelling the country training teachers to adopt the phonics scheme she had developed after leaving Kobi Nazrul, called Read Write Inc. In our subsequent meetings, Ruth suggested that I should attend one of her phonics training courses to enable me to really understand this debate. On 13 and 14 June 2004, I joined the Read Write Inc training session at Lansbury Lawrence Primary School in Tower Hamlets. During my two days, I saw how phonics teaching was anything but the dull, repetitive didacticism of caricature, but instead engaging, enjoyable, and—most importantly of all—effective. This immersion in the fundamentals of literacy teaching and the depth of understanding about the debate that it gave me would pay significant dividends once in office.

Clackmannanshire

As my interest in the reading debate snowballed, I became friendly with leading lights of the Reading Reform Foundation, such as Debbie Hepplewhite, Jennifer Chew, Elizabeth Nonweiler, and Sue Lloyd. Back in the early 2000s, they were all speaking with excitement about events north of the border, where a seven-year investigation into teaching reading was reaching its conclusion in Scotland. Clackmannanshire is an area of social deprivation situated in Scotland's old industrial heartland. To combat widespread pupil illiteracy, its council launched an Early Learning Initiative and—employing a level of evidential rigour that was rare in education reform at the time—conducted a controlled trial of three different reading schemes. Carried out across 19 local primary schools by two academics—Rhona Johnston of Hull University and Joyce Watson of St Andrew's University—it was one of the most authoritative trials of reading schemes ever conducted in Britain.

Around 300 children in their first year of primary school were divided into three groups. One group would be taught using an analytic phonics method with a whole-word basis, similar to the NLS.* The second group would be taught using the same analytic phonics method but supplemented with some direct teaching of phonemes. The third group would be taught using a 16-week systematic synthetic phonics programme. The pupils taught using the synthetic phonics programme pulled ahead immediately. At the end of the first 16 weeks, they were reading words around seven months ahead of their chronological age, whilst the two analytic phonics groups remained at their chronological reading age. In addition, the systematic, synthetic phonics group's spelling was seven months ahead of chronological age, some eight to nine months ahead of the other two groups.[20] Anne Pearson, headteacher of Park Primary School, Alloa, reported, 'The children are a year ahead of their

---

* Confusingly, by the time of the NLS, many fundamentally whole-word approaches had taken to calling themselves 'analytic phonics', because they were designed for pupils to read words 'analytically' and then link phonics with sounds. This led to a common misunderstanding that the NLS heralded a 'return to phonics'. To combat this misunderstanding, phonics advocates rebranded their favoured approach systematic, synthetic phonics to distinguish themselves from the analytic phonics camp.

chronological age. They have done two years' work in one year. It is fantastic.' She added, 'This is the most deprived school in Clackmannanshire. The teachers have learned you should not put a ceiling on children's learning abilities.'[21]

The Clackmannanshire study went public in November 1998 and was widely reported. 'Scots throw down literacy gauntlet', wrote the *TES*, adding, 'Pupils taught using the new method did far better than those following the one advocated by the Government.'[22] An editorial in the *Scotsman* dubbed systematic phonics 'the holy grail in education'. Its author suggested the success of this phonics scheme might spur an embrace of whole-class, teacher-led lessons more broadly but was clearly aware of the strength of ideological opposition. They sagely observed: 'The modern orthodoxy of child-centred education is a phrase with great power . . . even though the Clackmannanshire and other research begs the question of whether this method actually delivers.'[23]

As was predicted, the anti-phonics lobby dismissed the evidence from Clackmannanshire, claiming that the early advantage gained by pupils in the synthetic phonics group would be 'washed out' by the time they finished primary school. It was said those learning through other approaches would eventually catch up. To test this hypothesis, Joyce Watson and Rhona Johnston returned to the schools in question six years later, in 2004, when the pupils involved in the original trial were about to leave for secondary school. Far from being washed out, the early advantage of systematic, synthetic phonics had compounded over the years. Now aged 10 to 11, these pupils were three years six months ahead of their chronological age in word reading, one year nine months ahead in spelling, and three and a half months ahead in reading comprehension (a less dramatic increase, as comprehension relies on general knowledge as well as the ability to read words). These results suggested that systematic phonics gave pupils early confidence in reading, which helped them improve at a faster rate throughout primary school. In addition, systematic synthetic phonics teaching had narrowed the gap between Clackmannanshire pupils from disadvantaged homes and their peers, and—unusually for primary-age children—boys were outperforming girls.[24]

Teachers involved in the trial, many of whom had been initially sceptical, reported a Damascene conversion to phonics. Lorna Spence, headteacher of Deerpark Primary School, reported:

> Our heads are up—staff, pupils and parents. The feeling of professional satisfaction that comes from being part of an exciting and ongoing success story is the reason why each and every one of us came into teaching—to know that we can make a difference![25]

2005 Phonics Campaign

As a member of the Education and Skills Select Committee, I was electrified by the results of the Clackmannanshire study. In February 2005, I wrote to the Labour

Education Secretary Ruth Kelly, asking her to undertake an immediate review of the place of phonics in the National Literacy Strategy in light of this new evidence. I wrote to the Director of Education at West Sussex County Council, the education authority serving my constituency, enclosing a summary of the Clackmannanshire study and asking what action they intended to take. Finally, I wrote to every one of my fellow MPs suggesting they send similar enquiries to Directors of Education at Local Authorities serving their own constituencies. More evidence was coming from elsewhere. In 2000, a multi-million-dollar National Research Panel established by the United States Congress to investigate the teaching of literacy completed its work. The final report concluded that 'Findings provided solid support for the conclusion that systematic phonics instruction makes a bigger contribution to children's growth in reading than alternative programs providing unsystematic or no phonics instruction.'[26] Five years later, a report by the Australian National Inquiry into the Teaching of Literacy reached the same conclusion in favour of direct systematic instruction in phonics.[27]

Even more pleasingly, teachers who used phonics schemes were becoming more vocal back home. Speaking to the *Guardian* in 2005, Shahed Ahmed, the head of Elmhurst primary school in East London, praised Ruth's Read Write Inc programme. With 950 pupils, 25 languages spoken at home, and 40 percent of pupils on free school meals, Elmhurst was the sort of school where 20 percent of children would regularly leave each year below the expected standard. But systematic phonics teaching was ending that record. 'It is these struggling children who are making the most progress', Shahed reported, 'The change in self-esteem has been enormous.'[28] Shahed would go on to become a good friend and trusted adviser.

With increased national attention on phonics, I persuaded the Labour Chair of the Select Committee to hold an inquiry into the teaching of reading. It took place between November and December 2004, with both Sue Lloyd and Debbie Hepplewhite of the RRF giving evidence, as well as Ruth Miskin and Professor Rhona Johnston, the co-author of the Clackmannanshire Study. The Select Committee's report, published on 31 March 2005, recommended that the government review the National Literacy Strategy. During Prime Minister's Questions that week, I asked Tony Blair on the floor of the House of Commons whether he would ask his new Education Secretary, Ruth Kelly, to follow our recommendation. Perhaps knowing this was coming, Kelly had written an opinion piece for the *Guardian* defending the NLS the previous day. She argued that phonics must not be seen as a 'magic bullet' for illiteracy and concluded, 'we are clear that the way forward is not a prescriptive and reductionist approach to phonics, to the exclusion of all else.'[29] The anti-phonics lobby clearly had her ear, as this was one of their common lines of argument. Phonics advocates never insisted that literacy teaching should end with phonics; of course, reading books for pleasure would follow. But we did insist literacy teaching should start with phonics, 'first and fast'. This insistence led us to be accused of dogmatism, whilst our opponents could occupy the perceived moral high ground of pluralism with their arguments for 'mixed methods'.

However, these arguments were crumbling in the face of evidence. A general election was held that summer, and Conservative party leader Michael Howard made phonics a campaign issue, pledging to stipulate synthetic phonics teaching in all primary schools.[30] Three days before the election, on 2 May 2005, *The Times* leader celebrated that there was 'evolving acceptance' in both the Labour and Conservative parties of the importance of phonics, and attributed this development to 'the crusading efforts of one Tory MP, Nick Gibb'.[31] Labour won the election, but I won my own small battle. The following month on 3 June, Ruth Kelly launched a review of how reading is taught in England's primary schools. The government announcement stated that 'the debate now centres not on whether to teach phonics but how.'[32] The former Director of Inspection at Ofsted, Jim Rose, was appointed to conduct the review.

The Rose Review reported its findings in March 2006. Although the language was at times ambiguous, Rose clearly recommended that a new NLS should have the discrete teaching of phonics at its centre. It was my first real victory, and the campaign had taught me two important lessons. Firstly, the importance of following the evidence, even when opponents within the education sector insist 'the research' is on their side. Secondly, and more pertinently, it taught me the importance of forming relationships with members of the profession. Having never been a teacher, many sought to caricature my phonics campaign as the obsession of a nostalgic, backward-looking Tory. However, the knowledge that I was helping to give voice to teachers with decades of experience, such as Ruth Miskin, Sue Lloyd, and Shahed Ahmed, gave me the confidence and courage to push on with our campaign.

Backlash

As soon as Jim Rose's interim report was published in December 2005, the anti-phonics lobby took up arms. For the first time, I saw the full force of the education establishment at work, as teaching unions, university academics, local authorities, and even government agencies tried to derail the Labour government's backing of phonics. The General Secretary of the NUT, the UK's largest teaching union, set out his opposition, telling the *Guardian* that teachers should not be made to follow a single technique, concluding: 'They know that to teach reading effectively there must be a range of strategies to hand.' The ATL union followed suit, stating, 'Teachers and children do not need a new literacy strategy that dictates what to do on a daily basis.'[33] In December 2006, some 100 experts, including union leaders, university academics, national advisers, heads, and teachers, signed a joint letter to the *TES* expressing grave concern at the government's backing of phonics.[34]

Two years later, the NUT's executive committee proposed a motion to create their own reading scheme to rival the government approach, based on a range of strategies including whole word and picture books.[35] I am not sure it ever came to fruition. Most worryingly, officials at the government's own agencies worked to undermine the push on phonics. Mike Lloyd Jones was a former primary head-teacher and Regional Director for the National Literacy Strategy at the time and saw this process from the inside. He wrote in his 2010 book *Phonics and the Resistance to Reading*:

> The Labour Government had allowed an extraordinary position to develop in which a range of publicly funded bodies seemed able to pursue individual policies orthogonal to national policy. In some educational quangos—for example the chronically-dysfunctional Qualifications and Curriculum Authority—individual officials behaved at times as though they believed that they were entitled to issue whatever guidance they pleased.

Lloyd Jones went on to describe how responsibility for implementing the new National Strategy was given to Local Authority advisers and school improvement partners, who were 'actively opposed to phonics and colluded with poor teaching and low standards.'[36] It was an instructive, if depressing, lesson on how challenging it can be to achieve alignment when pushing against an orthodoxy.

Following the election, Michael Howard appointed me as Shadow Minister for Schools, a job I had long desired. Working alongside me would be the newly appointed Shadow Education Secretary, a young and impressive new MP named David Cameron. He was a leading advocate of the need for the Conservative Party to modernise if it was to get back into government, an analysis I shared. He was also passionate about education reform and firmly supported what he called my 'zealous' drive for academic standards. Of course, Cameron would soon become the Conservative Party leader, having led the shadow education team for just six months. However, he started the process of designing the reform programme which we were to adopt in government, and his steadfast commitment to that programme as Prime Minister would play a critical role in its success.

I took my appointment as Shadow Schools Minister in 2005 seriously. I was determined to understand not only the day-to-day challenges of teachers and head-teachers but also the underlying causes of the UK and England's low ranking in international surveys. I would visit at least one school a week across the country, a routine I maintained through the next five years in opposition and continued as a Minister, working on the basis that—if you are willing to get up early—you can arrive at any school in England by 11am. Normally, this was on a Monday, as that was when I would be freest from the Party whip (being required to vote in the House of Commons). Making such visits was the only way to gain a true understanding of the quality of education, including curriculum and teaching methods, in English schools. I also saw first-hand the dire behaviour challenges many schools were confronting. However, I still struggled to understand why school improvement was still proving so elusive despite the enormous injections of money and energy given to schools by the New Labour government. Thankfully, one year after my appointment, I discovered a writer whose insights would be fundamental to answering that question.

Notes

1 James Callaghan's 'Ruskin College speech', *Ruskin College Oxford*, 18 October 1976.
2 B. Plowden, *The Plowden Report: Children and their Primary Schools, A Report of the Central Advisory Council for Education*, vol. I, London: Her Majesty's Stationery Office, 1967, p. 460.
3 *New Labour: Because Britain Deserves Better*, London: Labour Party Sales, 1997.
4 Ruth Lupton and Polina Obolenskaya, 'Labour's record on education: Policy, spending and outcomes 1997–2010', *Social Policy in a Cold Climate Working Paper WP03*, 2013, p. 17.
5 The £290 million figure is the sum of annual spending figures on Education Action Zones, provided for me by the House of Commons Library.
6 'Gilbert lambasts specialist schools programme', *The Guardian*, 29 November 2007.
7 National Foundation for Educational Research (NFER), 'Excellence in cities: The national evaluation of a policy to raise standards in urban schools 2000–2003', *Queen's Printer and Controller of HMSO*, 2005. Figure for overall cost is the sum of annual spending figures on Excellence in Cities, provided for me by the House of Commons Library.
8 David Blunkett, *On a Clear Day*, London: Michael O'Mara, 2002, p. 52.
9 *Improving Literacy and Numeracy: A Fresh Start (The Moser Report)*, London: Department of Education and Employment, 1999, p. 16.
10 *The Moser Report*, p. 17.
11 Recounted in Tom Burkard, *After the Literacy Hour: May the Best Plan Win!*, London: Centre for Policy Studies, 2004, p. 1.
12 Hansard House of Commons Debate, vol. 480, 14 October 2008.
13 Plowden, *The Plowden Report*, p. 212.
14 G. Brooks et al., *What Teachers in Training are Taught about Reading*, London: NFER, 1992.
15 Martin Turner, 'Foreword: Educating the educators', in B. Macmillan (ed.), *Why Schoolchildren Can't Read*, London: Institute of Economic Ideas, 1996, p. 9.
16 *The National Literacy Strategy: Framework for Teaching YR to Y6*, London: Department for Education and Skills, 1998, p. 3.
17 Burkard, *After the Literacy Hour*, p. 6.
18 *Education and Skills Committee—Eight Report,* London: House of Commons, 2005.
19 For example, see 'Phonics' first lady sheds ex-factor', *TES Magazine*, 29 July 2005.
20 Rhona Johnston and Joyce Watson, *The Effects of Synthetic Phonics Teaching on Reading and Spelling Attainment: A Seven Year Longitudinal Study*, Edinburgh: The Scottish Executive, 2005.
21 'Scots throw down literacy gauntlet', *TES Magazine*, 6 November 1998.
22 'Scots throw down literacy gauntlet', 6 November 1998.
23 Leader, 'Dare we return to "traditional" teaching methods?' *The Scotsman*, 28 October 1998.
24 Rhona Johnston and Joyce Watson, *The Effects of Synthetic Phonics Teaching on Reading and Spelling Attainment: A Seven Year Longitudinal Study*, Edinburgh: The Scottish Executive, 2005.
25 Quoted in a case study of Deepark Primary School in Jolly Phonics's promotional material.
26 National Reading Panel, *Teaching Children to Read: An Evidence-Based Assessment of the Scientific Research Literature on Reading and Its Implications for Reading Instruction*, 2000, pp. 2–92.

27 National Inquiry into the Teaching of Literacy, *Teaching Reading: Reports and Recommendations*, Australian Government Department of Education, Science and Training, 2005.

28 Geraldine Bedell, 'When words fail them', *The Guardian*, 20 February 2005.

29 R. Kelly, 'Reading for purpose and pleasure', *The Guardian*, 5 April 2005.

30 H. Mulholland, 'Howard bets on phonics to improve literacy', *The Guardian*, 14 April 2005.

31 Leader, 'Knowledge and power', *The Times*, 2 May 2005.

32 M. Taylor, 'Unacceptable literacy level leads to teaching review', *The Guardian*, 3 June 2005.

33 R. Smithers, 'Teachers' anger at Kelly U-turn over phonics', *The Guardian*, 2 December 2005.

34 S. Gray, 'Experts slam the phonics enforcers', *TES Magazine*, 1 December 2006.

35 'Teachers call for return to the liberal 1980s', *The Guardian*, 24 March 2008.

36 M. Lloyd-Jones, *Phonics and the Resistance to Reading*, Howl Books, 2013, Chapter 9.

2 Peak Progressivism

> I would label myself a political liberal and an educational conservative, or perhaps more accurately, an educational pragmatist. Political liberals really ought to oppose progressive educational ideas because they have led to practical failure and greater social inequity.
>
> E. D. Hirsch, The Schools We Need and why
> We Don't Have Them (1996)

In the summer of 2006, I boarded a plane for a holiday to South Carolina with my now husband, Michael Simmonds, feeling frustrated by the backlash against the Rose Review and its endorsement of phonics. I kept asking myself: how could so many well-meaning educators, confronted with clear evidence on how best to teach children to read, particularly the disadvantaged, still side with ideology over evidence? The answer to that question, it would transpire, lay in my luggage. My researcher at the time was Edward Hardman, who also happened to be Michael's nephew. He had come across an American academic named E. D. Hirsch and suggested I read his books, in particular his 1996 work *The Schools We Need and why We Don't Have Them*. However, freed from the daily grind of life in Westminster, I spent my time on the beach reading a novel. Michael took it upon himself to read the book instead and, having finished it, insisted that I really had to read it. Once I started, I understood why. Reading Hirsch, I had the strange sensation that he had taken my own inchoate and disparate thoughts on education and turned them into an articulate plan of action.

Hirsch had begun his career as a Professor of English Literature at Yale University. However, it was at the University of Virginia that he became interested in studies of reading comprehension. In 1978, he gave a group of disadvantaged, predominantly African American, community college students a text to read on the theme of friendship and an extract on the American Civil War from a popular collection of historical essays. With the text on friendship, their reading comprehension was on par with their wealthier peers. However, they fared far worse with a passage on the Civil War. The challenge for the students was not the words but the knowledge that lay behind them. Consider the following sentence: 'Grant, the

DOI: 10.4324/9781003533474-3

son of a tanner on the western frontier, was everything Lee was not.' The students had no prior knowledge that Ulysses S. Grant was the general of the Union Army or that Robert E. Lee was his Confederate opponent, let alone what it meant to grow up on the 'western frontier'. Deprived of a knowledge-based education, these community college students were left struggling to comprehend a text about a pivotal moment in their nation's history.[1]

Hirsch had always taken such historical knowledge amongst students for granted, so this experience left him—in his words—'shocked into educational reform'. He let go of his career as a university academic and, in 1987, wrote a book entitled *Cultural Literacy*, arguing that American schools needed to teach a curriculum based on 'core knowledge'. This struck a chord with the American public, and *Cultural Literacy* stayed on the *New York Times* bestseller list for 26 weeks. Hirsch went on to develop his Core Knowledge Curriculum for grades K to 8 (aged 6 to 14), which still runs out of the Virginia foundation he established and is taught in over 600 American schools today.

On the beach that summer in South Carolina, I read Hirsch's 1996 follow-up book *The Schools We Need: and Why We Don't Have Them*. In this work, Hirsch widened his scope away from the need to place knowledge at the foundation of a school curriculum to a general critique of the damage caused by what he termed the progressive education 'thoughtworld' in America. This thoughtworld, it turned out, was almost indistinguishable from the progressivist ideology in Britain. Hirsch explained how the thoughtworld had taken over the American education establishment during the twentieth century, constantly rebranding itself with new names ('child-centred schooling', 'discovery learning', the 'project method') as old ideas were dressed up as new solutions to school failure. Throughout the twentieth century, progressive education had rebranded itself to provide a 'new' solution to overcome the issues it had itself caused. As Hirsch pithily described it, it was the 'orthodoxy masquerading as reform'.[2]

The book also helped to explain the ideological convictions which led teachers in America and Britain, *en masse*, to do something so counter-intuitive as abandoning knowledge from their school curriculum. He explained how what he termed 'educational formalism' had advanced the argument that inculcating formal skill is more important than transmitting knowledge; thus, school curriculums began attempting to teach all-purpose goals such as 'higher-order skills', 'self-esteem', 'metacognition', and 'critical thinking.'[3] In the view of progressive educators, knowledge was not a means of acquiring these skills but an impediment to doing so. As he wrote, '"Mere facts" are seen to be indissolubly connected to "rote learning", which may be the most disparaging phrase in the "progressivist" educationalists' glossary.'[4]

Reading this passage, I was taken straight back to an encounter I once had with a headteacher in Rotherham following my selection to contest its seat in a 1994 by-election. Visiting her school as a local Parliamentary candidate, she explained how she had completed an 'audit' of her school library, removing any old-fashioned books that simply conveyed information. She explained that education was not about equipping children to take part in general knowledge quizzes but instead 'learning for life'. At the time, I could not understand the thought process that had led to such a decision. Reading Hirsch, I was able to do so. What is more, through Hirsch's scrupulous reference to evidence from cognitive psychology, I better understood why such an aversion to knowledge would prove to be so damaging. The paradox of abandoning knowledge in favour of skills is that it is impossible to acquire skills such as 'critical thinking' without a fundamental grounding in knowledge. This argument was later developed by Hirsch's colleague at the University of Virginia, Daniel Willingham (see Chapter 5).

Alongside 'educational formalism', Hirsch argued the second pillar of progressive education was 'education naturalism'. This was the belief that the artificiality of formal school teaching, with its drill and practice, was detrimental to pupil learning. Instead, progressives believed that learning should—as far as possible—emulate the lifelike, thematic, holistic way in which we learn in the wider world. As he explained, 'In education, this optimistic cast of mind induces trust in the child's natural development, and suspicion of harsh discipline, bookish hard work, and other forms of artificial stimulation and constraint.'[5] Hirsch made the crucial observation that children from disadvantaged backgrounds suffer most from the optimism which leads schools to abandon formal approaches. Whilst pupils from advantaged backgrounds may have the parental support and cultural capital to do well in such an environment, those without such a head start simply fall further behind. It is the tragedy of progressive education, Hirsch argued, that those with the fewest advantages in society suffered the most.

Hirsch explained how this progressivist ideology had become a professional creed from which few American teachers—if they wished for career advancement—could dissent. He also explained how the frequently invoked 'research base' for this thoughtworld was, in fact, built on sand. One by one, Hirsch slayed the sacred cows of progressivist ideology with rigorous reference to empirical research. 'Critical thinking skills'? Impossible to exercise without specific contextual knowledge. 'Multiple Intelligences'? Never accepted by the psychological community. 'Learning Styles'? Probably don't exist either.

In Chapter 5, 'Reality's Revenge: Education and Mainstream Research', Hirsch summarised three sources of academic research which—when applied to child-centred approaches—found them wanting. They were controlled trials of different teaching methods, basic research in cognition and learning, and large-scale international comparative studies. These three different areas of research had all independently shown that teacher-led instruction brings better results for pupils than a child-centred approach. As Hirsch wrote, 'There are few or no examples in the history of science where the same results, reached by three or more truly independent means, has been overturned.'[6]

Reading Hirsch's critique of education progressivism was a revelation. Since the 1960s, there has been no shortage of voices within British society bemoaning modern education. However, sober-minded critiques of misguided teaching methods were all too easily conflated with nostalgic attacks on everything, from the spread of sex education to the end of corporal punishment. This meant that since the 1960s, anyone attempting to—for example—suggest classrooms should be laid out in rows or pupils should memorise timetables risked being dismissed as a swivel-eyed reactionary. However, here was a liberal university professor with a committed belief in social justice providing a rigorously evidence-based critique of progressive education. Pivotal to Hirsch's work was his insistence that curriculum debates must be depoliticised. He confronted the caricature of knowledge-based, teacher-led schooling as somehow 'right wing' and reactionary as nonsense, arguing that all educators, regardless of political leanings, should be led by evidence.

A Rosetta Stone

The Schools We Need has shaped my thinking more than any other book on education. Perhaps most importantly, Hirsch taught me to understand the language of the education debate, a vital tool for any reformer, particularly one determined to challenge entrenched orthodoxies. He explained why seemingly benign phrases such as 'learning to learn', 'critical thinking', 'developmentally appropriate', and 'personalised learning' should be received with caution. He also provided my first encounter with concepts such as 'working memory', the 'Matthew Effect', and the eminently pragmatic 'Principles of Instruction' devised by psychologist Barak Rosenshine—all of which have since played a central role in equipping teachers in England to devise alternatives to the progressivist ideology.

Reading Hirsch's critique of progressive education acted as a Rosetta Stone, gifting me with a code book to the progressivist lexicon. To aid his reader's mastery of this language, Hirsch even includes a glossary of education jargon in the back of his book, complete with wry definitions. For 'passive listening', Hirsch writes:

> a progressivist phrase caricaturing 'traditional' education, which makes children sit silently in rows in 'factory-model schools,' passively listening to what the teacher has to say, then merely memorizing facts.[7]

'Research has shown' is:

> a phrase used to preface and shore up educational claims. Often it is used selectively, even when the preponderant or most reliable research shows no such thing, as in the statement 'Research has shown that children learn best with hands-on methods.'[8]

Reading Hirsch's analysis gave me the vocabulary to identify, understand, and resist the progressivist ideology. Ideologies survive by making their ideas implicit in the everyday language adopted by institutions. Once I became a Minister in 2010, this insight from Hirsch emboldened me to be ruthless in editing every White Paper, policy position, and guidance document published by the Department. Without a concerted counter-effort at the Ministerial level to expunge the lexicon of progressive education, I knew it would inevitably seep back into government policy-making. As any official who sat in meetings with me from 2010 onwards might attest, my dog-eared, much-annotated copy of *The Schools We Need* made continual appearances.

Quango Unchained

Introducing his glossary, Hirsch describes his book as 'a kind of typhoid-tetanus shot' against the education establishment. I could not have received this treatment at a better moment. Despite the initial promise of David Blunkett's reforms and the valiant work of Andrew Adonis as Schools Minster (see Chapter 3), by the later years of the Labour Government the education establishment was firmly in control of policy. From 2006 onwards, the progressivist ideology went into overdrive. Newly inoculated, I was ready to understand the implications.

In 2007, the Department for Education and Skills was renamed the Department for Children, Schools and Families (DCSF). Education was no longer even in the name. Nobody could quite remember the order of the letters, so Schools Minister Andrew Adonis devised a handy mnemonic: the Department for Cushions and Soft Furnishings. The DCSF had indeed gone soft. During these years, the Labour government moved away from its initial drive on standards and allowed the advocates for the progressivist ideology to make the weather. These ideologues found a comfortable home in the quangos that were created or expanded during the New Labour years. Quangos, standing for quasi-autonomous non-governmental organisations, are government agencies overseen by departments and tasked with administering particular aspects of public life. Properly established, they can provide important stability in the running of our public services. However, left unguarded, they are easily captured by ideologues and used to subvert government policy. In size alone, it was clear that the educational quangocracy was out of control by the late 2000s.

- The Qualifications and Curriculum Authority (QCA), which was responsible for overseeing the National Curriculum and associated assessments, was given new powers and saw its budget more than triple from £54.8 million in 1999 to £180 million in 2010.

- The Training and Development Agency (TDA), responsible for overseeing the training of new teachers, was expanded and saw its budget increase from £230 million in 2000 to £782 million in 2010.

- Specialist Schools and Academies Trust (SSAT), perhaps the most extreme proponent of the progressivist ideology, ballooned in size and influence under

Labour, seeing its annual budget grow from £3 million in 2000 to £44 million in 2008.[9]

Like many of these organisations, the SSAT was originally established by a Conservative Government. It had its origins in a small Trust established to support City Technology Colleges (see Chapter 3), but it underwent a complete transformation during the 2000s. In 2002, David Hargreaves, a well-known educationalist of notably progressivist views, was appointed as the SSAT's Associate Director. He produced 23 pamphlets advocating the complete system-redesign of our schools. As a 2009 profile of David in the *Guardian* stated, 'If the mist cleared and politicians and newspaper editors fully understood what Hargreaves was up to, all hell would break loose.' It continued, 'Take any aspect of secondary schooling as we understand it—lessons, subjects, tests, year groups, the role of heads, the authority of teachers—and he challenges it.'[10]

A paper published in 2009 by the Centre for Policy Studies calculated that by 2007, the 11 largest education quangos had a combined annual budget of £1.2 billion.[11] And, together with the DCSF, they produced seemingly endless streams of guidance. A House of Lords committee report into the impact of guidance on schools recorded that in 2006–7, the Department and its agencies produced more than 760 documents for schools, almost four documents for every day of the school year.[12] Insulated from the impact of their ideas on the ground and seemingly free of ministerial or democratic control, quango officials could indulge in the furthest reaches of progressive education. Nowhere was this more evident than in the mania for 'personalised' learning, which played a central role in the Secretary of State Ed Balls's 2007 Children's Plan, pledging £1.2 billion of spending on personalised learning and special educational needs.[13] Talk of personalised learning sounded cutting edge, especially when accompanied by oft-repeated mantras about 'twenty-first century schools'. However, its implication was that lessons could be tailored to the interests and abilities of each child. In essence, this was the same child-centred attack on whole-class teaching that had been around since the 1960s, dressed up in the language of choice and modernity.

It is hard to convey just how voluminous the guidance to schools on personalised learning, and its various derivatives, became. Not just the DCSF, but quangos such as the QCA, TDA, and SSAT became mini-publishing houses, producing a stream of reports and pamphlets. The new Professional Standards from 2007 were just one example. Produced by the TDA, they were used to inform progression decisions throughout a teacher's career. These 33 separate standards were, in essence, the Department's official definition of what makes a good teacher. Standard 10 stated that teachers should 'Have a knowledge and understanding of . . . how to personalise learning'. Standard 19 stated that teachers should 'know how to make effective personalised provision for those they teach'. Standard 28 suggested that teachers 'support and guide learners to reflect on their learning . . . and identify their emerging learning needs'.[14] For any teacher wondering what 'personalisation' actually meant, the DCSF published 'Personalised Learning—A Practical Guide' in 2008. Its chapter on teaching and learning began with a quote from the 2007 Children's Plan, stating that effective teachers 'have the confidence to stand back and encourage pupils to become independent learners.'[15] It endorsed 'enquiry-based individual or group work', 'learning styles', and 'differentiation'—the idea that different lesson resources should routinely be produced for pupils of different abilities in the same class, a concept that became notorious amongst teachers for being as labour intensive as it was impractical. By searching for such terms on Google Ngram, one can see quite how prevalent these ideas became during the early years of the millennium. See Figure 2.1.

For many years, practically minded teachers in successful schools had been able to ignore publications promoting such concepts. However, no teacher could ignore Ofsted. Without a doubt, the school's inspectorate was the single most powerful enforcer of progressivist orthodoxy during the late 2000s. Like so many other agencies, Ofsted had been created by a Conservative government but became a very different animal during the New Labour years. From 2006 to 2011, the Chief Inspector leading Ofsted was Christine Gilbert. The year that she took the post, she published *2020 Vision*, a report commissioned by the then Secretary of State to establish how schools may look in 2020. Bringing together luminaries of the education quangos, it was a classic piece of education futurology, high on sweeping sentiment, low on evidence. It promoted the usual array of child-centred concepts: personalised learning, group work, project work, and pupils taking 'ownership' of their learning.[16]

From 2006 onwards, these concepts increasingly became the criteria by which schools and teachers were judged during inspections. Countless inspection reports from the time show Ofsted inspectors criticising successful schools where they observed teacher-led lessons whilst heaping praise on less successful schools which conformed to their progressivist ideology. This was a time when Ofsted inspectors still gave grades from 1 to 4 for individual teachers' lessons, so school

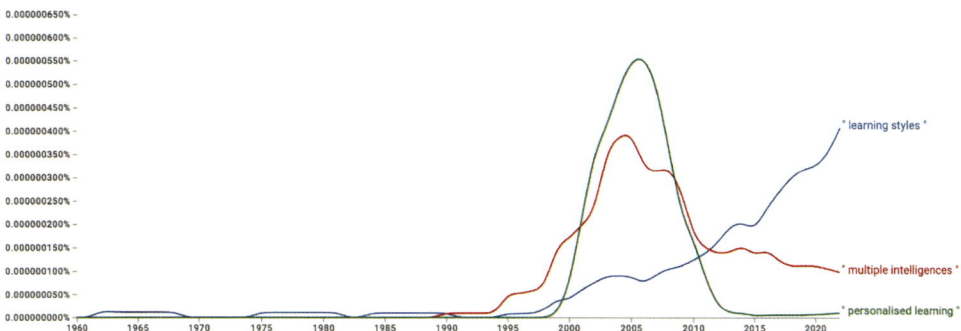

Figure 2.1 Google Ngram showing the increased popularity of key concepts from the progressivist ideology during the late 2000s, as measured by the incidence of appearances in Google's text corpora of published works in British English.

leaders felt forced to push their teachers towards child-centred approaches for the good of both them and the school. In 2010, a popular handbook entitled *The Perfect Ofsted Lesson* was published. Though not official guidance from the inspectorate, the authors were sure about what Ofsted wanted:

> a focus on learning, the development of thinking skills, opportunities for independent learning, a variety of strategies that take into account different elements of the individual learner's preferences, strengths and weaknesses, the use of positive emotions, great relationships, clear goals, metacognition, creativity and the willingness to take a risk or two . . .[17]

Since its creation in 1992, Ofsted has been synonymous in the public mind with school accountability and the drive for higher standards. Once in office, it took us some time to realise how far it had strayed from its original mission and become the education establishment's main means of enforcing the progressivist ideology.

Wacky Warehouses

In 2005, Tony Blair announced 'Building Schools for the Future' (BSF), a £55 billion programme to rebuild or renew every secondary school in England. A project of this type was undoubtedly needed, with many pupils still attending crumbling schools that had not been updated for decades. However, value for money was not a high priority, with superstar architects drafted in to build schools for three or four times the going rate: Norman Foster designed Bexley Business Academy in Kent (opened in 2003 at a total cost of £31 million)[18] and Capital City Academy in London (opened in 2008 at a total cost of £27 million),[19] whilst Zaha Hadid designed Evelyn Grace Academy (opened in 2008 at a total cost of £38 million).[20]

In many of these BSF projects, the progressivist ideology was built into the bricks and mortar of the school. A glossy 2004 guidance document produced by the DfES entitled 'Schools for the Future' was a worrying foretaste. The foreword by Schools Minister David Miliband promised that BSF would 'transform our secondary schools into innovative learning environments.'[21] Innovations described in the guidance included 'break out spaces', 'open plan learning areas', 'amorphous learning pods', and rooms of varying sizes with 'a variety of learning activities taking place within a single area'.

This marriage of architectural vanity and education ideology produced some disastrous results, and I still encounter teachers with horror stories about what came to be known as 'schools without walls'. Bexhill High Academy in East Sussex opened in 2010 at a cost of £38 million with 15 open-walled classrooms dubbed 'education pods', where 90 pupils would learn at a time. Two years later, it went into special measures, and five years later, *Schools Week* was reporting a £6 million grant from the DfE to add classrooms.[22] At the radically child-centred New Line Learning Academy in Kent (reported in 2010 to have the worst truancy rate in the country), pupils edited the school's Wikipedia page to complain that they could not learn in their open-plan classrooms.[23] At the £54 million Isle of Sheppey Academy,[24] one employee recounted on Twitter how staff gave the headteacher a standing ovation when he announced approval for classroom walls to be built.

The most notorious example was to the east of Liverpool in Knowsley, one of the most deprived boroughs in the country with consistently poor education outcomes. A new quango for delivering BSF called Partnerships for Schools led a project set upon the wholesale transformation of education in the borough. Eleven secondary schools were flattened, and in 2009, seven new schools were opened in their place, costing £157 million. Dubbed 'centres for learning', they had no classrooms but 'base areas' divided into different zones. The Knowsley Partnership was awarded 'best transformational learning strategy' at the 2008 'Excellence in BSF Awards'. Three years after the strategy was launched, Knowsley remained the worst performing Local Authority in the country on almost every measure, and many local residents had taken to calling their schools 'wacky warehouses'. In July 2013, only 381 of the 900 places at Christ the King Centre for Learning (cost £24 million) were filled. The school has since closed.[25]

Watching tens of millions of pounds being wasted on these vanity projects made me extremely angry. The education establishment seemed blind to the mistakes of the past—it was remarkable how closely the enthusiasm for classroom-free schools resembled the first flush of enthusiasm for open-plan classrooms during the 1970s. As a result, in each school, dozens of teachers struggled to keep control, and hundreds of pupils seethed with frustration at their inability to learn. It pains me to think not only how much better those millions of pounds could have been spent but also how many children were let down. There are no more concrete examples of the destructiveness of the progressivist ideology during the tail end of the New Labour years than these follies of educational futurism.

Pious Nothing-In-Particular

This resurgence of progressive education reached a new peak in 2007 when the QCA published a new national curriculum for England's secondary schools. They had resisted the pressure from many in the education establishment to abolish subject distinctions entirely. However, there was little else to be thankful for. Armed with an understanding from my reading of E. D. Hirsch about the dangers of a 'skills' or 'competency' based curriculum, I was aghast at what it contained. Subject content, the knowledge and understanding of the world with which pupils should be empowered by a school, was almost entirely absent; in its place was endless, for want of a better word, fluff. The 'Aims' of the National Curriculum were to enable young people to become three things: 'successful learners who enjoy learning, make progress and achieve'; 'confident individuals who are able to live safe, healthy and fulfilling lives'; and 'responsible citizens who make a positive contribution to society'.[26] All laudable aims, but rather beside the point when it comes to the nuts and bolts of planning a school curriculum. As Chris Woodhead, the former Ofsted Chief Inspector wrote in his 2009 book, *A Desolation of Learning*:

> [T]he underlying belief is that it is more important to teach children 'how to learn' than it is to open their eyes to the magic and mystery of the world that lies beyond their immediate experience. A curriculum that starts from the 'whole person' aim that children should become 'successful learners, confident individuals, and responsible citizens' is bound to result in a set of requirements that is anti-educational.[27]

His prediction was correct. For secondary school Geography, the 2007 National Curriculum did not name a single Geographical area with the exception of the European Union. Instead, it focused on 'Concepts' such as 'Physical and human processes' and 'Cultural understanding and diversity', and 'Processes' such as 'Geographical enquiry'. In 'History', it made no mention of any specific historical events aside from the two world wars and the Holocaust, and—in an explanatory note—the French Revolution and the Rise and Fall of the Roman Empire. Again, it focused instead on 'Concepts' such as 'Chronological understanding', 'Change and continuity', and 'Cause and consequence', and 'Processes' such as 'Using evidence'. As the journalist and author Phillip Hensher wrote in the *Independent* following the publication of the 2007 National Curriculum:

> Can the government really complain if the general public has the impression that education in schools nowadays appears to consist of a lot of pious nothing-in-particular? Nobody understands what their children are supposed to be learning, or how these ludicrous aims are supposed to be achieved.[28]

In truth, although the 2007 competence-based curriculum was the apotheosis of a progressivist anti-knowledge movement, the trend away from teaching a solid body of factual content had been in place for many years in Britain's schools. In a 2009 paper by an economics lecturer at Cardiff University, entitled 'The Strange Death of History Teaching', Derek Matthews reported the results of a short history quiz he had set for 284 undergraduates over a three-year period. In that test, 60 percent did not know Brunel's profession; 65 percent did not know who the reigning monarch was when the Spanish Armada attacked Britain; 83 percent did not know that Wellington led the British army at Waterloo, and a staggering 88 percent could not name a single nineteenth-century Prime Minister—not Disraeli, not Gladstone, not Peel. Matthews attributed this to the way history is taught in schools, as he wrote: 'children playing games, role playing, drawing pictures, engaging in group discussion, trying to imagine what it feels like to be a medieval peasant, or studying a range of historical source materials.' He identified the drive to teach 'historical skills' rather than history itself as a key cause of the problem.[29] Indeed, I remember visiting a secondary school in West Sussex (thankfully, not in my constituency) where a 12-year-old boy, wearing a toy princess's crown and wielding a plastic sword, was standing on a desk re-enacting some element of the Battle of Hastings. I bade a hasty exit from the classroom lest my ill-disciplined tongue let rip at my concern at what I was witnessing.

The Department for Education attracted much criticism from commentators, teachers, and parents for the 2007 curriculum, but I doubt whether the Department and its Ministers actually had much of a role in its creation. Such was the size and power of the education quangocracy New Labour had created; the Department was no longer at the helm of its own policy-making. This democratic deficit was further exacerbated by the constant churn of Ministers. During my five years shadowing the Department in opposition, there were three Secretaries of State for Education and four MPs as my opposite number as Schools Minister. Launched into the fray with little or no understanding of the education debates, they were powerless to resist the establishment's ideology, even if they wanted to. This was particularly the case for the National Strategies, which were outsourced to Capita, a private company. In retrospect, it is staggering to consider that Capita was given responsibility for a central plank of the government's reforming agenda. With almost no ministerial oversight, they sent out detailed guidance on how individual lessons should be taught in schools and contracted school improvement partners to advise on change across the country.

As I learnt more about this situation, I could not believe it was being allowed to happen. To try and bring some level of accountability to the QCA's work, I asked a series of Written Parliamentary questions of the QCA. I asked them about the evidence base for their new curriculum, comparisons of their curriculum with those in high-performing foreign countries, membership of their curriculum review committee, meeting minutes and agendas, and the salaries of their highest-paid employees. As a consequence, in April 2007, I was invited to a meeting at the QCA's salubrious offices in Piccadilly with both the CEO of the QCA and its chairman who told me in what I considered to be an aggressive tone to, in effect, stop wasting their time. I was furious that a public body had asked me not to hold them accountable to Parliament. To have attempted to do so was, I suspected, a breach of parliamentary privilege. I ignored their request, and instead asked even more Parliamentary questions over the ensuing months. This upfront encounter with the 'get off our lawn' attitude that the education quangos had developed would be an instructive lesson for government. The gates to the Secret Garden that James Callaghan had sought to prise open were well and truly sealed shut by a bureaucracy politicians had created.

As part of the research for this book, I spoke to Charles Clarke, who had been Education Secretary between 2002 and 2004. He said it was a point of principle for him not to interfere with the independence of the QCA. I took the view, however, that while it would not have been appropriate to intervene in regulatory matters relating to the conduct of exam boards or the standards and grading of public examinations and tests, it was important for ministers to be involved in policy matters relating to the content of the curriculum. Curriculum content is a contested area of public policy with significant ideological issues at stake and, as we have seen in Scotland and Wales with their precipitous falls in the international league tables of educational standards, has a huge impact on standards and the outcomes for children, for which ministers are held directly accountable by the public. My thinking on this issue was greatly influenced by David Cameron's seminal speech as Leader of the Opposition in July 2009 about the governance arrangements for arm's length bodies (see Chapter 3), which determined that both policy and administrative matters should be decided by departmental ministers accountable to Parliament, with only regulatory and highly technical matters reserved for bodies outside the political process.

For policy-makers in other countries looking to reform their education systems, ensuring the political process allows ministers to determine one of the most important levers in driving up standards, namely the curriculum, is an important precondition for success.

Michael Gove

With an election on the horizon, we needed to start moving our thinking from critiques of the status quo to actual policies we would pursue if we formed a government. Following David Cameron's election as Leader of the Party in 2005, the education brief passed to David Willetts, one of the Conservative Party's deepest thinkers. David established a series of reviews, led by sympathetic outside experts, and made a number of thoughtful speeches which began to sketch out an agenda for government.

Our policy on grammar schools, however, needed to be clarified. The policy position at that time was that new grammar schools could be established if local authorities, or indeed new providers through the Free School programme, wished to establish them. And we would legislate to allow that. In practice, we didn't think there would be many such proposals. This was an odd policy with which to go into an election where the possibility of returning to the 11-plus could well become a controversial issue. With Steve Hilton, we conducted a series of focus groups in a number of counties that had abolished selection in the 1970s. These overwhelming revealed no appetite amongst parents of primary-age pupils for the return of selection at 11 years old and convinced us that the policy had to be abandoned.

In May 2007, David Willetts made a speech saying he did not support the creation of new grammar schools and expressed his level of opposition in language that caused a huge row to break out within the Conservative Party. David's criticism of selection struck a raw nerve, and the Party's vociferous grammar school lobby went into action. A well-liked shadow frontbencher resigned in protest (he later went on to be elected Chairman of the powerful 1922 Committee), and other MPs and party activists fuelled weeks of debate and argument, all eagerly reported across the media. Shortly afterwards, David was moved on to shadow the newly created post of Secretary of State for Innovation, Universities, and Skills, but the Party's position that we should not extend grammar-school selection remained.

David Willett's replacement was one of the most talked about new MPs in Parliament, a former leader writer for *The Times*, with a reputation for fierce intelligence and being scarily well read: Michael Gove. In opposition, Michael fizzed with ideas and reforming energy. He was a leading moderniser within the Conservative Party and a close friend of David Cameron, so his appointment suggested education would be a significant focus in the election campaign. I was excited to work with him. In our first meeting, I gave Michael a copy of E. D. Hirsch's *The Schools We Need*, confident that he was the sort of enquiring politician who might actually read it.

Notes

1 Hirsch recounts this experience in E. D. Hirsch, *Cultural Literacy: What Every American Needs to Know*, New York: Random House, 1988, Chapter 2.
2 E. D. Hirsch, *The Schools We Need and Why We Don't Have Them*, New York: Doubleday, 1996, p. 48.
3 Hirsch, *The Schools We Need and Why We Don't Have Them*, pp. 218–222.
4 Hirsch, *The Schools We Need and Why We Don't Have Them*, p. 59.
5 Hirsch, *The Schools We Need and Why We Don't Have Them*, p. 76.
6 Hirsch, *The Schools We Need and Why We Don't Have Them*, p. 159.
7 Hirsch, *The Schools We Need and Why We Don't Have Them*, p. 262.
8 Hirsch, *The Schools We Need and Why We Don't Have Them*, p. 265.
9 Figures taken from T. Burkard and S. Talbot Rice, *School Quangos: An Agenda for Abolition and Reform*, London: Centre for Policy Studies, 2009, and provided for me by the House of Commons Library.
10 P. Wilby, 'Intellectual guru seeks "system redesign" of secondary education', *The Guardian*, 22 September 2009.
11 Burkard and Talbot Rice, *School Quangos*, p. 8.
12 House of Lords, *Merits of Statutory Instruments Committee, the Cumulative Impact of Statutory Instruments on Schools*, London: The Stationery Office Limited, 2009, p. 10.
13 Department for Children, Schools and Families, *The Children's Plan: Building Brighter Futures*, London: The Stationery Office Limited, 2007, p. 65.
14 *Professional Standards for Teachers,* London: TDA, 2007.
15 Department for Children, Schools and Families, *Personalised Learning—A Practical Guide*, Nottingham: DCSF Publications, 2008, p. 9.
16 C. Gilbert, *2020 Vision: Report of the Teaching and Learning in 2020 Review Group*, Nottingham: DFES Publications, 2006.
17 J. Beere, *The Perfect Ofsted Lesson*, Carmarthen: Crown Publishing, 2010, p. iv.
18 E. Heathcoat-Amory, 'Scandal of Blair's £31m flagship school', *Daily Mail*, 14 October 2010.
19 R. Morrison, 'The good, the wise and the very boring', *The Times*, 24 January 2006.
20 C. Scott, 'Inner-city academy that's a blueprint for the future', *The Telegraph*, 16 May 2011.
21 Department for Education and Skills, *Schools for the Future: Exemplar Designs, Concepts and Ideas*, London: DfES, 2004, p. 1.
22 N. Phillips, 'Two academies get £7m to go back to the wall', *Schools Week*, 1 May 2015.
23 R. Garner, 'Revealed: The schools where 1 in four play truant', *Independent*, 13 January 2010; 'Pupils' website attack on school was "silly prank"', *KentOnline*, 12 May 2006.

24 'Multi-million pounds windfall for two Kent academies', *KentOnline*, 7 April 2011.

25 I. Cobain, 'The making of an education catastrophe—schools in Knowsley were dubbed "wacky warehouses"', *The Guardian*, 29 January 2017; and 'Christ the King: Four-year-old £24m Huyton school to close', *BBC Online*, 10 July 2013.

26 QCA, *The National Curriculum*, London: QCA, 2007.

27 C. Woodhead, *A Desolation of Learning: Is this the Education Our Children Deserve?*, Chippenham: Pencil Sharp Publishing, 2009, p. 94.

28 P. Hensher, 'Does anyone really understand the National Curriculum?', *Independent*, 3 April 2009.

29 D. Matthews, *The Strange Death of History Teaching: Fully Explained in Seven Easy-to-Follow Lessons*, published online, 2009.

3 Laying the Foundations

> One of the central goals of David Cameron's Conservative Party is the breaking up of bureaucratic control, and establishment power, when bureaucracies and establishments are thwarting the commons sense of the people. And nowhere is common sense more flouted than among the education establishment and by education bureaucracies. . . . The British people's common sense inclines them towards schools in which the principal activity is teaching and learning, the principal goal is academic attainment, the principle guiding every action is the wider spread of excellence, the initiation of new generations into the amazing achievements of humankind.
>
> Michael Gove, Speech to the Royal Society of Arts,
> 30 June 2009

David Cameron had great faith in Michael Gove and gave him licence to 'think big' on education. Once we began working together, I was struck by Michael's desire to understand schools in the context of an education *system*. The piles of books and papers in his office grew ever higher as he studied each component part of the system, from curriculum to exam boards and inspections to university education faculties. He put considerable intellectual legwork into his time in opposition, learning precisely what role each part of the education system played, how they influenced one another, and—crucially—which could be reformed first.

In doing so, Michael had some formidable assistance. Advising him from the Conservative Research Department was Rachel Wolf, the daughter of Alison Wolf (see Chapter 6). In July 2009, Rachel left to become the founding director of the New Schools Network, laying the groundwork for the success of the Free Schools policy from 2010 onwards, and was replaced by the equally capable Elena Narozanski. Michael's principal adviser was Dominic Cummings, a figure who was—even then—something of an acquired taste in Conservative circles. He had already earned a reputation as a brilliant political organiser, leading campaigns against the UK joining the Euro and against Labour's plans for a Regional Assembly in the Northeast of England. He had also had a brief, unhappy, stint as Director of Strategy to Iain Duncan Smith as Party leader. Although he was idiosyncratic in many of his views and ways of working, I was a fan: Dominic brought fresh thinking, was

DOI: 10.4324/9781003533474-4

unafraid to challenge conventional opinion, and had rare organisational and motivational skills. Temperamentally, we were very different: whilst Dominic relished confrontation, I erred on the side of caution. Nevertheless, I supported Michael's view that Dominic's skills would be crucial to the success of our reforms.

In many ways, Education was the perfect role for Michael. His impassioned belief in the importance of schooling was significantly influenced by his own upbringing in Aberdeen. He was adopted at four months and never knew his birth parents. A precocious child, his parents scrimped and saved to send him to Robert Gordon College, one of Aberdeen's most prestigious independent schools. There, he thrived. When his father lost his business, and it looked as if his parents would no longer be able to afford the fees, Michael won a full scholarship, going on to become school vice-captain. Throughout his life, Michael was trailed by an awareness that his subsequent achievements—University of Oxford, leader writer at the *Times*, Member of Parliament, Cabinet Minister—owed much to the random twists of fate that had placed him at that school. It was impossible to hear Michael speak of his upbringing and not believe the authenticity of his desire to help underprivileged children. To borrow a phrase he used often in his early speeches: a good school can empower children to become 'authors of their own life story.' How can we provide as many children as possible with a good school? That was the question with which we grappled each day whilst in opposition.

As covered in the previous chapter, the answer reached by most of our New Labour predecessors had been money, energy, and a stream of centrally directed initiatives. The emblematic New Labour initiatives were the Primary Literacy and Numeracy Strategies, which combined in 2003 to form the Primary National Strategy, at the eventual cost of £2 billion.[1] However, there were endless smaller strategies, covering everything from pupil behaviour to healthy eating. These strategies followed a similar lifespan: national concern about an issue; headline-grabbing initiative to 'solve' it, hundreds of millions of pounds spent on armies of consultants, advisers, and 'school improvement partners' (a fixture of the New Labour years), public interest moving onto a new issue, and the strategy petering out with little lasting change. To take one infamous example, the Department spent more than £1 billion on strategies to combat truancy from 1997 to 2008, during which period truancy rose by a third.[2]

Most of these initiatives failed because they were not addressing the fundamental causes of educational failure in our school system: an ideological approach to teaching that had no basis in evidence and—wherever tried—led to a weakening in school standards. All key institutions of the education establishment, including local authorities, university education faculties, government quangos, and even the Department for Education itself, were dominated by true believers in this ideology. Its orthodoxy crowded out competing thoughts and ideas, most powerfully through the reluctance or refusal to employ, promote, or appoint those expressing or holding challenging viewpoints. For this orthodoxy to be short-circuited, we would have to move the balance of power away from these ideologically driven institutions and hand it to schools themselves. We needed to weaken or sever the control and influence the education establishment had over schools. Whether it was early reading, pupil behaviour, truancy, or any of the other myriad challenges schools faced, Michael Gove and I shared a conviction that headteachers, not members of the education establishment, were best placed to find the solutions. Surprising as it may seem, a key inspiration for this belief came from someone within the Labour Government itself. His name was Andrew Adonis.

The Adonis Academy

Andrew Adonis was a controversial figure within the Labour Party. He was a committed Blairite who led the Number 10 Policy Unit from 2001. Whilst many Labour education reformers have been stymied by their close ties, both personal and professional, with the education establishment, Adonis—a former Liberal Democrat and determined reformer—had no such hang-ups. Adonis had a similar zeal for school reform to Michael Gove, and I doubt it is a coincidence that they share a similar life story. Like Michael, Andrew Adonis never knew his birth mother. As a consequence, he was partly brought up by his father in North London and partly in a children's home outside the capital. His life chances were transformed when he received a fully funded place at Kingham Hill, an independent boarding school in Oxfordshire. Similarly to Michael, this twist of educational fate propelled him to the University of Oxford, journalism, politics, and education reform. During the early 2000s, Andrew provided a counter-current against the mainstream of Labour thought on education, favouring autonomy over central direction. He became a key figure in the Labour Government, progressing from Downing Street adviser to Minister for Schools and Learners from 2005, and then a Cabinet Minister under Gordon Brown from 2008 (although, sadly, not at Education).

It cannot be stated clearly enough that the revolution we undertook whilst in office began with Andrew Adonis. He, in turn, found inspiration in a small, and by then largely forgotten, Conservative Party reform of the late 1980s. During Margaret Thatcher's final years as Prime Minister, her Education Secretary, Kenneth Baker, established a series of secondary schools, independent of local authority management, sponsored by private business, and with a specific focus on technology and the vocations. They were known as City Technology Colleges (CTCs). Ken Baker fought the education establishment tooth and nail to get his CTCs established, originally aiming for 100 but managing only 15. The policy was later abandoned, having been seen as—in the words of one of his Conservative successors—'maximum aggro and huge expense for minimum reward.'[3]

During the intervening decade, these CTCs disappeared from the national education debate. However, in areas generally away from the gaze of Westminster politicians (such as Derby, Bradford, and Middlesborough), they quietly flourished. In his 2012 book, *Education, Education, Education*, Andrew Adonis details how he chanced upon the story of CTCs in October 1999 while attending a meeting at a CTC called Thomas Telford in the West Midlands. On entering the school, he was taken aback by its smartly dressed pupils, huge sixth form, and motivated teachers. He met the school's charismatic headteacher Kevin Satchwell, who—according to Andrew—combined 'a tough no nonsense style' with 'sky high ambitions for his pupils.'[4] Andrew returned home and began researching outcomes at the other CTCs. As he wrote, 'Virtually every CTC was both very high performing and demonstrated exceptional student academic progress.'[5]

Amongst the roughly 3,600 secondary schools in England, these 15 relics of a forgotten Conservative reform had become hidden beacons of success. Inspired by this discovery, Andrew used his place as Tony Blair's policy adviser to develop an updated Labour Party version of Baker's City Technology Colleges. Andrew envisaged schools that would be like CTCs in that they would be free from local authority control, have sponsors, and serve areas of deprivation. But unlike CTCs, their focus would be broader than technological and vocational education, and their sponsors could be from a wider range of areas, such as charitable foundations, religious organisations, and other schools. In the early days, sponsors would all have to stump up a £2 million contribution towards the school's conversion. Crucially, the headteachers of these schools would have the freedom to break from existing orthodoxies and pursue new approaches to classroom teaching and school management. But what to call them? Andrew searched for a snappy term that could be incorporated into a school's name and imply high standards but not enrage the left of his party. At the very last minute, before David Blunkett announced the policy in March 2000, he found his answer: 'academies'.[6]

Some policies emerge through growing consensus and the collective effort of a political party. The academies policy was not one of them. Within the Labour Party, it began as the almost singular mission of Andrew Adonis, helped—of course—by the backing of his boss, Tony Blair. After David Blunkett announced the policy, Andrew had to fight constantly against the inertia of the Department for Education and the Labour Party to get the first such schools off the ground. As policy adviser to the Prime Minister, Andrew had no official responsibility for implementing the academies programme, but he took charge regardless. He became the self-appointed 'persuader in chief' for academies, completing the seven-minute walk between Downing Street and the Education Department multiple times a day to keep the wheels of reform whirring.[7] The first three academies opened in 2002, followed by nine in 2003, five in 2004, and ten in 2005. As the policy gained increased acceptance within the Labour Party, it began to accelerate. Nineteen academies opened in 2006, 37 in 2007, 47 in 2008, and 70 in 2009, bringing the overall number by the time of the 2010 election to 203.[8] The majority of this number were existing but struggling schools (including one in my constituency), which converted to academy status and were given new management, new leadership, and (often) a new building. However, 20 of these academies were entirely new schools—what we, from 2010 onwards, would call 'Free Schools'.

Looking on from the opposition benches, it was gratifying to see the Labour government seek inspiration from a Thatcher-era education reform. In October 2005, Tony Blair published his flagship education White Paper, 'Higher Standards, Better Schools For All'. It set out a series of proposals to create more autonomy for schools; as Blair wrote in the Foreword, 'Our aim is the creation of a system of independent non-fee paying state schools.'[9] Specifically, the White Paper said that 'All new schools will be self-governing Foundation, voluntary aided, Trust schools or Academies.'[10] In other words, local authorities would no longer be able to establish new schools. And most incendiary of all to many MPs within Blair's Labour Party, the role of local education authorities 'will change from provider to commissioner.'[11] As such, Blair's White Paper presaged many of the structural reforms we introduced in 2010.

Labour backbenchers saw this White Paper and the Education and Inspections Bill that followed as an attack on the 'comprehensive ideal', and began to plan a rebellion. David Cameron made the brave decision to announce his support for this Labour policy. Dismissing the arguments of many senior Conservatives that it was the opposition's job to oppose and take any opportunity to defeat the Government in the House of Commons, he made it clear to Blair's Government that they could count on Conservative support for the Bill. This decision, it turned out, was critical to its success. 46 Labour MPs voted against the Education and Inspections Bill—the largest rebellion on Third Reading for any Labour government since 1924—and so it required the support of Conservative MPs to proceed.[12] I was delighted, not only because I supported the academies policy but because this was proof that the Conservative Party was ready for government. We could be trusted to do the right thing rather than play cynical political games, an approach to politics I had long argued for and written about.[13]

In our minds, there was a direct line of continuity joining Kenneth Baker's Conservative reforms, the New Labour academies driven by Andrew Adonis and Tony Blair, and our nascent reform programme. Michael Gove endlessly praised Andrew Adonis in public (much to his annoyance, I am sure). He even used an interview with the *Guardian* in 2008 to offer Andrew a role in a future Conservative government, claiming, 'I have yet to find a speech of Andrew's outlining policies that I disagree with'.[14] The 203 academies he helped to create gave us a glimpse of how a future school system in England might look.

For supporters of the academies policy on both the Labour and Conservative benches, evidence appeared to be in our favour. Research from the National Audit Office in 2010 suggested that results and attendance were improving at a faster rate in academies compared to the rest of the sector, stating in its 'Key Findings' that 'Most academies are achieving increases in academic attainment for their pupils compared with their predecessor schools.'[15] There were some on the structures side of the education debate who believed that academies were likely to improve simply because they had more freedom. For such 'structuralists', autonomy was a good in and of itself. This was because, compared to local authority schools, academies were free to make many more of their own decisions. Amongst other things, academies could:

- independently procure services such as staff training previously provided by the local authority;

- devise their own performance management procedures;

- choose their own term dates;

- diverge from the National Curriculum; and

- set their own pay and conditions.

Structuralists believed that, freed from the dead hand of local government, and with the energy of new sponsors, schools converting to academy status were almost fated to improve. I was not so sure. The average direction of travel for academies may have been positive, but this masked significant variation. In 2005, Ofsted placed one of the first three academies to open into special measures, the worst category available. The inspectors cited the school's low attendance, poor behaviour, and inadequate building—a £19 million folly modelled, extraordinarily, on a 'Tuscanmountain village'.[16] That summer, this pioneering academy recorded the 11th worst GCSE results in England.[17] By 2009, two more academies had been placed by Ofsted in special measures, and many others were failing to live up to their initial promise.[18] These early failures demonstrated that autonomy did not automatically improve schools. It was what schools did with their autonomy that mattered.

The Mossbourne Miracle

Founded in 2004, Mossbourne Academy was built on the site of a former school named Hackney Downs, once said to have been the worst secondary school in England. Located in a deprived area of East London blighted by gang activity, this new academy was built opposite a road known as 'murder mile'. In such areas, many claimed that poverty and deprivation made running a successful school impossible. The founding headteacher at Mossbourne Academy, Michael Wilshaw, set out to prove such claims wrong. Wilshaw was a veteran of inner-London comprehensives, with a reputation from his previous headship—an all-boys Catholic school in Newham—for holding a firm line on behaviour. He saw in Mossbourne the opportunity to create a new type of school where routines, structure, and clear sanctions for poor behaviour would create an environment where all pupils, no matter how underprivileged, could learn. In a 2011 interview with the Daily Telegraph, he explained his philosophy as follows:

> Mossbourne is a grammar school within a comprehensive intake. I realised a long time ago that if you work with disadvantaged children you can't be

woolly. It's about meticulous standards, standing up for teachers, using 'Sir' and 'Miss', lots of homework, very clear boundaries, no excuses and high expectations. In return, all the students get the very best of what we can offer.[19]

This was not a typical way to run a school back in the mid-2000s. Michael Wilshaw's many critics labelled him a 'sergeant-major' and accused him of running a 'prison camp' in place of a school. However, nobody could accuse him of letting down his pupils when they gained their first set of GCSE results in 2009. That summer, 84 percent of Mossbourne pupils reached the government's defined level of success, five or more GCSEs above a C, including English and Maths. This was compared to a nationwide average of 47 percent. These results placed Mossbourne in the top 1 percent of schools in England for pupil progress. What made these results truly remarkable was that they were achieved in an area of significant social deprivation, where 40 percent of their pupils received free school meals, compared to a national proportion of 13 percent.[20] Two years later, Mossbourne pupils received their first-ever A-level results: 70 students gained places at the UK's top-tier Russell Group Universities, with nine admitted to the University of Cambridge.*

I remember visiting Mossbourne Academy for the first time in 2007. It was a revelation. Pupils were conscientiously working or paying attention to their teacher in every lesson I visited. Far from an atmosphere of mirthless oppression, the warmth that teachers exuded towards their pupils was palpable. For headteachers who visited Mossbourne Academy, the experience was just as profound. Here, in a deprived area of East London, they could see a school achieving extraordinary results with a radically different approach to behaviour and school culture. Before long, these methods were trickling into other schools across the country. For me, this was the real power of academies: not autonomy but emulation. Some academies used their autonomy well; some used it poorly. But, those academies that did use it well provided a model to inspire change in other schools. This process of autonomy, example, emulation, and further innovation, as successful approaches were developed and honed elsewhere, gave me confidence that school improvement at scale might be possible.

Autonomy was, of course, the first step in this process. Put simply, Michael Wilshaw could never have implemented his approach to the same extent that he did at Mossbourne at a local authority school. The progressivist ideology requires that schools should try to achieve good behaviour through positive relationships and

---

* Many books on education reform feature schools which then burn out after their brief blaze of glory. This has not been the case with Mossbourne Community Academy. Twenty years after its foundation and 13 years since Sir Michael departed, Mossbourne remains one of the best schools in the country. In 2024, it ranked 9th out of 3,600 secondary schools in England for the progress of pupils between the ages of 11 and 16 years old. The previous year, it was named 'London School of the Year' by the Sunday Times Good Schools Guide.

engaging lessons rather than the use of sanctions. Local authorities propagated this belief through the training they offered schools, the policies they promoted, and the headteachers they helped appoint. However, academy freedom allowed head-teachers such as Michael Wilshaw to disprove these tenets, not through abstract reasoning, but through demonstration. In 2010, the Guardian ran an interview with Wilshaw beneath the title, 'Is Mossbourne academy's success down to its traditionalist headteacher?' For any fair-minded visitor to the school, it was hard not to answer with a resounding 'yes'.[21]

Andrew Adonis opened his book *Education, Education, Education* with an account of Mossbourne's success. The front cover of his book is illustrated with a photograph of its smartly uniformed pupils in their grey blazers with red trim, lined up in ranks so they could walk in silence from the playground to their lessons (this approach, called 'line up' was rare in English schools at the time, but has since become commonplace). This photograph is emblematic of the power academies had to challenge the progressivist thoughtworld. Although Adonis has always studiously avoided using such language, I long suspected he was a traditionalist at heart. Why else would he dub Mossbourne 'the flagship of the national academy movement' and 'the vanguard of a revolution in secondary education'?[22]

Michael Wilshaw attended the Conservative Party Conference in October 2009 and was surprised when Michael Gove singled him out for praise in his conference speech. Michael Gove paid Michael Wilshaw the following tribute: 'If you want to know what Conservative education policy is in a nutshell, it's taking what has made Sir Michael's school excellent and spreading it to every school.'[23] But could Mossbourne's excellence be spread to every school in the country when progressivist ideology still held such sway? For me, this was the most significant question our reforms had to answer. More than anything else, we had to create a system where the thoughtworld's power was weakened, and ideas from schools such as Mossbourne could spread unimpeded by ideology.

The Co-Option Machine

Michael Gove and I were by no means the first prospective ministers hoping to challenge the orthodoxy of progressivist ideas. We were keenly aware that many previous ministers, both Conservative and Labour, had sought to do similarly but with limited success. One of the key reasons for this disappointing record was that their reforms had been co-opted by the education establishment and ended up reinforcing the very ideas they were meant to challenge. Such a story can be told of Conservative reforms such as the National Curriculum (1988) and Ofsted (1992), and early Labour reforms such as the National Strategies (1998) and the National College for School Leadership (2000).

Studying the history of education reform whilst in opposition, the National Curriculum provided an instructive case study. Created by the Conservative Education Secretary Kenneth Baker in 1988, he hoped it would codify the fundamental knowledge that should be taught in English schools. However, the process of its design and implementation was invariably put into the hands of members of the education establishment who were ideologically opposed to such an idea or whose ideas about the curriculum were antithetical to his. Thus, the National Curriculum ended up reinforcing, not countering, the anti-knowledge agenda. As Ken Baker recalled in a recent interview:

> I set up committees for each subject, expecting some, like history, to be more controversial than others, like maths. But I was wrong—I soon discovered that feudal armies marched across the plains in the process of trying to agree the correct approach to maths. Some would say you don't need to learn times tables at all; others would say abandon fractions as quickly as you can. The armies formed up on either side, and I had to reappoint new members to the committee. English was even more difficult. Some of the first people I appointed recommended abandoning grammar altogether.[24]

Michael and I knew that any attempt to overturn the progressivist ideology from Whitehall had to be approached with caution. Centrally directed strategies would always run the risk of being subverted by those figures in whose hands their implementation would have to be placed: in a word, the 'educationalists'. In our minds, an increasingly clear distinction could be drawn between those who educated children and those who 'worked in education'. This latter category encompassed the phalanx of educationalists, whose initial careers in teaching had led them to the offices of local authorities, quangos, and university education departments. With the freedom to indulge in sentimentally attractive notions of teaching but little accountability for their results, educationalists had—I came to believe—an inbuilt bias towards progressivist ideology, which I did not come across when speaking to the education pragmatists (read, teachers) I met every week in classrooms across England.

It was these teachers and school leaders in whose hands Michael and I wanted to put power, as we were convinced that they were best placed to find solutions. Successful approaches to teaching were most likely to prosper if they grew organically from within schools, succeeded on their own merits, and spread to other schools. The question was how this could be achieved at scale and at a speed that would deliver a real improvement in the life chances of those for whom the status quo was so clearly failing.

Structures Beget Standards

In implementing education reform, there are—broadly speaking—two approaches you can take. Do you rely on structural reform, taking schools away from the influence of sclerotic institutions wedded to failed ideas? Or do you engage in debate, challenge failed ideas, and ultimately insist that different approaches to teaching and the curriculum are adopted? This was the essence of the standards versus structures debate, which we spent time in opposition thrashing out. Dominic Cummings believed strongly that the answer was widespread structural reform through a radical expansion of the academies programme. Teachers, he believed, should be given professional autonomy combined with strong accountability to allow new ideas to flourish and evidence to replace ideology.

Whilst not disagreeing with this diagnosis, I argued that we also had to address and challenge the ideas themselves. It was my view that we should understand in detail the approaches to education that these failed ideas were prescribing. We needed to look at how reading and maths were being taught, how classrooms were configured, and how approaches to behavioural management differed between schools. We needed to look carefully at the content of the curriculum and how teachers were trained. In other words, we as politicians needed to enter what had long been described as the 'Secret Garden', and engage in debate with the education establishment, arguing not just about the way in which schools were organised, but also the way in which lessons were taught. In March 2005, before I joined the shadow front bench, I had set out my thinking on this in an article in *The Times*:

> At the heart of the problem in schools is an old-fashioned ideology that insists that the majority of lessons take place in mixed-ability classes, and which eschews rigour, competition and rote learning. Until politicians engage with the teaching profession and educational academics on these issues, and unless we challenge the education orthodoxies that are the cause of decline, we will make no progress in improving standards.[25]

I wrote this article one year before my epiphany when reading Hirsch, so my definition of failed educational orthodoxies wasn't quite as well developed as it would become, but my conviction that standards mattered as much as structures was already evident. The contradiction between these two approaches formed the basis of the debates I had with Dominic Cummings in the Opposition years prior to the 2010 General Election. They were resolved by Michael Gove, who took the view that structural reform and interventions on standards had to work together for lasting change to be achieved. In doing so, he was echoing Tony Blair's 2010 memoir *A Journey,* in which he wrote:

> We had come to power in 1997 saying it was 'standards not structures' that mattered. . . . Unfortunately, as I began to realise when experience started to shape our thinking, it was bunkum as a piece of policy. The whole point is that structures beget standards. How a service is configured affects outcomes.[26]

Our experience in government proved that both Blair and Gove were right. Without a change in structures, any push on standards would founder on the inertia and resistance of local authorities, where the prevailing orthodoxies of progressive education were so deeply entrenched. I remember in my first years as an MP visiting a primary school in my constituency and asking the head teacher whether the school taught children multiplication tables. She said they didn't but that she would ask West Sussex (the Local Authority) whether she might. I was appalled that a teacher with over 20 years' experience would need permission from the Local Authority about her school's teaching methods. However, without tackling the debates over standards, most newly autonomous schools would continue to be run largely as before, with no significant change to the curriculum or teaching methods. There was no guarantee that every school freed from local authority oversight would automatically become Mossbourne Academy. In fact, it took a remarkable leader like Michael Wilshaw to have the bravery and independence to establish a school in such direct contradiction to prevailing orthodoxies. Thus, those orthodoxies would also have to be challenged head-on.

2010 Manifesto

The period from 2007 to 2010 was hugely exciting. Michael visited America to learn more about their equivalent to Academies, known as the Charter School programme, and Singapore to find out more about their highly ambitious school curriculum. Michael, Dominic, and I went to Sweden to learn about friskolor, the Swedish free schools programme. Back in England, we travelled up and down the country talking to teachers and spending endless hours in airless rooms sharing what we had learnt. By the time the Conservative Party's General Election Manifesto was published in April 2010, the section on education was one of the most detailed and eye-catching. Much of the standards agenda was to be delivered through a new National Curriculum, which would be 'more challenging and based on evidence about what knowledge can be mastered by children at different ages.'[27] In particular, we promised to promote systematic synthetic phonics by providing teachers with proper training on using the approach. On structures, we committed to an expansion of the academies programme and, influenced by our experience in Sweden, the introduction of free schools.

Both structures and standards would be underpinned by stronger accountability measures based on reformed qualifications and robust school performance metrics. This was a crucial aspect of our policy: during the 13 years of New Labour government, the English exam system had become critically devalued. Their time in office had seen year-on-year increases in the number of pupils passing National Curriculum assessments aged 11, GCSEs aged 16, and A-levels aged 18. However, employers and the public doubted whether this reflected genuine improvement, and—as I will explain in Chapters 5 and 6—they had every right to be suspicious. What is more, school accountability measures were poorly designed and far too easy for schools to manipulate, breeding cynicism within the profession. Prior to 2010, it was difficult to promote successful schools because any claim that one school was outperforming its peers would provoke the question, 'How have they played the game?' We needed fundamentally to redesign the metrics that measured school success, ensuring that they reflected genuine pupil achievement across all ability levels. Our vision was that if you defined success correctly, set a high bar, and gave schools more freedom to reach that bar, the holy grail of a self-improving school system could be the result. Amongst education reformers in both Conservative and Labour circles, the 'high autonomy, high accountability' mantra emerged to describe this vision.

More generally, David Cameron's 2010 Manifesto promised to 'cut the Quango State', which it calculated had grown to over 700 unelected public bodies delivering government policy, at the cost of some £46 billion per year. The manifesto promised that by closing many of these agencies, £1 billion a year could be saved whilst also bringing political decision-making closer to the people.[28] This had significant implications in education, one of the areas of government in which the quango state's expansion had been most costly. A year previously, in July 2009, David Cameron had developed his thinking on this topic in a speech to the Reform think tank. This was a landmark speech in which he set out three tests that a Conservative government would apply to all non-governmental bodies once in power to ascertain their usefulness:

- Is the role being carried out by the organisation necessary or can it be scrapped?

- If there is a need for it, should any or all of its functions be carried out within a government department under ministerial control and for which the minister would be accountable to Parliament?

- Are the functions of a technical nature where non-political expertise and judgement are required (such as the Nuclear Installations Inspectorate); or where clear political independence is required (such as in awarding funds to Research Councils); or where information provided must be impartial (such as the Office for National Statistics).

With regard to education quangos, David Cameron announced that a future Conservative government would abolish the QCDA (as the QCA was renamed in 2009) and that the Education Department would take direct responsibility for a streamlined National Curriculum.[29] However, he promised to retain the Office of Qualifications and Examinations Regulation (Ofqual), a new arm's-length body also created in 2009 with responsibility for regulating qualifications. This decision was based on the fact that Ofqual, in overseeing qualifications, needed to be seen to be independent of ministers and the political process which would benefit from rising numbers of top grades. Therefore, Ofqual had a structural reason for needing always to remain politically impartial. In addition, we were—to be frank—confident our reforms would lead to higher standards being reached, and we needed those metrics to be credible. For those of us working on education policy,

David Cameron's speech on quangos was an important intervention which set the course of our thinking for the next decade of reform.

In preparing for the manifesto, Michael Gove and I decided early on not to entertain two education policies that, for decades, had animated education thinking within the Conservative Party. The first was a return to academically selective state secondary schools, grammar schools, which had been largely discontinued during the 1960s and 1970s. Many within the Conservative Party still saw grammar schools as a silver bullet for education reform. Having attended a grammar school myself, I was sympathetic. However, in 2010, a commitment to opening more grammar schools beyond the 164 that already existed would not only have been a major political distraction, it would have undermined the rest of our reforms (see Chapter 2). The political capital needed to introduce new grammar schools would have made any wider reforms all but impossible, so we concluded grammar schools were a distraction we needed to avoid.

The second policy we chose to jettison was marketisation of the education system, most commonly advocated through a 'voucher' scheme. First popularised by the American economist Milton Friedman during the 1960s, vouchers had, for decades, been something of an obsession amongst free-market reformers. The idea was that all parents would be given a voucher roughly equivalent to per pupil state expenditure on education—say £5,000 per child, per school year—and they would be free to spend it on any school they wished. It could either pay a child's school fees in its entirety or supplement fees paid for a place they already had at an independent school. However, we had no intention of introducing such an approach, which would have been hugely expensive and failed to address the fundamental issues of how to improve the state schools, which educated 93 percent of children. What is more, I firmly believed that teachers—the great majority of whom enter the profession through genuinely altruistic impulses—did not need a profit-motive to ensure they did a good job.

Although both Michael and I were and are passionate free marketeers, we did not believe that the private sector or marketisation was the right approach for reforming public services such as education. As Conservatives, we had to find out why and how state services could and should be improved and empower those working within them—like Michael Wilshaw—who we believed held the answers.

Notes

1 R. Alexander et al., *The Cambridge Primary Review: Children, their World, their Education*, London: Routledge, 2009, p. 42.

2 G. Paton, 'Truancy rates rise despite £1bn campaign', *Daily Telegraph*, 27 February 2008.

3 A. Adonis, *Education, Education, Education: Reforming England's Schools*, London: Biteback, 2012, p. 32.

4 Adonis, *Education, Education, Education*, p. 54.

5 Adonis, *Education, Education, Education*, p. 56.

6 Adonis, *Education, Education, Education*, p. 61.

7 Adonis, *Education, Education, Education*, p. 74.

8 Figures provided by Will Driscoll, publications editor at the Institute for Government.

9 Department for Education and Skills, *White Paper: Higher Standards, Better Schools For All*, London: The Stationery Office, 2005, p. 4.

10 *White Paper: Higher Standards, Better Schools for All*, p. 10.

11 *White Paper: Higher Standards, Better Schools for All*, p. 11.

12 'Education bill passes with smaller rebellion', *The Guardian*, 24 May 2006.

13 N. Gibb, 'For too many politicians, 'politics' is a sport. It's as if we were a football team, not a political party', *Independent*, 25 January 2003.

14 G. Hinsliff, 'Gove invites key Blairites to join a future Tory cabinet', *The Guardian*, 28 September 2008.

15 National Audit Office, *The Academies Programme*, London: The Stationery Office, 2010, p. 5.

16 R. Smithers, 'Failed academy has not got better, says Ofsted', *The Guardian,* 20 March 2006.

17 W. Mansell and W. Stewart, 'Academies among worst performers', *TES Magazine*, 20 January 2006.

18 W. Mansell and P. Curtis, 'Third academy fails Ofsted inspection', *The Guardian*, 13 September 2009.

19 R. Fowler, 'Mossbourne Academy: A tale of high expectations . . . and no excuses', *The Telegraph*, 23 February 2011.

20 Adonis, *Education, Education, Education*, pp. 6–7.

21 P. Wilby, 'Is Mossbourne academy's success down to its traditionalist headteacher?', *The Guardian*, 5 January 2010.

22 Adonis, *Education, Education, Education*, p. 7.

23 M. Gove, *Speech to the Conservative Party Conference*, 7 October 2009.

24 K. Baker, quoted in E. Dorrell, *From the Office of the Secretary of the State*, Public First, 2022.

25 N. Gibb, 'No more flights of fancy', *The Times*, 30 March 2005.

26 T. Blair, *A Journey*, London: Random House, 2010, p. 265.

27 *The Conservative Party Manifesto: Invitation to Join the Government of Britain*, London: Pureprint Group, 2010, p. 52.

28 *The Conservative Party Manifesto*, p. 70.

29 D. Cameron, *Speech to the Reform Think Tank*, 6 July 2009.

4 Creative Destruction

It should be clear that the primary responsibility for improvement rests with schools. Government cannot determine the priorities of every school, and the attempt to secure compliance with its priorities reduces the capacity of the system to improve itself. Instead our aim should be to create a school system which is more effectively self-improving.

'The Importance of Teaching', Schools White Paper,
November 2010

The 2010 election was held on 6 May. The Conservatives won 306 seats in the House of Commons, 20 seats short of an overall majority, with 48 more seats than the Labour Party. It was clear that David Cameron was likely to be Prime Minister, but the question remained whether he could form a stable government or whether there would have to be another election in a few months' time. In a bold move, David Cameron approached the Liberal Democrats, who had won 57 seats, with a 'big, open and comprehensive offer' to form a coalition government. Nick Clegg and the 'Orange Book' Liberal Democrats (those on the right in the centre-left Liberal Democrats) put country before party in agreeing to the Coalition with the Conservative Party, a decision which I have admired them for ever since. Smaller parties rarely do well electorally after joining a coalition government, but the severe state of the public finances as the UK emerged from the consequences of the 2008 banking crash made stable government vital. Nick Clegg and his senior team understood this.

For the next week, the party leaders negotiated a coalition agreement behind closed doors, and an agonising wait ensued. A natural pessimist, I was convinced that my role in the Education team would be offered up for sacrifice, particularly as the Liberal Democrat Education Spokesman David Laws, a close ally of Nick Clegg, had been given a seat at the negotiating table. However, to my delight, I was appointed Schools Minister with Michael Gove as Education Secretary. Dominic Cummings was not so fortunate. He and Michael travelled together to Downing Street for Michael's appointment, no doubt expecting that from there, they would

DOI: 10.4324/9781003533474-5

head straight to the Department to begin the revolution. However, as Michael emerged from the Prime Minister's office with Dominic waiting outside, he brought bad news: David Cameron's Communications Director had ruled Dominic a liability and blocked his appointment.[1]

With the exception of banning Dominic from the Department, David Cameron gave us maximum freedom to hit the ground running. A natural delegator, the Prime Minister never sent anyone from Downing Street to man mark us. On the contrary, he trusted Michael, believed in the need for radical reform, and—from the very start—left us to get on with it. The subsequent success of our reforms rested on this trust and support from a Prime Minister who understood what we were trying to do. It was a remarkable opportunity and one that Michael embraced with alacrity. During our years of preparation, Dominic had convinced Michael that if he did not make significant inroads at the Department during his first 100 days, stasis would ensue, and he would achieve little of note over the next five years. So, Michael arrived brimming with enthusiasm, ambitious to deliver immediate change. We had already been meeting regularly with the Permanent Secretary David Bell whilst in opposition, so civil servants had some idea of what to expect from our programme. Nothing could have prepared them, however, for the speed with which we planned to pursue it.

On his first day in office, Michael returned the Department for Children, Schools, and Families to its original name: the Department for Education. Covering the walls of the Department's seven-story office block in Westminster were garish children's book-style cartoon characters of children, nicknamed 'the munchkins' by the civil servants. Michael ordered they be taken down immediately. Seriousness, not sentimentality, was our aesthetic. Redecorating over, we started work on the Academies Bill. This arrived pre-prepared thanks to the assistance of a former teacher and the then Pro Chancellor of Brunel University, Sir Bob Balchin. A campaigner for school autonomy since the 1980s, Bob had been a senior adviser to four Education Secretaries and two Conservative opposition leaders and had been instrumental to the Grant Maintained Schools policy (a forerunner to Academies) during the previous Conservative Government. His experience was invaluable to us, and, thanks to his hard work in opposition and that of a team of Conservative lawyers, the Academies Bill was ready to be debated in Parliament just two weeks into the new government. Bob was a constant support throughout those first years in government, and his influence on education policy cannot be overstated.

With the pressure of new legislation in the early months of the new government, it was decided to start the Parliamentary process of the Academies Bill in the House of Lords rather than the Commons. The Second Reading debate on 7 June 2010 was opened by our Education Minister in the House of Lords, the Conservative Peer, Jonathan Hill, a highly experienced political operator who had headed Prime Minister John Major's political office in Number 10 during the 1990s. The Academies Bill sought to expand radically the academies programme:

- Existing schools, including for the first time the roughly 17,000 primary schools in England, were given the chance to convert to academy status, with those rated by Ofsted as 'outstanding' pre-approved to do so. These became known as 'Converter Academies'.

- Schools eligible for intervention due to underperformance could be converted to academy status, provided they worked in partnership with a high-performing academy. These were to be known as 'Sponsored Academies'.

- Groups such as charities, parents, or existing schools could set up new academies from scratch. Inspired by the schools we had visited in Sweden, these would be known as 'Free Schools'.

We made no secret of our motivation: we wanted the power of local authorities to diminish and new, more dynamic groups of schools to emerge in their place. As I said in my speech in the House of Commons, concluding the Second Reading debate before the vote on 19 July:

> The Academies Bill is not simply about the nuts and bolts of the conversion process for maintained schools to become academies or for groups of teachers or parents to establish new free schools. It is about changing the deeply unsatisfactory and, for many parents, highly distressing situation where schools in an area are not of a standard and quality they want for their children . . . Central to our drive, however, is liberating professionals to drive improvement across the system. We want all our schools to be run by professionals rather than by bureaucrats or by bureaucratic diktat.[2]

The Academies Bill received Royal Assent on 27 July, just 76 days into the coalition government. Later that day, Parliament broke for its six-week summer recess. The Act had passed just in time, giving school leaders the summer holiday to reflect on the invitation Michael Gove had made to headteachers across the country to consider academy conversion. By the time the new school year began in September, 181 schools had submitted applications to convert. Some critics suggested this figure was low and showed that we had overestimated the desire amongst school leaders for academisation.[3] However, it was early days. By January 2011, there were 409 academies, consisting of 138 Converter Academies and 271 Sponsored Academies, including the 203 Sponsored Academies inherited from the Labour Government. This was double the figure at the start of our government, and already covered one in ten English secondary schools.[4] From then on, the number of schools converting to academies grew and grew, from hundreds to thousands, to the overwhelming majority of the sector today. Though no one could be sure of this outcome at the time, the Academies Act would change the structure of English state schooling more than any other measure since Circular 10/65 and the beginning of the process of comprehensivisation in 1965.

The Importance of Teaching

By the autumn of 2010, mass academisation was underway, but we knew any benefits of this grand structural change would take years, perhaps decades, to be felt. To articulate other aspects of our reform agenda, we published a White Paper on 24 November 2010. Entitled 'The Importance of Teaching', it was a programme of fundamental education reform and the culmination of years of painstaking work in opposition. It was accompanied by a further paper, 'The Case for Change', which set out in more detail the arguments for and the evidence supporting our reform agenda.

The centrality of education reform to the government's ambitions could be seen in the Foreword to the White Paper, penned jointly by the Prime Minister and the Deputy Prime Minister. Michael Gove's own Foreword reflected his passionate belief in the power of a good education, 'It is only through reforming education that we can allow every child the chance to take their full and equal share in citizenship, shaping their own destiny, and becoming masters of their own fate.' He cited the lamentable statistic that in 2009, out of the 40,000 pupils eligible for free school meals, only 40 made it to Oxbridge—fewer than the individual number achieved by some private schools.[5] The White Paper's title, with its nod to Oscar Wilde, was intended to reflect the admiration that Michael Gove and I have for those who devote their careers to teaching, as well as the importance of the teacher being the focal point of a classroom, rather than the child-centred conception of a facilitator, or 'guide on the side'.

'The Importance of Teaching' set out a blueprint for fundamental change to the prevailing philosophy of state education, replacing the progressivist ideology with new evidence-led approaches, from the curriculum, to qualifications, to behaviour policies. It built on the structural changes that had been introduced in the Academies Act by extending the automatic ability of schools graded 'Outstanding' by Ofsted to convert to academy status to schools graded 'Good' but with some 'Outstanding' features. The White Paper also promised a National Curriculum that embodies children's 'cultural and scientific inheritance, the best that our past and present generations have to pass on to the next.' It stated that the curriculum should be a benchmark 'outlining the knowledge and concepts that pupils should be expected to master to take their place as educated members of society.'[6] The White Paper also promised a reform of GCSEs and A-levels to ensure their standards were on par with similar qualifications in the highest-performing education systems around the world. We promised to legislate so that the regulator, Ofqual, had a specific objective to secure international comparability of our qualification standards.

The 2010 White Paper was also where we first introduced our idea of the English Baccalaureate, an accountability measure designed to encourage schools to enter more pupils for a core of academic subjects. I had always assumed that the majority of pupils in England taking their GCSEs would be studying English, Maths, two or more sciences,* a foreign language, and either History or Geography. Pupils tend to go through the options-choosing process during Year 8 or Year 9, and in my experience, most good schools stipulated these sorts of combinations. However, in 2010, the proportion of pupils nationwide taking such a combination of subjects was just 22 percent, and amongst pupils eligible for Free School Meals, it was 8 percent.[7] I was determined to encourage schools to enter more pupils for this combination of subjects, as it gives pupils the broadest range of opportunities post–16. In England, this struck many as controversial but, as the White Paper pointed out, 'In most European countries school students are expected to pursue a broad and rounded range of academic subjects until at least the age of 16.'[8] To emphasise this fact, we termed such a combination of subjects the English Baccalaureate (EBacc) and promised to publish annual data on the proportion of pupils entering and achieving the EBacc at each secondary school in the country.

It was a direct challenge to the unacceptable culture in schools at the time, where an academic curriculum was believed to be unsuitable to most children from poorer backgrounds. Michael and I were determined to eliminate the 'soft bigotry of low expectations' which claimed subjects such as History, Spanish, or Physics weren't right for 'these kids'. Closing the attainment gap between disadvantaged children and their more affluent peers was our guiding mantra in everything we were to do at the Department, and our disdain for such soft bigotry appeared in multiple speeches and policy documents. Of course, the pervasive idea that some pupils will always struggle as readers was another example of this pernicious thinking. In the White Paper, we stated in no uncertain terms that systematic synthetic phonics is the most effective way of teaching young children to read, particularly for those at risk of having problems with reading. We promised to provide high-quality phonics training and approved resources for primary schools, explaining why this was an exception to our general mantra of autonomy on the following grounds: 'As this is an area of such fundamental importance, we will go further than in any other area in actively supporting best practice.'[9] The White Paper also committed us to ensuring children 'master the core arithmetic functions by the time they leave primary school', including, in my own mind but not presaged in the White Paper, ensuring pupils know their times tables by heart by the age of 9.[10]

Sanctioning Strictness

We knew that none of the changes promised in the White Paper would succeed if poor pupil behaviour in schools was left unaddressed. Since at least the 1970s, reports of worsening behaviour in schools had been something of a constant in

---

* Confusingly, the majority of pupils in English secondary schools take 'Combined Science', where you study all three sciences but receive 2 GCSEs. Around one in four pupils take the more academically challenging option of studying Biology, Chemistry, and Physics as separate sciences, commonly known as 'Triple Science'.

British life. By 2010, eye-watering stories of pupil defiance were commonplace amongst teachers, frequently in the news, and vividly laid bare by hidden camera TV shows set in schools. A 2008 survey from the National Foundation for Education Research found that two-thirds of teachers believed pupil behaviour was driving colleagues out of the profession.[11] In 2010, major assaults on teachers in schools reached a five-year high, with 44 being taken to hospital with injuries sustained from their pupils.[12] When, in 2008, the British Social Attitudes survey asked the public whether they agreed with the statement that 'the behaviour of young people today is no worse than it was in the past', 69 percent disagreed, and only 24 percent agreed. The reputation of English schools for terrible behaviour was costing the profession dearly. Among undergraduates considering becoming teachers, the most commonly cited reason for choosing an alternative profession was 'feeling unsafe in the classroom'.[13]

The Labour government had responded to this mounting concern by doing what governments always do when they can't think of a solution: it commissioned a report. Completed in 2005, the Steer Report, entitled *Learning Behaviour,* offered little reassurance to the profession. Instead, it claimed that incidents of serious misbehaviour were 'exceptionally rare', and repeated the tired old nostrums of child-centred behaviour management: sanctions should not be relied upon, and poor pupil behaviour is most often caused by bad teaching.[14] We were determined not to make the same mistake. Fundamentally, pupil behaviour is dictated by the policies put in place by headteachers and their willingness to enforce them. I was well used to visiting out-of-control schools where headteachers sat you down in a meeting room and shut the blinds because they knew that pupils controlled the corridors. I had also been to schools where a sense of adult authority pervaded the institution, such as Mossbourne Academy led by Michael Wilshaw, Burlington Danes Academy led by Sally Coates, or Twyford High School led by Alice Hudson.

Our White Paper pledged 'to restore the authority of teachers and head teachers so that they can establish a culture of respect and safety, with zero tolerance of bullying, clear boundaries, good pastoral care and early intervention to address problems.'[15] In addition, it supported the power of headteachers to exclude disruptive children, safe in the knowledge that their decision was not at risk of being overturned. In opposition, our conversations with the profession consistently raised five measures which they claimed could improve teachers' authority over pupils. All five were included in the White Paper and made statutory by the 2011 Education Act.

Firstly, we took away the requirement to give families 24 hours' written notice before setting an after-school detention, empowering teachers to give decisive and timely sanctions—something crucial to the functioning of any effective school. Second, we gave teachers new rights to search pupils for unauthorised items, such as weapons or video cameras, and to find and delete offensive content from phones. Third, we offered clarification on whether school staff could use 'reasonable force' when fights or severe disruption occurred, reassuring school staff that they absolutely had the right to restrain pupils physically in such circumstances. Fourth, we gave teachers accused of wrongdoing by pupils or their parents the right to anonymity until they were charged, preventing innocent teachers from being hounded out of the profession by pernicious allegations published in local and national newspapers.

Finally, we made it impossible for review panels convened by the local authority to make schools take back pupils they had permanently excluded. Fundamentally, if a headteacher and their governing body had determined that a pupil's violent or disruptive behaviour disqualified them from membership of their community, we did not want that decision to be undermined. The state compels children to go to school and fines families who do not comply. We were not going to change this, but we felt deep unease that some children are compelled to go to a school where behaviour is out of control, and they do not feel safe. You cannot overestimate the ongoing sense of hopelessness, unhappiness, and trauma that children attending such schools experience.

Our 2011 reforms on behaviour gave headteachers significantly more power to make their schools calm and safe. On a philosophical level, this was inspired by an acceptance that children, though wonderful in countless ways, are not always on the side of angels. School-age children can be brilliant, inventive, and compassionate. However, just like the rest of us, a very small minority can also be violent and malign. We allowed headteachers to create behaviour policies which recognised that truth and ensured consequences were upheld. The ultimate consequence of the most serious bad behaviour has to be the right of schools to permanently exclude a pupil whose behaviour was unacceptable. Of course, within every story of an excluded pupil, there is a personal tragedy, and I would never suggest headteachers take those decisions lightly. However, if a school rules out entirely the possibility of ever making the decision to exclude, the greater tragedy of pupils failing to learn because their school is disruptive and unsafe will be the consequence.

School Guidance

When we talked in speeches about school autonomy, we never meant just academisation: we also meant freedom from bureaucracy. As well as costing huge sums of money, the constant stream of New Labour initiatives cost a lot of teacher time. Each new initiative came with additional paperwork and bureaucracy, which could distract teachers from the fundamental purpose of their job: to teach. For any public sector worker, the frustration of bureaucracy which aims to make you better at your job but actually makes you worse is palpable. We wanted as little of it as possible to come from the Department. Visiting a headteacher's office during the 2000s, you were reliably faced with a desk flanked by ring-bound files of government guidance (which was still regularly posted by mail, as opposed to published online). These were symbolic of a command-and-control approach to school improvement. We wanted to take the time that headteachers had to spend reading such guidance and give it back to them, allowing them to spend more time walking the corridors, talking to their colleagues, and working out what they—not we—believed would improve their school.

Perhaps the most infamous example of unnecessary workload came from the schools' inspectorate, Ofsted. Known as the 'self-evaluation form', its abbreviation 'SEF' sent shudders down the spine of teachers. It was introduced in 2005 to give schools the chance to present themselves in their best possible light before Ofsted inspectors arrived and either verified or countered school leaders' own verdict. However, this seemingly benign process had given birth to a monster document, often hundreds of pages long. There were 24 sections for evaluating school performance, 70 sections for factual details, sections for compliance with statutory requirements, and so on. According to one primary head we spoke to, she would spend every summer holiday updating her SEF and then hold multiple senior management meetings at the start of each term to discuss it.[16] Weeks of executive time were being wasted on making schools successful on paper as opposed to in reality. Three months into the new government, Michael Gove asked Ofsted to scrap the SEF process, a decision that won the support of all the main teaching unions.

Our drive to reduce paperwork led to a day-long meeting at the Department for Education, for which Michael asked officials to compile an exhaustive spreadsheet of school guidance. Every civil servant responsible for such guidance assembled in a large meeting room, and I went through the spreadsheet line-by-line so that the civil servant responsible for each item could justify its existence. If they could not do so adequately, the guidance was scrapped. Looking back, it was an exhausting day and no doubt viewed by civil servants as a considerable absorber of their time. However, it sent an important message: staff time is a school's most valuable resource, and a very high bar had to be set for any impositions made upon it. In addition, we stopped sending fortnightly Department emails to headteachers; cut the Performance Management guidance by three-quarters, radically simplified teacher capability procedures, which made it simpler and quicker to dismiss poor-performing teachers, and cut behaviour and bullying guidance from 600 pages to just 52.[17] By 2013, Michael Gove could boast that we had scrapped or simplified 50 unnecessary duties or school guidance, cutting the volume of paperwork issued to schools by 75 percent, some 21,000 pages.[18]

Of course, some guidance will always be needed, indeed demanded, by schools and headteachers, particularly in challenging and legally fraught areas of a school's functioning. However, where we did produce new guidance, we imposed upon civil servants a self-denying ordinance to avoid jargon or officialese, and embrace the gospel of plain English. A testing ground for this principle was the new Teachers' Standards document. This would replace the 33 Professional Standards introduced in 2007, which emphasised a plethora of voguish concepts such as 'personalised learning'. In contrast, we wanted our Teachers' Standards to be pragmatic, evidence-led, and shorn of any promotion of the progressivist ideology. The convention in the UK is for such documents to be composed by panels of professionals so that they win buy-in from the sector. We appointed Sally Coates to chair the independent review of the Teachers' Standards. She was the headteacher of one of the most successful academies in the country, Ark Burlington Danes. Since its conversion in 2006, it had been providing a rigorous curriculum and high standards of behaviour to the children living on the White City Estate, one of the largest and most challenging housing estates in London. She was aided by 15 panel members, mostly successful headteachers, all chosen for their pragmatic, non-ideological views on classroom practice.

Our brief for the panel was simple: the new Teachers' Standards had to fit onto as few pages as possible—ideally, no more than one page of A4 paper. We wanted to be sure that the new standards reflected the emerging evidence of what constituted an effective teacher, including setting high expectations for pupils and delivering the best possible outcomes, the importance of teacher subject knowledge, planning well-structured lessons and assessment, and, of course, behaviour management. They fulfilled this request admirably, replacing a sprawling document of 33 standards with one page of eight clearly written standards which genuinely reflected the skills and knowledge teachers needed to be successful professionals.[19] This document is still in use today and will have informed countless conversations regarding teachers' career progression since 2011. We were indebted to Sally Coates and her two panel members who took charge of the drafting—John McIntosh (former Headteacher of the London Oratory School) and Professor Antony O'Hear—for getting it right the first time.

The positive experience of working with Sally and her panel taught me that selecting the right people for any official post deserved hours of time and research. If I could share one piece of advice for a new government Minister, it would be that the power of appointment is your single most effective lever for bringing about change. There is always a temptation simply to appoint people recommended by DfE officials, fellow Party members, or people you know who support the government. However, I never forgot advice from a former Conservative Education Secretary, John Patten, who, over lunch in the House of Lords, said to me, 'When making appointments, beware of your friends: they have views too.' In other words, what mattered was not their closeness to the Government or Party affiliation but their views on education.

A Bonfire of the Quangos

The ruthlessness we brought to cutting regulation we also brought to cutting quangos. Following David Cameron's landmark 2009 speech on the 'Quango State', we scrutinised the role of all non-governmental bodies involved in Education. Wherever a quango existed to address a concern that could plausibly be addressed in schools, our conclusion was the same: dissolve the quango and redirect the money to headteachers. During our first year in office, we closed the Teenage Pregnancy Independent Advisory Group (TPIAG), the General Teaching Council for England (GTCE), the British Educational Communications and Technology Agency (BECTA), Teachers TV, the School Support Staff Negotiating Body (SSSNB), as well as the notoriously bloated and dysfunctional Qualifications and Curriculum Development Agency (QCDA). In 2012, we stopped government funding for the Specialist Schools and Academies Trust (SSAT) and in 2013 the National College for School Leadership (NCSL) was merged with the Teaching Agency to become the National College for Teaching and Leadership (NCTL).

Today, very few of these quangos are lamented within the profession. The ensuing 14 years have shown us that this alphabet soup of arm's-length bodies was fundamentally superfluous to the effective running of schools. What is more, many of them had been actively damaging, becoming as they were a natural home for exponents of the progressivist ideology. By 2013, we had abolished or merged with other agencies nine quangos, thus saving money, reducing bureaucracy, and neutralising major sources of proselytising for bad ideas in education.

Following the 2008 financial crisis and the ensuing recession, our annual budget deficit had reached 11 percent of GDP by 2010. Faced with this crisis, the Chancellor of the Exchequer, George Osborne, vowed to eliminate the government's deficit by 2015. In order to achieve this, huge spending cuts had to be found, although the NHS, overseas aid, and school funding were largely protected. These cuts were spread unevenly between different departments, with some, such as local government, asked to make cuts of 40 percent. Over the course of 2010 to 2015, per pupil funding for schools (up to the age of 16) remained constant in real terms. Total spending in schools, in fact, increased from £35 billion to £39.6 billion over the period due to an expanding pupil population.[20] Though per-pupil funding for schools was protected, we still had to deliver hundreds of millions of pounds worth of education spending cuts elsewhere. This was less painful in some areas than others—we already believed that Labour's ancillary spending on strategies, quangos, and other initiatives was delivering little value for money. In addition, we were critical of the wastefulness of Labour's multi-billion pound 'Building Schools for the Future' programme. Nonetheless, telling around 700 schools that the new buildings they had been promised would not be delivered was painful and difficult.

Despite the climate of austerity, we were still able to introduce the pupil premium, one of the coalition government's most enduring reforms. This policy had featured in both the 2010 Liberal Democrat and Conservative manifestos and involved changing the funding for schools so that pupils from disadvantaged backgrounds gave rise to significant extra money for schools. We introduced the pupil premium in 2011, giving schools an extra £488 for every pupil in receipt of free school meals they admitted, amounting to some 1.2 million children from the UK's least well-off households. By 2015, we had increased the premium to £1,320 for primary pupils and £935 for secondary pupils, at which level it remained for the next seven years (to give some context, the average per pupil funding in English schools that year was £5,600). In addition, the reach of the pupil premium was expanded to all pupils who received, or ever had received, free school meals, amounting to almost 2 million children.[21]

Changes to school funding can sometimes be a thankless game of robbing Peter to pay Paul, but the pupil premium was different. It has fundamentally changed the behaviour of school leaders, giving them the motivation to change their admissions codes and proactively recruit the least advantaged children in their community into their schools. It also helped counter any argument that claimed a school's results were weak because their intake was poor. I would meet any such excuse with the rejoinder that we were giving schools significant extra funding through the Pupil Premium to ensure that a school's intake would no longer be given as a reason for educational failure. In recent years, there have been squabbles between the Conservatives and Liberal Democrats over who originated this policy. However, we should celebrate that it was jointly pursued and agreed upon by the Treasury, despite all the pressures on them to reduce the size of the deficit.

A Man in a Hurry

By the end of our first two years in government, there were few areas of the education landscape that had not been touched. Mass academisation begun, phonics screening check introduced, guidance reduced, quangos abolished, and school funding reformed, not to mention the areas to be covered in later chapters, such as Ofsted, free schools, new accountability measures, a revised National Curriculum, and qualification reform. This rate of change could not have been achieved without an exceptional team. Despite being blocked by the Prime Minister, Dominic Cummings continued to offer advice in an unofficial capacity. Then, when David Cameron's communications director had to resign for activities in his past life as a journalist (for which he was subsequently jailed), the ban was lifted. Dominic became Michael's Special Adviser proper in February 2011.

Dominic joined the brilliant policy adviser Sam Freedman, a supporter of the Blair and Adonis reforms and former head of education at the think tank Policy Exchange. Whereas Dominic was a radical, Sam was a pragmatist whose mastery of the details of any given policy was extremely useful. In charge of communications was Henry de Zoute, another former think-tanker with an uncanny ability to articulate our vision for reform. Their office on the seventh floor of the Department seemed to typify our wider way of working: it was highly energetic and very messy. Clothes and discarded food containers covered the floor like a teenager's bedroom, whilst drawers were crammed with sugary sweets to power their long hours of work. Tellingly, none of these three advisers were Conservative Party members. They had all been chosen for their passion for school reform rather than party political loyalty. Our reforms were being powered by an unusually talented and driven team of advisers.

Those first two years of frenetic activity laid the groundwork for a revolution in the English school system. It was hard work and far from plain sailing. Michael has always been a man in a hurry, and the speed with which he wanted to move made mistakes inevitable. As David Cameron said of him, he is 'a bit of a Maoist—he believes that the world makes progress through the process of creative destruction.'[22] Michael embraced this perception, hanging in his office alongside a photograph of Margaret Thatcher those of Lenin and Malcolm X.[23] He had been given a once-in-a-career opportunity to transform English education and would not let caution dim our momentum. As Secretary of State for Education and in his future roles at Justice and the Environment, Michael has proven to be the most effective Cabinet minister of his generation. It was a pleasure and a privilege to work with him during those early days.

Notes

1 This is recounted in more detail in O. Bennett, *Michael Gove: A Man in a Hurry*, London: Biteback Publishing, 2019, pp. 224–225.
2 Hansard House of Commons Debate, vol. 514 col 25–6, 19 July 2010.
3 Bennett, *Michael Gove: A Man in a Hurry*, p. 237.
4 Department for Education, *Academies Annual Report 2010/11*, London: The Stationery Office, 2012, p. 11.
5 Department for Education, *White Paper: The Importance of Teaching*, pp. 4–6.
6 *White Paper: The Importance of Teaching*, p. 41.
7 'The English Baccalaureate: Fifth report of session 2010–12', *House of Commons Education Committee*, 19 July 2011, pp. 6, 16.
8 *White Paper: The Importance of Teaching*, p. 44.
9 *White Paper: The Importance of Teaching*, p. 43.
10 *White Paper: The Importance of Teaching*, p. 44.
11 *White Paper: The Importance of Teaching*, p. 32.
12 Department for Education, 'Press release: School discipline: New guidance for teachers', 11 July 2011.
13 S. Freedman, B. Lipson, and D. Hargreaves, *More Good Teachers*, London: Policy Exchange, 2008, p. 15.
14 A. Steer et al., *Learning Behaviour: The Report of the Practitioners' Group on School Behaviour and Discipline*, Nottingham: DfES Publications, 2005, p. 5.
15 *White Paper: The Importance of Teaching*, p. 32.
16 Department for Education, 'News story: Education Secretary Michael Gove sets out the next stage in a programme of reducing bureaucracy', 23 September 2010; and 'Unions back Gove's call to scrap Ofsted self-evaluation forms', *Children and Young People Now*, 24 September 2010.
17 Department for Education, 'Press release: School discipline: new guidance for teachers', 11 July 2011.
18 M. Gove, 'On the importance of teaching', *Speech to the Policy Exchange Think Tank*, 13 September 2013.
19 Department for Education, 'Teachers' standards: Overview', 2011.
20 Figures taken from Department for Education, 'School funding in England, 2010–11 to 2020–21', 2020; and National Audit Office, 'Financial sustainability of schools', 2016.

21 Figures taken from N. Roberts, *Research Briefing: The Pupil Premium (England)*, House of Commons Library, 2023, pp. 10–11; and N. Roberts, *Research Briefing: School Funding in England*, House of Commons Library, 2022, p. 11.
22 R. Sylvester, '"Maoist" Gove—rebelling against the reactionaries', *The Times*, 30 June 2016.
23 Bennett, *Michael Gove: A Man in a Hurry*, p. 229.

5 Primary Basics

> The evidence submitted to the Review overwhelmingly accepts that, as public bodies, schools should be held accountable for the education of their pupils. This is an important point of principle which we wholeheartedly support.
>
> Independent Review of Key Stage 2 testing, assessment
> and accountability (The Bew Report), June 2011

Over the years, I developed something of a stock lesson that I would wheel out whilst visiting primary schools. I call it a lesson: it was really just me asking a class of pupils lots of questions. I am sure some teachers found me taking over their class a bit surprising, but I found it instructive and a good opportunity to interact with the children. I would start with their times tables, beginning with the easy ones, and move on to the more challenging, the seven times table always, in my mind, being the hardest. I would then ask pupils what they were reading, something that gradually changed over time. Common responses were Horrible Histories, Michael Morpurgo, and Jacqueline Wilson, with Enid Blyton and Roald Dahl still gaining occasional mentions (though never, to my sadness, C. S. Lewis). Sometimes, the class show-off would say George Orwell.

I would then ask how many of them could drive, prompting some uncertain laughter from pupils, followed by which sea they would end up in if they drove directly south from where we were located. Then what country would they reach having crossed the sea? And what was its capital? And if they went east, what country came next? Then, some general knowledge. Who is the monarch? Who was her father? What county are we in? And which counties do we border? Then, I would end with some science and geography. Name the planets. Name the oceans. I liked to ask how many miles we are from the moon and the sun, which would generate some entertaining guesses.

My stock lesson was focused on trivia, but the implications were not—to my mind—trivial. As Hirsch had written about so extensively from an American perspective, the tide of curriculum thinking over the past two generations had been against knowledge and towards more nebulous concepts such as skills,

 DOI: 10.4324/9781003533474-6

competencies, and critical thinking. In all areas of schooling, from the knowledge of phonics in Year 1 to the content of A-level exams in Year 13, I saw this approach as a fundamental cause of educational underachievement in England. Following the election in May 2010, it was my mission to oversee a wholesale review of the National Curriculum. I set myself the overriding aim to restore knowledge as a central component of curriculums in English schools.

Working Memory

At my first meeting with officials in the Department for Education, they arrived bearing copies of Hirsch's Core Knowledge curriculum from America, which his Foundation had developed following the landmark publication of *Cultural Literacy* in 1987. It was an encouraging start, suggesting that our attempts to spread these ideas whilst in opposition were cutting through to the civil service at least. In America, Hirsch's *Cultural Literacy* and his 1996 critique of modern American schooling, *The Schools We Need* helped to inspire a colleague at the University of Virginia, the cognitive psychologist Daniel T. Willingham, to write more directly for teachers. Willingham's wife, Trisha Thompson-Willingham, herself a teacher, also pushed him to do so. As an expert on the latest research on memory and cognition, Willingham set about applying cognitive science to classroom practice, resulting in *Why Don't Students Like School?: A Cognitive Scientist Answers Questions About How the Mind Works and What it Means for the Classroom.* Published in 2009, this is—to my mind—the most significant work written for teachers in the last 20 years.

Prior to Willingham, it was habitually claimed by educationalists that the consensus from academia or 'the research' was that knowledge is less important than more generic skills. Particularly in the age of the internet and, latterly, the smartphone, it was a widely held truth that knowledge stored in one's long-term memory no longer mattered. Willingham called such thinking into question by popularising two concepts. The first was 'working memory'. Cognitive scientists have long known that our working memory, where we manipulate information and produce thought, is limited. As a general rule, our working memory can only hold between five and seven new pieces of information before experiencing 'cognitive overload'. In Chapter 2 of his book, Willingham illustrates this point with maths. Most of us can multiply 19×6 in our heads because we have in our long-term memory the facts that $10 \times 6 = 60$, and $9 \times 6 = 54$. We also have enough knowledge in our long-term memory of number bonds to add the two separate numbers, $60 + 54 = 114$. However, hardly anyone can multiply $184,930 \times 34,004$ in their heads, and the reason is working memory. As Willingham writes, 'The processes are the same, but in the latter case you "run out of room" in your head to keep track of the numbers.'[1]

What is true of mathematics is also true of reading. If you encounter too many unfamiliar words or concepts whilst reading a text, your cognition will overload, and you will have to revisit the sentence multiple times in order to understand its meaning. To illustrate this point, Willingham includes the following sentence:

> Ashburn hit a ground ball to Wirtz, the shortstop, who threw it to Dark, the second baseman. Dark stepped onto the bag, forcing out Cremin, who was running from first, and threw it to Anderson, the first baseman. Ashburn failed to beat the throw.[2]

If you are a baseball fan, the sentence makes immediate sense: it describes a double play (apparently). If you are not—the experience for most of Willingham's British readers—the sentence makes no sense whatsoever. Incidentally, multiple studies show that school children score better for reading ability if they have some background knowledge of the text in question, and sport is often used to illustrate this point. Most readers of this passage on baseball will experience cognitive overload, and the solution to cognitive overload is knowledge and memory. Knowledge committed to long-term memory gives complex thought on any given topic a far greater likelihood of being achieved.

This leads to Willingham's second key concept, domain specificity. One of the much-vaunted qualities of skills such as 'critical thinking', 'problem-solving', and 'creativity' is that they are, supposedly, transferable. If school equips you to be good at problem-solving, modern educationalists claim, you can turn that skill to multiple areas of life, from resolving a dispute at work to fixing your car engine after a breakdown. Such claims are not necessarily new: English public schools during the nineteenth century liked to boast that the style of thinking developed by an education in Latin and the Classics was transferrable to the demands of later life, particularly high office. Willingham challenges these claims, arguing instead that thinking is 'domain specific'. Due to the limitations of working memory, your ability to think about a topic, what Willingham terms a 'domain', is heavily dependent on your long-term memory of its context. Whenever I visit a school and move from one lesson to the next, I experience the reality of domain specificity. Having spent 13 years as an accountant, I can still hold my own in a relatively high-level maths lesson. Problem-solving when faced with an algebraic equation is still—just about—within my reach. However, problem-solving during a computer science lesson (which hardly existed as a subject when I was at school) remains beyond me. I will watch in mute admiration as 11-year-old pupils use Boolean logic to design a circuit or critique the relative merits of different programming languages.[3]

Working memory also explains why the 'learning by doing' ethos so popular in many English schools at the time was misplaced. Progressive educators have long worked on the principle that to ensure children learn in a deep and authentic fashion, we should study how experts generate knowledge and encourage pupils to emulate those methods. So, pupils are encouraged to read historical sources like a historian, conduct experiments like a scientist, and compose music like a musician. However, expecting pupils to learn effectively through such activity is misguided, as experts learn in a way that is fundamentally different from novices. This is because experts have decades of knowledge and experience stored in their long-term memory, which they can readily deploy when faced with a problem to solve. As Willingham wrote,

> It turns out that those years of practice make a qualitative, not quantitative, difference in the way they think compared to how a well-informed amateur thinks. Thinking like a historian, a scientist, or a mathematician turns out to be a very tall order indeed.[4]

Willingham provided a significant contribution to what teachers often refer to as the 'knowledge versus skills' debate. Sometimes, those who engage in this debate are accused of offering up a false dichotomy, and a favourite riposte is, 'Surely, schools should just teach knowledge *and* skills?' Willingham agrees with this up to a point but emphasises that any curriculum, scheme of work, or even individual lesson needs to be sequenced so that knowledge comes first. 'Critical thinking', 'problem-solving', and 'creativity' are all laudable aims that are important for an advanced economy like Britain's, but they cannot be taught in isolation: they have to emerge from a bedrock of domain-specific knowledge. What is more, knowledge—in Willingham's description—encompasses so much more than 'mere facts'. Yes, facts are a component of knowledge, but in any curriculum subject, knowledge also includes concepts, principles, and approaches to analysis and learning. My reading of Willingham suggested that the way forward in this debate was not to argue for knowledge *over* skills nor for knowledge *and* skills. Instead, I would argue that successful teaching should offer knowledge, *then* skills. This particular insight from Willingham's work loomed large in my thinking as we undertook the curriculum review.

Illusory Gains

Whether our government's contention that the National Curriculum at the primary level needed a wholesale review could easily have been called into question by the test scores of primary-aged pupils. From 1997 to 2010, these suggested that English primary schools were not just working but working wonders. All pupils in England take National Curriculum assessments in English and Maths at the end of primary school, aged 10 or 11 (the end of Key Stage 2). The 'expected standard' for pupils to reach in their Key Stage 2 assessments, in order to be ready for secondary school, was a Level 4. Introduced by a Conservative government, these assessments were taken for the first time in May 1995. That year, 48 percent of pupils reached Level 4 in English, and 44 percent reached Level 4 in Maths. Over the years that followed, this figure shot up to 75 percent for English in 2000 and then to 79 percent by 2005, after which it plateaued. In Maths, the figures rose to 72 percent by 2000 and to 75 percent by 2005, after which, again, the figure plateaued (see Figure 5.1).[5]

These outcomes enabled the then-government to boast of 'record results in schools', as Gordon Brown did in his 2009 speech at the Labour Party conference.[6]

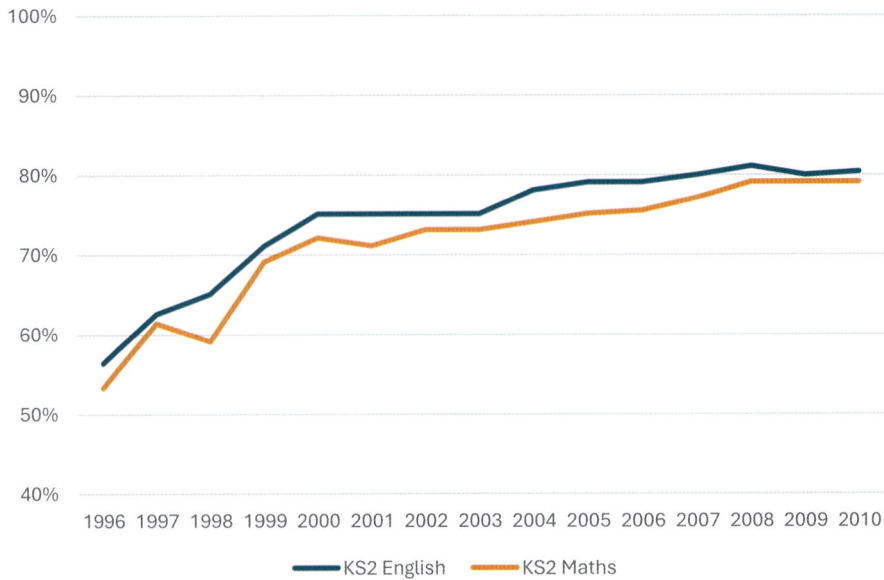

Figure 5.1 The proportion of English primary school pupils reaching the expected standard in English and Maths at the end of Key Stage 2 (aged 10 or 11).

However, the scale of this improvement did not correspond with what the public, or their children, were experiencing. Labour's claim in their 2010 manifesto that almost 100,000 more primary-age pupils were reaching the expected standard in reading, writing, and maths—quite simply—rang hollow.[7] And with good reason. In 2001, two academics from Durham University, Professors Carol Taylor Fitz-Gibbon and Peter Tymms, reviewed the improved scores of England's 11-year-olds and concluded: 'the changes seen between 1995 and 1999 are so dramatic and so out of step with the other longitudinal data as to raise questions about their being true representations of changes in standards.'[8] Further research by Tymms was validated by two of the government's own bodies, the QCA and the Statistics Commission. To quote the conclusion of the Commission's 2005 report,

> The Commission believes that it has been established that (a) the improvement in KS2 test scores between 1995 and 2000 substantially overstates the improvement in standards in English primary schools over that period, but (b) there was nevertheless some rise in standards.

Troubled by the implications for her government's reforms, Education Secretary Ruth Kelly did not accept these conclusions and told the Permanent Secretary at the Department to write a rebuttal, asking the Commission to 'revisit your conclusions and set the record straight.'[9]

There were multiple reasons why this overestimation occurred. As with any new assessments, marks improved as primary teachers became more familiar with the test, and their ability to teach 'exam technique' improved. In addition, pressure to improve results led teachers to focus on pupils at the 'borderline' of a Level 4, to the detriment of those pupils at the higher and lower end of the achievement spectrum. A simpler answer was that pass marks were allowed to drop without any corresponding rise in the difficulty of the papers. The total number of marks required to make the 'expected standard' of a Level 4 in English fell from 51 to 43 between 1998 and 2003 and from 52 to 45 in maths.[10]

A more reliable measure of changes in pupil attainment over time came from the Department of Business, Innovation and Skills, who were conducting their own surveys of literacy in the adult population in 2003 and 2011. Amongst adults attending primary school during the first phase of Labour reforms, the level of functional illiteracy in the 16–24 age bracket hardly moved, from 16 percent in 2003 to 15 percent in 2011.[11] The same stagnation in English reading was suggested by the international education survey, the Progress in International Reading Literacy Study (PIRLS), which is carried out every five years, and suggested that England's soaring improvement in reading at the end of primary school was an illusion. In PIRLS, England's 10-year-olds scored 553 in 2001 (placing England 3rd out of 35 participating countries), scored 539 in 2006 (15th out of 41 countries), and then returned to 552 in 2011 (11th out of 45 countries). Similarly ambivalent results were recorded by the PISA surveys into the attainment of English 15-year-olds in Reading, Mathematics, and Science. Attainment remained stable in mathematics and only improved marginally in reading, keeping England's children educated at primary schools during the New Labour years firmly in the mid-tier of international performance (see Figure 5.2).

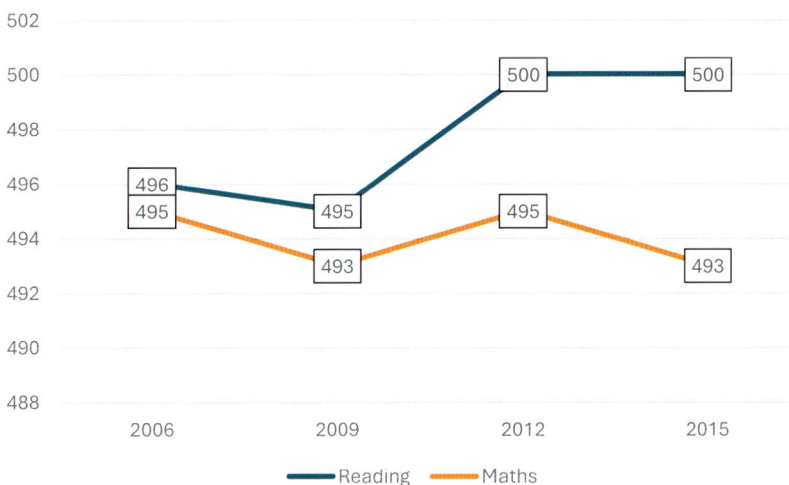

Figure 5.2 The scores for English pupils aged 15 years old in Reading and Mathematics, according to the OECD's Programme for International Student Assessment (PISA), 2006 to 2015.

In 2013, the OECD published an international survey of adult skills, including literacy. Far from 'record results', it found that the UK (constituting England and Northern Ireland) was the *only* nation amongst the 24 jurisdictions surveyed where literacy levels amongst 16 to 24-year-olds were worse than amongst 55 to 66-year-olds.[12] Reading that finding in 2013 left me aghast. Put another way, in 23 participating nations, you could be confident that young adults were more literate than those educated in the decades immediately following the Second World War. But not in England. We knew that claims of breakthrough improvements were based on inflation-induced data, and there remained a significant need for change.

National Curriculum Review

We launched our review of the National Curriculum on 20 January 2011, with the stated aim of replacing 'the current substandard curriculum with one based on the best systems in the world.'[13] This chapter will focus only on the primary school curriculum. Before going on, I should provide an overview of the different stages through which English children's schooling progresses. Generally speaking, the National Curriculum looms larger in English primary schools (5 to 11 years old) than it does in secondary schools (11 to 16 years old). This is for two reasons. Firstly, the National Curriculum covers almost all subjects at primary school, but only some subjects at secondary school. From the age of 14 onwards, the National Curriculum is only in place for English, Maths, Science, Citizenship, and Physical Education.

Secondly, pupils at primary school are assessed in English and Maths using National Curriculum assessments, which are overseen directly by the Department for Education. However, at secondary schools, pupils are assessed through GCSE exams, which are set by independent exam boards (an unusual quirk of the English system covered in the next chapter). Therefore, in most subjects at the secondary level, independent exam boards play a larger role in dictating what content pupils learn compared to the National Curriculum. Table 5.1, I hope, offers some clarity:

Table 5.1 Chart summarising the different stages of the National Curriculum in England

	Primary School		Secondary School	
	Key Stage 1	Key Stage 2	Key Stage 3	Key Stage 4
Age	5–7	7–11	11–14	14–16
Year Groups	1,2	3,4,5,6	7,8,9	10,11
English	✓*	✓**	✓	✓†
Mathematics	✓*	✓**	✓	✓†
Science	✓*	✓*	✓	✓†

(Continued)

Table 5.1 (*Continued*)

	Primary School		Secondary School	
	Key Stage 1	**Key Stage 2**	**Key Stage 3**	**Key Stage 4**
Art and Design	✓	✓	✓	
Citizenship			✓	✓
Computing	✓	✓	✓	
Design and Technology	✓	✓	✓	
Languages	✓	✓	✓	
Geography	✓	✓	✓	
History	✓	✓	✓	
Music	✓	✓	✓	
Physical Education	✓	✓	✓	✓

✓ Contained in the National Curriculum
* Teacher assessment of the National Curriculum
** Compulsory National Curriculum Assessments
† Compulsory subject assessed by GCSE

The National Curriculum review was conducted in two phases: the first concentrated on the core subjects of English, Maths, and Science, plus PE. The second phase, starting a year later in 2012, would cover the remaining subjects of Geography, History, Languages, Art and Design, Citizenship, Computing, and Design and Technology. The aim of the review was for a curriculum that 'properly reflects the body of knowledge all children should learn.' It should 'embody rigorous and high standards and create coherence in what is taught in schools.' That principle of coherence was vital: one of the main roles of a curriculum is to provide the optimal sequence for ensuring that the order in which components of a subject are taught minimises pupils' cognitive overload. On launching the curriculum review, we also referred to the important distinction between the National Curriculum and the school curriculum. As it stated, the National Curriculum should be 'a guide to study in key subjects, which gives parents and teachers confidence that students were acquiring the knowledge necessary at every level of study to make appropriate progress.' The school curriculum, on the other hand, is much wider and incorporates the whole curriculum as experienced by pupils in school.

To oversee our National Curriculum review we appointed a four-member Expert Panel and a 15-member Advisory Panel. Of course, who we appointed to these panels remained crucial, and I laboured over membership of the Advisory Panel to ensure it contained school leaders with a proven track record of success. Many names already encountered in earlier pages were present, such as the phonics expert Ruth Miskin, the primary school headteacher, Shahed Ahmed, and the secondary headteachers, Sir Michael Wilshaw and John McIntosh. I also included the primary school headteacher, John Martin of Castle Hill Junior School in Basingstoke, which I had recently visited and thought was a superb school. My school visits during our years in opposition and in government were hugely important, not least in being able to meet some exceptional teachers and school leaders who might, in the future, help with our reforms.

I also thought it important to include an independent school head on the panel and chose Bernice McCabe, the headmistress of the North London Collegiate College, a leading girls' public school. Bernice also ran the Prince's Teaching Institute, a charity established in 2006 by the Prince of Wales, as he then was, to offer teachers professional development based on enhancing their subject knowledge, an unusual aim at a time when the trend was towards child-centred and cross-curricula teaching.

To chair the four Members of the Expert Panel, we appointed Tim Oates. Since 2007, Tim had been the Director of Research and Assessment at Cambridge Assessment, a non-teaching department of the University of Cambridge which runs its exam boards. Prior to that, Tim had been Head of Research at the QCA, the quango responsible for developing the 2007 National Curriculum. However, Tim left the QCA out of disillusionment at what he saw as the declining standard of GCSE and A-level exams. Tim came to our attention in 2009 when he publicly attacked the new 2007 National Curriculum in the *Guardian* for being 'too vague', pointing out that it no longer even mentioned 'photosynthesis' in Biology.[14] Tim was a rare beast—a career educationalist who had not swallowed the hokum of skills-based curriculum theorising. When we first met, it did not take much to bring his righteous anger at the paucity of knowledge being taught in English schools to the surface. A philosophy graduate prone to citing technical academic papers as if they were common knowledge, Tim was soft of speech and a stickler for detail. I knew we would get on.

Global Leaders in Education

As an expert in global education systems, Tim Oates brought to our review a rigorous appraisal of what the highest-performing countries around the world were doing. Before the curriculum review was even announced, he had compiled his thinking into an influential essay entitled *Could do better*, published by Cambridge Assessment in November 2010. It had a particular focus on the leading lights of the PISA and PIRLS education league tables, such as Singapore, Shanghai, and Hong Kong. In 2012, I went to Hong Kong to see first-hand how maths is taught and how students achieve such high scores in the TIMSS and PISA international rankings. In the results of a PISA study published for that year, Hong Kong was third in the world in maths (behind just Shanghai and Singapore) and second in reading. By contrast, in 2012 England was 25th in maths and 23rd in reading.* My experiences on the ground whilst visiting Hong Kong schools firmly corresponded with this statistical evidence. I remember asking a 10-year-old pupil when his class learned their times tables. He told me the second year of primary school. When I asked if he could add 1/7 and 1/8, within a few seconds, he responded with the correct answer of 15/56. The same 2012 PISA survey revealed that 22 percent of English 15-year-olds were set to leave school functionally innumerate.[15] This means they were unable to carry out simple tasks such as recognising that a cyclist travelling 4km in ten minutes is going at the same speed if travelling 2km in five minutes.[16] The corresponding proportion of low attainers in Hong Kong was 9 percent, Singapore 8 percent, and Shanghai 4 percent.[17] Visiting schools in countries such as Hong Kong, I would ask myself, if such states could come so close to eliminating educational failure, why couldn't we?

Of course, you can point to any number of culturally contingent factors to explain away the educational performance of East Asian countries, such as greater social respect for authority, parental pressure, a more competitive job market, and so on. I would give such arguments credence were the classroom practice and curriculum design in East Asia largely the same as ours, but they were not. They were fundamentally different. In classroom after classroom that I have visited in such countries, desks are in rows, lessons are teacher-led, and pupils work from textbooks. When faced with such a fact, to refuse the possibility that classroom practices might play a role in pupils' success seems a particularly wilful form of denial.

In December 2011, the Expert Panel published its report and recommended a set of seven 'Key Principles.' These included:

- 'The National Curriculum should set out only the essential knowledge (facts, concepts, principles and fundamental operations) that all children should acquire, and leave schools to design a wider school curriculum that best meets the needs of their pupils and to decide how to teach this most effectively.'

- 'Our National Curriculum should compare favourably with curricula in the highest performing jurisdictions, reflecting the best collective wisdom we have about how children learn and what they should know.'

- 'The National Curriculum should embody rigour and high standards and create coherence in what is taught in schools, ensuring that all children have the opportunity to acquire a core of knowledge in the key subject disciplines.'

- And, in dealing with the conundrum that academies were exempt from the National Curriculum, we included the principle that: 'The National Curriculum

---

* These figures vary slightly from those included in the introduction, where only those nations involved in five consecutive surveys from 2009 to 2022 were included in the rankings.

will continue to be a statutory requirement for maintained schools [i.e. non-academies] but will also retain its importance as a national benchmark of excellence for all schools.'[18]

Accompanying the Expert Panel report were two key evidence documents that Tim Oates was instrumental in creating, aided by the exemplary work of around 20 DfE officials as well as the National Foundation for Educational Research (NFER). One paper published in February 2012 was entitled, 'What can we learn from the English, maths and science curricula of high performing jurisdictions?', which included a review of curricula from countries such as Australia, Canada, New Zealand, Singapore, Hong Kong, Finland, and Belgium. We wanted to include Japan and South Korea but could not source a good enough translation of their curriculum materials in time.[19] The other paper was a 'Report on subject breadth in international jurisdictions', published in December 2011, which included most of the previously mentioned countries together with Japan, South Korea, and the Netherlands.[20]

From these reports, three conclusions emerged. Firstly, our curriculum needed to be more challenging. This was particularly clear in Mathematics, where curriculums were easiest to compare. For example, Singapore, Hong Kong, Massachusetts, and Finland all expected more from pupils in terms of numbers and algebra by the end of primary school, with Singapore and Hong Kong expecting pupils to be able to complete calculations with both fractions and decimals using all four functions (add, subtract, multiply and divide) by the age of 12. By contrast, our 1999* National Curriculum expected 11-year-old pupils to understand fractions on a conceptual level but did not specify any use of them in calculations. Secondly, our curriculum needed to be more specific, with a coherent and detailed sequence of knowledge in each subject. The aversion to knowledge that influenced our 1999 Curriculum was reflected by the generic nature of its stated pupil outcomes. It was generally built around high-level statements which focused on skills and ways of thinking, but with very little elaboration of the building blocks which would allow pupils to reach such a point. For example, for Writing at Key Stage 2, it stated, 'pupils should be taught to: broaden their vocabulary and use it in inventive ways', but with no detail on what might constitute a broad vocabulary.[21]

Lastly, we needed the curriculum to specify fewer things in greater depth. Tim's favourite term for describing a good curriculum was 'parsimonious'. He wanted our new curriculum to contain little guidance, but what guidance it did contain, he wanted to be extremely well thought through. Previous iterations of England's National Curriculum had chosen to be eclectic, offering a range of content from which schools could pick. Instead, Tim argued, a good curriculum would be specific, providing a common curriculum which schools could then embellish and

---

* Whilst the Secondary National Curriculum had been updated in 2007 (see Chapter 2), the same Primary National Curriculum had remained in place since 1999.

augment. This lack of specificity about what schools should teach was compounded by the multiple curriculum documents which emerged from the Department during the late 1990s and 2000s. At the primary level, there was the 1999 National Curriculum, but also the various versions of the National Strategies, and (from 2005) the 'Every Child a Reader' and 'Every Child Counts' programmes, designed—at the cost of £144 million—for pupils who were falling behind.[22] All three were backed by the Department but offered competing and sometimes contradictory guidance. In contrast, the curriculums of high-performing jurisdictions such as Singapore and Hong Kong contained single, precisely thought-through sequences of knowledge. Pupils' education was too important to be left to randomness and chance.

The 2014 Curriculum

After various phases of consultation and drafts, the government published its new National Curriculum for England in September 2013. Schools were given a year to prepare for first teaching in September 2014. By the time of its publication, I had been out of office for a year (see Chapter 7). However, when I left office for the first time in September 2012, most of the work on the new Primary National Curriculum had been completed. When it was published a year later, the details that I had been developing were—to my relief—largely intact.

At the time of writing, the 2014 National Curriculum has now been in place for ten years, with minimal revision. In maths (based on the 2007 Singapore curriculum), pupils are expected by the age of 7 to know their 'number bonds' up to 20. These are simple addition and subtraction facts that they should know and recognise instantly (e.g. 16–7 = 9). By the age of 9, they are expected to know their timetables up to 12 x 12, whereas previously, pupils were only expected to know up to 10 x 10 by the age of 11. By the age of 11, pupils are expected to multiply and divide fractions, allowing them to progress to more advanced topics like algebra when they get to secondary school. The mathematics curriculum also makes it clear that facility in these number bonds and times tables is secured by practice.[23] However, when the first draft of the curriculum was sent out for informal consultation amongst maths subject associations, it returned with all 64 mentions of the word 'practice' expunged from the document. I was furious and rang Tim, who was on holiday in France at the time, to ask what was going on. From a layby outside Pontarlier, he gave me a crash course on the progressivist ideology when applied to maths. Essentially, members of the mathematics education establishment had long perceived practice as 'boring drudgery' and sought to find ways to teach maths without it. Tim gave me the courage to stick to my conviction, and we restored 'practice' as a fundamental principle of primary mathematics.

This was in tune with all the evidence that Daniel Willingham and others had provided about the importance of ensuring both procedures and number facts are secure in long term memory. In his book *Why Don't Students Like School*, Willingham writes persuasively to rehabilitate the idea of practice, and remove it from the negative connotations of the military term 'drill', or worse still, 'drill and kill'. The cognitive benefits of practice far outweigh the concerns some teachers have for the impact it might have on pupils' motivation and sense of fun. Willingham concludes it is 'virtually impossible to become proficient in a mental task without extended practice.'[24] Willingham argues that because our working memory has limited capacity, many of the more complicated tasks we perform, such as driving a car or playing the piano, rely on long term memory and practice. In applying this notion to maths, he argues you need to be fluent in both procedural knowledge (the algorithms) and the basic number bonds. Or as Malcolm Gladwell writes in his book *Outliers*, 'Practice isn't the thing you do once you're good. It's the thing you do that makes you good.'[25]

In English, the 2014 curriculum includes lists of words that all children should be able to use and spell by the end of primary school, words such as 'famous', 'favourite', and 'February' in Years 3 and 4, and 'temperature', 'thorough', and 'twelfth' in Years 5 and 6. We also added a greater focus on grammar, with a year-by-year explanation of what grammatical terms pupils should be able to use, starting with terms such as 'word', 'sentence', 'singular', and 'plural' in Year 1, and progressing to 'relative clause', 'the subjunctive', and 'use of the passive' in Year 6.

In retrospect, we may have given too much ground to the grammarians in our advisory group, who pushed 'fronted adverbials' to be included in the Year 4 Curriculum. This particular detail was frequently cited by critics of our reforms, as—to be fair—very few adults know, or have even heard, of a 'fronted adverbial'.* In later years, I did consider tweaking the grammar element of the English curriculum, but I was persuaded by advice from officials who said that children don't find concepts such as 'fronted adverbials' difficult, once they've been told about them. It's only the adults who have never heard of them before who are fazed.

Though we may have overreached in some areas, my confidence in the fundamental arguments behind the teaching of grammar remained. All children should be able to write prose where verbs agree with subjects, commas separate independent clauses, and pronouns agree in number with the nouns to which they refer. Now, for children from homes which are suffused with reading and complex language, it may be possible to assimilate such rules indirectly. But for a great number of pupils in our schools, the best way to learn the rules that govern our language is through explicit teaching. In order to teach in that way, you need a shared language of how language works—what academics call a 'meta-language', and we call 'grammar'. When pupils come to learning a foreign language, the benefit of having a 'meta-language' of grammatical terms pays out again. It would amuse me that the comment pieces attacking the grammatical terms in the new Primary Curriculum were always written using perfect grammar by writers who would be appalled to

---

* For those of you scratching your heads, a 'fronted adverbial' is a term used at the start of a sentence (hence 'fronted'), which modifies the following clause. For example, 'Later that day, I heard the bad news'.

do otherwise. It was beyond me why these writers would want to take away from children the ability to write with the accuracy that they displayed. Perhaps grammatical knowledge, as with knowledge more generally, is like money: it tends to be those who have it who are complacent enough to deny its importance.

Another feature of the 2014 primary Curriculum that distinguished it from its 1999 predecessor is that it specifies when content in English, Maths, and Science should be taught on a year-by-year basis. The 1999 Curriculum broke content down according to the longer timescales of Key Stage 1 (ages 5 to 7) and Key Stage 2 (ages 7 to 11). This vagueness was seen as a virtue, allowing teachers to decide what to teach and when, according to the abilities, interests, and needs of their pupils. However, I wanted more specificity, as did Tim Oates. As Tim has recently written: 'While the autonomy argument drove towards retaining the larger content blocks of the key stages covering two to three years of teaching, evidence pointed towards the greater clarity and support to schools of year-by-year specification, particularly in primary.'[26] As the subject content at Key Stage 2 covers a four-year period, there is a significant difference in what is taught to an 11-year-old compared to a seven-year-old. This became a major source of disagreement in the Advisory Panel. In June 2012, one member—a Professor at the Institute of Education—wrote a blog post on his university website attacking the approach as 'fatally flawed', which was widely covered in the national media. He argued that the curriculum would rob primary teachers of the ability to exercise 'professional judgement' and contained insufficient thinking on the needs of those who fall behind.[27]

In reading his criticism, I feared he had misunderstood the intention of the National Curriculum. It is, fundamentally, guidance as to the optimal sequence of teaching that should be followed. However, it is very far from being the last word on what the enacted curriculum in every English school should be. As its aims explain, 'The national curriculum is just one element in the education of every child. There is time and space in the school day and in each week, term, and year to range beyond the national curriculum specifications.'[28] Of course, for pupils with Special Educational Needs and Disabilities, English as an additional language, or for those who simply struggle to keep up with their peers, the Primary Curriculum should not be a restriction. Teachers should exercise professional judgement in catering for pupils who move less quickly through content than their peers. The curriculum is not an exclusive path that all pupils must take in tandem, but an optimal path that the majority of pupils in a good school should be expected to achieve. As we wrote in our 2011 White Paper, 'We want the National Curriculum to be a benchmark not a straitjacket, a body of knowledge against which achievement can be measured.'[29] Today, this is the spirit in which I see it being used in any good school I visit.

Beyond the core subjects of English, Mathematics, and Science, the rest of the Primary Curriculum focuses on the traditional subjects of Art and Design, Computing, Design and Technology, Geography, History, Languages, Music, and Physical education. However, our guidance for those subjects is very light touch. Whilst

English covers 85 pages, Mathematics 44 pages, and Science 31, the remaining subjects are all just three or four pages long. For such subjects, there is less need for year-by-year prescribed content, as the path that pupils take to build an understanding of the subject is more cumulative than hierarchical. Whilst in Maths, it is generally accepted that you need to have mastered your times tables before trying to simplify fractions, in Geography, it makes little difference whether you start Year 4 by studying cities or coastlines.

That being said, the curriculum for subjects such as Geography still included more specified subject knowledge than had previously been the case. At Key Stage 1, I was delighted that pupils were required to name and locate the seven continents, the five oceans, the four countries of the UK, and their capital cities and surrounding seas. It also requires them to use simple compass directions of north, south, east, and west. At Key Stage 2, there is the requirement to teach the countries and major cities of Europe, North America, and South America (with Africa, Russia, Asia, and the Middle East saved for Key Stage 3). I was less sanguine about the Primary History curriculum, which failed to put into statute some of the specific content in early British history that I believed should be taught. Episodes such as Caesar's invasion of Britain or the death of Edward the Confessor were left as non-statutory suggestions in the notes and guidance. For this reason, in 2022, I commissioned a non-statutory Model History Curriculum to be written, setting out in detail and on a year-by-year basis the history that should be taught in primary schools and Key Stage 3 of secondary school (see Chapter 6).

Nevertheless, the 2014 National Curriculum was a significant improvement on what it replaced. Provided schools were getting the basics right in literacy, numeracy, and science, we were broadly happy with a high degree of autonomy in the rest of the curriculum. Even with the core subjects, we had few prescriptions about how those subjects should be taught. In our minds, the National Curriculum provided the accountability side of our reforming equation: it was the Department for Education's role to specify *what* primary pupils should know by the end of each year or Key Stage, but schools gained increased autonomy to decide *how* they got there. There was, however, one exception.

Phonics First, Fast, and Only

During the early years of the curriculum review, I remember meeting Mary Bousted, the General Secretary of the ATL, one of the UK's main teaching unions. On the topic of curriculum reform, she noted the government's inconsistent messaging in preaching the virtues of school autonomy with one breath whilst prescribing phonics teaching with the next. It was a fair challenge and one that—at the time—I could only answer by saying, 'Just give me this one pass; let me be prescriptive about phonics!' Which, by and large, she did.

Thinking back to that conversation, I believe there was a good reason for treating phonics as an exception. Firstly, phonics is unusual in the clarity of its evidence base. There are many other areas of the school curriculum where teaching methods are contested. But, whether a pupil can read by age 6 is very binary, allowing the evidence base to be conclusive. The evidence base was also growing, particularly in Scotland, where the most rigorous early reading studies in the UK were being conducted. West Dunbartonshire, close to Glasgow, is Scotland's second poorest council area. As an area of severe social deprivation, it had for decades suffered from the blight of adult illiteracy. Starting in 1997, its council pioneered a project to eradicate illiteracy, involving almost 60,000 pupils in 50 schools. Ten years later, the number of pupils leaving West Dunbartonshire's primary schools with low literacy had dropped from 28 percent to 6 percent. Central to their approach had been systematic synthetic phonics. What is more, the West Dunbartonshire programme cost only £13 per pupil, showing that effective teaching does not have to cost a fortune.[30] The West Dunbartonshire studies added to the previous study from Clackmannanshire, as well as large-scale government reviews in Australia and America (see Chapter 1), all of which confirmed the primacy of systematic synthetic phonics as the best approach for teaching young children to read.

I also pleaded exceptional status for phonics because early reading is, quite simply, too important to be left to chance. It is sad for pupils to leave school having underachieved in French or without much historical understanding. However, it is a tragedy for them to leave unable to read. A true believer in the structuralist approach to school reform would claim that primary schools, given high autonomy and strong accountability, would naturally gravitate towards phonics as the most effective approach available. However, I was not willing to wait and see whether or not this came to be. Our curriculum was not going to give systematic, synthetic phonics equal billing amongst a range of strategies for early reading: it had to be phonics first, fast and only, because that is where the evidence unequivocally lay. For this reason, we—very unusually—made a market intervention. From 2011, the Department provided match funding for any primary school looking to purchase resources or training in a new phonics programme. With the help of the former primary headteacher Gordon Askew, we created a list of programmes, with only those that used a systematic synthetic phonics approach approved. By 2013, more than 14,000 primary schools received the funding for new reading programmes (out of 16,500 in England), at an overall cost of £23.7 million.[31]

However, match funding for programmes was never going to be enough; we had to ensure they were being used successfully. Whilst in opposition, my conversations with Ruth Miskin and members of the Reading Reform Foundation led us to develop a test that could ensure children were making progress with their phonics and that their schools were teaching phonics correctly. This test would become the 'phonics screening check', which we introduced in 2012 for Year 1 pupils in all English primary schools. I wanted this check to be a model of simplicity. It required a Year 1 teacher to take five to ten minutes to assess each pupil when they asked them to read out 40 words. If a pupil could correctly read 32 or more of the words, they passed. The 40 words contain 20 actual words and 20 'pseudo-words', such as 'elt', 'bain', and 'girst'. These 'pseudo-words' do not exist in the English language and, therefore, help to distinguish between pupils decoding words through phonetic knowledge and pupils recognising familiar words having been taught to read by sight through a 'whole-word' approach, as this latter group would be more likely to struggle with made up words. To ensure that pupils have some context for reading the pseudo-words, they are told the word is the name of a monster and it is accompanied by a cartoon creature (see Figure 5.3).

There were long debates about the age at which children should sit the test. Jon Coles, the Director General of Schools at the DfE, argued for the end of Reception to ensure schools embarked on the teaching of phonics as soon as they started school. Others argued for the end of Year 2. In the end, I decided that Year 1 (age 6) was the best time, both educationally and politically. We determined the pass mark by assembling a panel of teachers to discuss and recommend a suitable number of correctly read words to constitute a pass. They advised 32 out of 40. I thought this was a high threshold, so I established another panel of teachers and asked them the same question. Independently, they came up with the same figure, so 32 it would be.

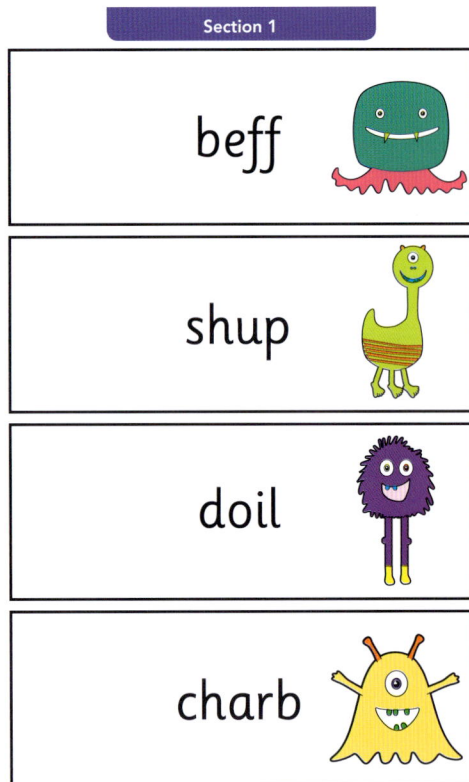

Figure 5.3 An example monster from the 2016 Phonics Screening Check, named 'Charb'. Contains public sector information licensed under the Open Government Licence v3.0.

Although the phonics screening check does help teachers identify pupils needing extra help, its fundamental purpose is school accountability. This aspect required careful negotiation with the profession, as National Curriculum assessments had only just been boycotted in 2010 (see further on). We agreed that results from the screening check would not be published on a school-by-school basis but would be shared with the local authority and Ofsted through RAISE-online (and later the Assessing School Performance intranet site). The aggregated figures would also be published at local authority level and nationally. Schools are encouraged to provide extra help to pupils who did not pass, and those pupils are tested again at the end of Year 2 to ensure that no child slips through the net with their struggles in reading unidentified. In 2016, we piloted a requirement for those pupils who failed the check for the second time (at the end of Year 2) to retake the check in Year 3. The pilot was a success in identifying a small minority of children who were still struggling with phonics decoding. But, I was unable to persuade the then-Secretary of State to support my desire to introduce the requirement permanently.

The Phonics Screening Check was ready to go in June 2011, but we decided to pilot it in just 300 schools that year. Only 33 percent of pupils in those schools passed. In 2012, the Phonics Screening Check became compulsory, and in that year, 58 percent of 6-year-olds passed. Nationwide, the most easily read word was 'jump' with a 95 percent facility, whilst the most easily read pseudo-word was 'yop' with a facility of 94 percent. The most difficult word was 'portrait' and pseudo-word 'yune', with facilities of 45 and 44 percent, respectively.[32] From 2012, the proportion of pupils meeting the expected standard in phonics increased every year to 2018, when 82 percent of pupils passed the check, representing 205,000 more pupils being on course to become good readers by the age of 6 compared to 2012.[33] In 2020 and 2021, the check was not carried out due to Covid, and as with so many areas of schooling, outcomes have slipped. However, with 80 percent of pupils passing the check in 2024, rising from 75 percent in the immediate post-Covid year, we are almost back on track (see Figure 5.4).

Though we gave a clear assurance that a school's results would not be published, there was nothing stopping us from publicly celebrating those who did well. Every year, I wrote a letter of congratulation to each primary school that achieved 100 percent in the phonics screening check, and successful schools and their pupils would often proudly display their letters in local newspapers and on social media. One borough which repeatedly celebrated exceptional results was Newham in East London. In 2011, Robin Wales, the directly elected mayor of the London Borough of Newham, came to see me in my office in Sanctuary Buildings. He had a proposal to teach every primary school child in Newham to play a musical instrument and was seeking government funding. Although I was in favour of the scheme, this was a period of severe restrictions on discretionary spending and, sadly, no funds were available. Instead, I suggested to Robin that he might like to pilot a scheme promoting high-quality phonics teaching in all 67 Newham primary schools. I had been trying, unsuccessfully, to find a local education authority

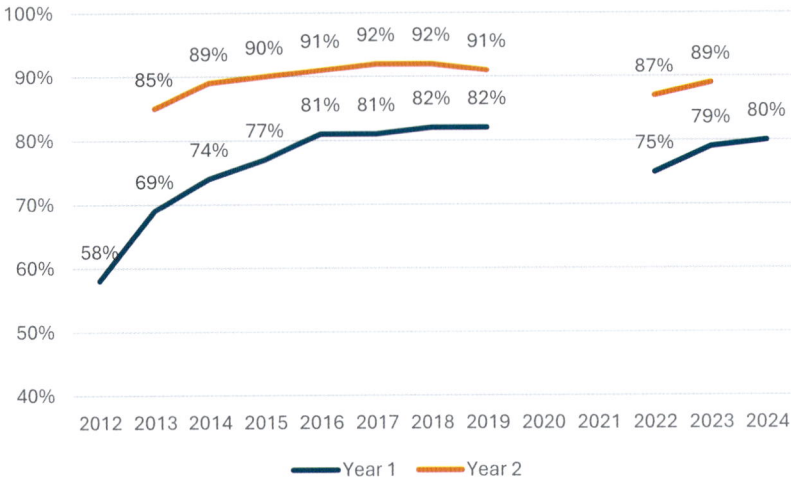

Figure 5.4 Percentage of pupils meeting the expected standard in the phonics screening check, 2012 to 2023.

that made systematic, synthetic phonics a major priority, and would eventually find only one: Newham.

Robin is one of those politicians driven by conviction and a genuine desire to improve the life outcomes for those living in his borough. The fact that he was a Labour mayor and I a Conservative minister did not matter in the slightest to him. He later told me that my passion about the vital importance of phonics teaching and encouragement as Schools Minister for him to roll it out across his entire borough gave him the impetus to do so. 'You led it', he told me. In Newham's budget for 2012/13, he secured £693,000 for that year and £495,000 for the following year to fund the pilot. Robin got to know Ruth Miskin, who was already involved with two schools which used her scheme, Read Write Inc in the borough: Elmhurst Primary School with Shahed Ahmed as head and Maryland Primary School with Lorna Jackson as head. The borough increased the number of primary schools trained in Read Write Inc, and by 2011, 45 of the 67 primary schools in Newham had signed up and were benefiting from regular borough-wide Development Days. In 2015, 83 percent of 6-year-olds in Newham passed the Phonics Screening Check compared to 77 percent nationally. By 2018, that figure had risen to 88 percent compared to 82 percent nationally. In 2017, Newham was joint first in England for its phonics results despite being one of the most disadvantaged boroughs in the country.[34]

However, not everyone showed the same support as Robin Wales did for our drive on phonics. In June 2014, the General Secretary of the United Kingdom Literacy Association (UKLA) wrote an open letter to Michael Gove opposing the phonics check. He warned:

The phonics check is methodologically flawed, undermines confidence of children, particularly some of the more able, is negatively impacting on how reading is taught and is an inefficient, and expensive and time consuming, way of assessing an aspect of children's reading ability.[35]

The letter was counter-signed by the doyens of the education establishment: education professors, chairs of subject associations, and the General Secretary of England's second-largest teaching union. Ten years on, we can say with some confidence that the UKLA's predictions have not come true. Since the introduction of the phonics screening check, England has risen in the PIRLS international league tables for reading ability amongst 10-year-olds from tenth place in 2011 to eighth place in 2016 and to fourth place in 2021. This placed only Singapore, Hong Kong, and Russia ahead of us out of 43 participating jurisdictions that tested children of the same age. Whilst pupils' scores in most participating nations saw sizeable falls between 2016 and 2021 due to Covid, the performance of English pupils fell by just one point.

Analysing the data, academics from the University of Oxford found a positive correlation between pupils' performance in the Year 1 phonics screening check and performance in PIRLS 2021 at Year 5. What is more, the gender gap in reading performance amongst English pupils participating in the PIRLS survey has narrowed every five years. In 2001, the difference between boys and girls was 22 points, but in 2021, it was just ten points. Most gratifying of all, it is in the results of the lowest-attainers where the greatest improvements have been made.[36] We can now confidently claim, as *The Times* front page did in May 2023, that English pupils are 'the best readers in the western world'.[37] Of all the reforms I was able to introduce in government, the promotion of systematic, synthetic phonics teaching in primary schools has been the most important.

Testing Times at Primary

As our cautious implementation of the phonics screening check showed, assessment at the primary level had long been a vexed issue. Prior to the 1990s, there was no national testing of pupils in English primary schools. When the National Curriculum was introduced in 1989, it was meant to be accompanied by assessments. However, the nature of these assessments—initially known as Standard Assessment Tasks (SATs)—proved to be highly controversial, causing teacher strikes and a government review in 1995. The newly designed National Curriculum assessments were only taken for the first time in 1995.* A decade of stability ensued, as Year 6 Assessments were taken every May by 10 and 11-year-olds, consisting of three English tests (writing, spelling and reading), three mathematics tests

---

* The botched introduction of SATs during the early 1990s and the subsequent media attention they gained firmly implanted the term 'SATs' in the national mind. Thus, 'SATs' has stuck as a colloquial term to describe primary school assessment, even though it was officially retired almost 30 years ago.

(calculator, non-calculator, and mental maths), and two science tests. These externally set, standardised tests for primary schools were a crucial first step in the long story of English education reform. Before the 1990s, there was no way in which primary schools could reliably compare their outcomes, meaning that identifying effective and ineffective practices was never much more than educated guesswork. Once comparable data on pupil outcomes was made publicly available, parents could make informed choices about where to send their child to school. Given the fact that schools are funded on a per-pupil basis (another change made by the 1988 Education Reform Act), the survival of a school depends on parents choosing it for their children. In creating a system of high autonomy and high accountability at the primary school level, the existence of standardised, national assessments since the mid-1990s was an important starting point.

However, when we entered government in 2010, this whole architecture of primary assessment was under threat due to a fiasco of epic proportions that had happened in the final months of the previous Labour Government. The QCA had contracted out the administration of National Curriculum Assessments to an American company named ETS, which—it turned out—was ill-equipped for the job. In 2008, everything unfurled: their computer system malfunctioned, markers began quitting, and enormous delays ensued. In August, one month after the deadline for returning marks to schools, almost 200,000 pupils' results were unavailable. By October, many were still outstanding, and in March 2009, it was reported that up to half of all grades were incorrect in some papers. The ETS contract was cancelled, and, to much embarrassment for all involved, the previous contractor (Edexcel) had to be called in to sort out the mess. An official inquiry was launched. One immediate outcome was that in 2009, the Science Key Stage 2 Assessments were cancelled, to be replaced with internal teacher assessments. This led to calls within the profession to abolish all external Key Stage 2 Assessments.[38] Over the next year, this anti-testing campaign gained ground, and in the spring of 2010, the main teachers and headteachers unions, the NUT and NAHT, balloted their members to boycott the Key Stage 2 National Curriculum Assessments that summer. This was the summer of the 2010 election, so one month after the coalition government was formed, some 4,005 primary schools (more than a quarter of the total number in England) did not administer the government's tests, leaving thousands of pupils without grades. Unsurprisingly, the 'SATs boycott' gained significant media attention.[39] Teachers in England had never taken widespread action against a statutory duty before, and we urgently needed to ensure that it did not happen again.

Following the 2010 'SATs boycott', Michael Gove launched a fresh review into the future of primary assessment. Unusually, he asked someone from outside the world of education, the historian Paul Bew, to act as its chair. Lord Bew was assisted by a panel of experts, and I ensured that school leaders with a successful track record—such as Kate Dethridge and Sally Coates—were included on the panel. Published in June 2011, Lord Bew's Report was a masterstroke of compromise and clear thinking. From the start, his review disappointed the teaching unions and the anti-testing lobby by affirming the need for external assessments of pupil attainment at primary school. Schools are public bodies, receiving tens of billions of pounds a year, and as the Bew Report argued, they must be held accountable for the job that they are doing. However, this came with some important concessions.

Surveying primary teachers, it became clear to Bew and his panel that one assessment was a far more significant cause of anger and frustration than all the others—the 65-minute-long English writing assessment. There was a widespread perception amongst primary teachers that whilst Maths, Reading, and Science (until it was discontinued in 2009) assessments were quite empirical and easy to mark, English writing was far more subjective. It is not surprising that this was the case: reliably assessing a generic skill such as 'writing' is always a challenge. The mark scheme for the English writing assessment attempted to do so via prose descriptions of different levels of writing quality, but these are difficult to interpret consistently. For example, in 2008, pupils were asked to write an imaginary story about a young man called Pip Davenport, who became famous for inventing a new kind of funfair ride. According to the mark scheme, a Band 3 answer would see 'some straightforward stylistic features used to support purpose', whereas a Band 4 answer would see 'Some stylistic features add emphasis and interest'. In a Band 2 answer, 'the handwriting is regular with some flow and movement', in a Band 3 answer, 'the handwriting is consistent and fluent'.[40] For teachers and examiners to distinguish between such descriptors with any sort of consistency is extremely difficult, some would say impossible. What is more, such prose descriptors encourage dispiriting 'teaching to the test', as Year 6 teachers spend much of the year teaching their class formulaic ways in which to perform the requirements in the prose mark.

The Bew Report concluded that there should be no more external assessment of pupils' writing at Key Stage 2, and teachers would provide their own 'teacher-assessed' judgements instead. There would, however, be a new assessment of the more empirically measurable skills of grammar, punctuation, and spelling, to be taken for the first time in 2015. Many had hoped for a full abolition of external testing at Key Stage 2, to be replaced by teacher assessment in every subject. Teacher assessment involves class teachers using their overall knowledge of a pupil's working level to decide on a grade. Its supporters argue that the judgement of teachers who know their children well is more holistic and, therefore, more fair. In a 2010 joint policy statement, three of the major teaching unions—the NAHT, NUT, and ATL—argued that teacher assessment 'is a more valid form of assessment, because a much wider range of pupils' learning, over a much longer time period, can be evaluated by the teacher than is possible through a few short, one-off, tests.'[41]

The Bew Report held a firm line against such thinking. Firstly, there is an inevitable bias towards generosity when teachers assess the outcomes of pupils they have themselves taught. This is particularly the case when those results feed into national league tables, making any objective, external accountability impossible. You only have to look at the runaway grade inflation that took place due to two years of teacher assessment during the Covid-19 pandemic in 2020 and 2021 to see recent evidence of this phenomenon. Secondly, the Bew Report contained fascinating (if depressing) research from Professor Burgess at the University of Bristol regarding bias in teacher assessments. By comparing the marks that Year 6 pupils achieved in external National Curriculum Assessments from 2002–05 against the marks their own teachers gave them through teacher assessment, Burgess discovered systematic bias against particular racial groups. As he wrote, with teacher assessment, 'On average, Black Caribbean and Black African pupils are under-assessed relative to white pupils, and Indian, Chinese and mixed white-Asian pupils are over-assessed.'[42]

This stereotype effect is a consistent finding in much academic research into teacher assessment. In 2015, Dr Tammy Campbell from the Institute of Education found a similar effect with teacher assessment of pupils aged 6 to 7 years old at the end of Key Stage 1, compared to tests carried out by the Millenium Cohort Study. Low-income pupils, pupils with SEN, non-white pupils, and pupils speaking English as an additional language were underrated via teacher assessment. When it came to reading, teachers underrated boys. When it came to maths, they underrated girls. Teachers cannot be relied upon to provide accurate assessments of the pupils because of the human tendency towards stereotypes. As Campbell emphasises in her paper, this is not because teachers are prejudiced; it is because they are human. As she wrote, 'all individuals have a propensity to enact this function to some degree: there is no reason that teachers should be exempt, nor unusually prone. Bias in judgements of pupils is just one manifestation of the human tendency to stereotype.'[43]

One of the most important principles I gleaned from the Bew Report was that external tests are a significantly fairer way to grade pupils, particularly those from minority backgrounds, than teacher assessment. External tests may be high-stakes and, at times, stressful, but they are a great equaliser. Like blind auditions for musicians, they strip out all possibility of bias and stereotype. For this reason, I would ultimately like to see a return to external National Curriculum assessments in Science at Key Stage 2, as well as English and Maths at the end of Key Stage 1. However, as with all areas of politics, the art of the possible had to prevail. Following the 'SATs boycott' that took place in 2010, annual assessments in Reading and Maths were successfully resumed. In addition, we introduced the phonics screening check in 2012, the grammar, punctuation, and spelling test in 2015, and the Multiplication Tables Check for Year 4 pupils in 2020 (delayed to 2022). Over this period, there has been no further teacher action against primary assessment.

Evidence-Led Policy

Reforming the Primary National Curriculum was beset with controversy. At every step, prominent educationalists criticised the direction we were taking. In March 2013, the education establishment made their most public intervention against our reforms when 100 university academics sent a joint letter to the *Independent* attacking our proposed National Curriculum. Its signatories represented most of the teacher training colleges in England. The opening to their letter read as follows:

> We are writing to warn of the dangers posed by Michael Gove's new National Curriculum which could severely erode educational standards. The proposed curriculum consists of endless lists of spellings, facts and rules. This mountain of data will not develop children's ability to think, including problem-solving, critical understanding and creativity.[44]

They went on to predict, 'Inappropriate demands will lead to failure and demoralisation.' Other predictions were even more melodramatic. In July 2013, Professor Terry Wrigley of Leeds Metropolitan University told the BBC that our new Primary Curriculum 'sets up the majority of children to fail.' Wrigley concluded, 'This is the Pied Piper curriculum: it abolishes childhood.'[45] Ten years on, international league tables show that educational standards in England are improving, not eroding. Childhood has not been abolished, nor yet—at the time of writing—has our curriculum. Instead, it has been generally accepted by teachers who prove to be far more pragmatic and accommodating than the educationalists who chose to speak for them.

In developing our curriculum reforms, we let evidence lead our approach, including international comparisons, empirical trials on teaching initial reading, and academic research regarding teacher assessment. This evidence led us to design a curriculum which was radically different from what came before. That, I believe, helps explain why the response from the English education establishment was so extreme. It also explains why so much had to change.

Notes

1 D. T. Willingham, *Why Don't Students Like School?*, San Francisco: Wiley, 2009, p. 107.
2 Willingham, *Why Don't Students Like School?*, p. 34.
3 Willingham writes about transfer and domains in *Why Don't Students Like School?*, but addresses the question of domain specificity more directly in D. T. Willingham, 'Ask the cognitive scientist: How can educators teach critical thinking?', *American Educator*, Fall 2020.
4 Willingham, *Why Don't Students Like School?*, p. 128.
5 Figures taken from Ruth Lupton and Polina Obolenskaya, 'Labour's record on education: Policy, spending and outcomes 1997–2010', *Social Policy in a Cold Climate Working Paper WP03*, 2013, p. 35.
6 Gordon Brown, *Speech to the Labour Party Conference*, 29 September 2009.
7 *The Labour Party Manifesto 2010: A Future Fair for All*, 2010, p. 32.
8 Quoted in T. Richmond and S. Freedman, *Rising Marks, Falling Standards: An Investigation into Literacy, Numeracy and Science in Primary and Secondary Schools*, London: Policy Exchange, 2009, p. 21.
9 Quoted in Richmond and Freedman, *Rising Marks, Falling Standards*, p. 24.
10 Richmond and Freedman, *Rising Marks, Falling Standards*, pp. 22–23.

11 A. Heath et al., 'Education under new labour, 1997–2010', *Oxford Review of Economic Policy*, vol. 29, no. 1, 2013, p. 237.

12 OECD, *OECD Skills Outlook 2013: First Results from the Survey of Adult Skills*, OECD Publishing, 2013, p. 107.

13 Department for Education, 'Press release: National curriculum review launched', 20 January 2011.

14 W. Mansell and J. Shepherd, 'Secondary school curriculum is "too vague", exam assessors warn', *The Guardian*, 20 October 2009.

15 OECD, *PISA 2012 Results: What Students Know and Can Do—Student Performance in Mathematics, Reading and Science*, vol. I, OECD, 2013, p. 406.

16 *PISA 2012 Results*, p. 68.

17 *PISA 2012 Results*, p. 298.

18 Department for Education, *The Framework for the National Curriculum: A Report by the Expert Panel for the National Curriculum Review*, 2011, p. 6.

19 Department for Education, *What Can We Learn from the English, Mathematics and Science Curricula of High Performing Jurisdictions?*, 2012.

20 Department for Education, *Report on Subject Breadth in International Jurisdictions*, 2011.

21 QCA, *The National Curriculum: Handbook for Primary Teachers in England*, 1999, p. 56.

22 Department for Education, *Every Child Counts: The Independent Evaluation—Technical Report*, 2011, p. 1.

23 All details can be found within Department for Education, *The National Curriculum in England—Framework Document*, 2014.

24 Willingham, *Why Don't Students Like School?*, p. 107.

25 M. Gladwell, *Outliers: The Story of Success*, London: Penguin, 2009, p. 42.

26 T. Oates, *Preparing for Power: Policy Making Around the School Curriculum from 2010*, London: Institute for Government, 2024.

27 See coverage in W. Stewart and H. Ward, 'Split down the middle', *TES Magazine*, 15 June 2012 and J. Vasagar, 'Michael Gove's curriculum attacked by expert who advised him', *The Guardian*, 12 June 2012.

28 *The National Curriculum in England—Framework Document*, p. 6.

29 *White Paper: The Importance of Teaching*, p. 40.

30 Summarised in T. Burkard, *A World First for West Dunbartonshire: The Elimination of Reading Failure*, London: Centre for Policy Studies, 2006.

31 N. Gibb, *Speech to the Reading Reform Foundation*, 28 March 2015.

32 Standards and Testing Agency, *Phonics Screening Check: 2012 Technical Report*, London: STA, 2012, p. 15.

33 Figures compiled from Department for Education statistical releases.

34 Figures taken from *Case Study: London Borough of Newham Narrows Attainment Gap in Phonics Screening Check*, Ruth Miskin Training, 2018.

35 'Open letter to Michael Gove: "Why the Year 1 phonics check must go"', *TES Magazine*, 27 June 2014.

36 A. Lindorff, J. Stiff, and H. Kayton, *PIRLS 2021: National Report for England Research Report*, London: Department for Education, 2024, pp. 6–7.

37 N. Woolcock, 'Children in England are best readers in the western world', *The Times*, 16 May 2023.

38 The history of national curriculum assessments and the 2008 ETS marking 'fiasco' is covered in detail Richmond and Freedman, *Rising Marks, Falling Standards*, Chapter 3.

39 G. Paton, 'Sats results: quarter of schools boycott tests', *Daily Telegraph*, 3 August 2010.

40 *English Tests Mark Schemes: Reading, Writing and Spelling Tests*, London: QCA, 2008.

41 Quoted in *The Bew Report*, p. 48.

42 Quoted in *The Bew Report*, p. 49.

43 T. Campbell, 'Stereotyped at seven? Biases in teacher judgement of pupils' ability and attainment', *Journal of Social Policy*, vol. 44, no. 3, 2015.

44 'Letters: Gove will bury pupils in facts and rules', *Independent*, 19 March 2013.

45 H. Richardson, 'Gove primary curriculum "abolishes childhood"', *BBC News*, 11 July 2013.

6 Qualification Reform

> GCSEs are, as they stand the walking wounded. 30 years of grade inflation. Years of lunatic BTEC equivalence. Successive, incremental, Darwinian dilution of content in favour of vapid, vague skills that rely on content to exist but ironically are starved of it. Reform or replace, the outcome is the same. The system needs to change.
>
> Tom Bennett, 'The Behaviour Guru' blog, January 2013

A good primary education can put pupils on a positive trajectory that lasts for the rest of their education, but it is at secondary school where pupils gain the qualifications that stay with them for the rest of their lives. However, by 2010 the English exams and qualifications system was in dire need of reform, having been debased by almost two decades of grade inflation, dumbed-down content, modularisation, and 'equivalent' qualifications. The previous chapter covered assessment problems at the primary level, but these paled in comparison with the horror show that was the secondary examination system.

Following Key Stages 1 and 2 at primary school, English secondary education begins at Key Stage 3, which encompasses pupils ages 11 to 14. During these three years, pupils study a full sweep of compulsory subjects detailed in the National Curriculum, and there are no external examinations. At Key Stage 4, which pupils start at age 14, their studies lead to examinations, which they take at age 16, most commonly the GCSE (General Certificate of Secondary Education). At Key Stage 4, pupils can, for the first time, make choices about which subjects to continue and which to drop. Mathematics, English Language, and at least two Science GCSEs are compulsory, leaving pupils to choose around four remaining subject options. In 2023, English pupils, on average, studied for eight GCSEs, in addition to a much smaller number of other non-GCSE qualifications.

At Key Stage 5, ages 16 to 18, students may choose to continue their academic study with the Advanced Level (A-level) qualification or take a more technical or vocational pathway. In 2024, 33 percent of 18-year-olds studied the traditional combination of three or more A-levels, 13 percent took one or two A-levels (commonly in combination with other qualifications), and the remainder studied from a wide range of other post-16 qualifications.[1] England is unusual in the level of specialism

DOI: 10.4324/9781003533474-7

afforded to students at this stage, as there are no compulsory subjects. The norm in most other nations is to study perhaps six or seven subjects at the upper secondary stage, compared to the norm of just three in England. This approach is often called into question, but I have always favoured it, as I believe academic specialisation at 16 enables more able students to develop intellectually, as well as providing a better transition from school to university.

A System in Need of Reform

GCSE and A-level qualifications have a long history and international reputation, with A-levels having been taught in English schools since 1951. The GCSE was introduced in 1986, replacing the previous two-tier system, where a minority of pupils sat Ordinary Levels (O-levels), whilst everyone else sat the less academic Certificate of Secondary Education (CSE).

However, by 2010, these qualifications were at risk of losing their reputation for academic rigour. Ever since the first GCSEs were taken in 1988, and school performance tables were introduced in 1992, the government measure for assessing schools was the proportion of pupils achieving at least five GCSE passes at grade C or above. This was seen as the basic, or 'expected standard' for being able to access a wide range of post-16 courses. Following the introduction of the A star (A*) grade in 1994, this 'expected standard' became known as '5 A* to C' measure. From 1988 to 2010, the proportion of pupils reaching this 'expected standard' improved every year, without exception. This improvement accelerated under the Labour government. When they took office in 1997, 45.1 percent of secondary pupils gained five A*-C grades at GCSE. This figure improved by one to two percentage points each year until 2004. At this point, it shot up from 53.7 percent of pupils in 2005 to 75.6 percent in 2010 (an average improvement of 3.7 percentage points each year). This represented a 67 percent increase in the proportion of pupils reaching the 'expected standard' in 13 years (see Figure 6.1).[2]

Such dizzying improvements were simply not credible: in nobody's mind had teaching in secondary schools become that much better. Trying to get to grips with these statistics, the BBC used a Freedom of Information request to ask the Education Department what the 5 A* to C measure would look like if the two most important GCSEs—English and Mathematics—had to be included. Reporting in October 2005, they found that with English and Maths included, the A* to C measure reduced from the provisional figure of 55.7 percent (later adjusted to 56.3 percent) to just 44.1 percent. What is more, one in six schools that had seen an improvement in their 5 A* to C measure from 2001 to 2004 saw a fall in their English and Maths results over the same period.[3]

In 2007, the government introduced a new measure which was 5 A* to C, including English and Maths. Once these more robust qualifications had to be included in school headline figures, the improvement in secondary school performance was much less pronounced, and many schools saw a significant drop in their headline figures

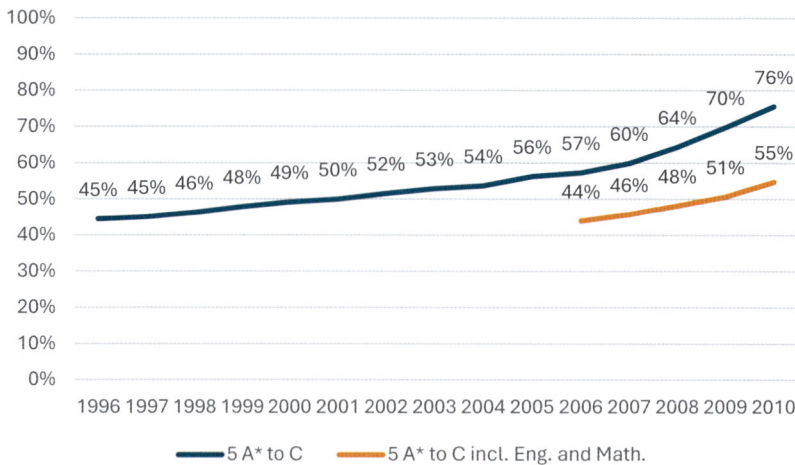

Figure 6.1 The proportion of pupils achieving 5 A* to C, and 5 A* to C incl. English and Maths, from 1992 to 2010.

(see Figure 6.1). Although in opposition at the time, I fully supported this simple but revealing change to the headline measure. It taught me how easily manipulated poorly designed performance measures can be, and I started to turn my mind to how we might redesign these metrics to influence more positive behaviours in schools.

In opposition, it was clear to us that grade inflation was at work. Each August, when exam results were released, similar lines of argument were followed: the government would boast of 'record improvements'; the opposition would argue that exams were becoming easier; in turn, the government would accuse the opposition of 'rubbishing the achievements of young people', as Ed Balls wrote in the *Guardian* in August 2009.[4] Though I believed the argument had to be made, I was aware it was not a good look for Conservative politicians to talk about grade inflation. We were simultaneously telling young people their qualifications were not worth as much as they thought and that exams were harder 'back in our day'. Though the argument was difficult to make politically, that did not make it untrue.

Talking to teachers and schools, we accumulated reams of anecdotal evidence about exams getting easier, or—in the more popular phrase—'dumbed down'. However, the Department had no official measure to prove or disprove whether grade inflation was taking place. We needed to find some other statistical evidence to test this widely held suspicion, and thankfully, a team at Durham University was developing exactly that. For nearly 30 years, the Curriculum, Evaluation, and Management (CEM) Centre at Durham has provided schools with baseline tests of pupil ability. This gave them consistent historical data on the academic abilities of English pupils, starting with the A Level Information System (ALIS) in 1983, followed by the Year 11 Information System (YELLIS) in 1994.

In 2007, Professor Robert Coe of the CEM wrote a report for the Office of National Statistics comparing the data his institution held with GCSE and A-level results.

He calculated that pupils achieving a typical YELLIS score in 1996 had an average GCSE grade on the D/E borderline, but by 2006, this had risen to a high D-grade.[5] In 2013, he updated this study, finding that such pupils were achieving an average C-grade at GCSE by 2012. In other words, pupils of roughly the same level of academic ability and knowledge saw their average GCSE rise by over a grade between 1996 and 2012. Coe concluded that it was 'very problematic' to interpret the recent improvement in GCSE grades as reflecting a genuine rise in standards. 'The question,' he wrote, 'is not whether there has been grade inflation, but how much.'[6] Coe also compared the soaring pupil achievement at GCSE to England's stagnant place in international league tables, observing that the two sets of data 'are not remotely compatible.' He observed, 'Even half the improvement that is entailed in the rise in GCSE performance would have lifted England from being an average performing OECD country to being comfortably the best in the world.'[7] Which, needless to say, we were not.

A-levels also saw year-on-year improvement, with the proportion of entries awarded at C-grade or higher rising from 55.7 percent in 1997 to 75.6 percent in 2010 and the proportion at A-grade rising from 16.0 percent to 26.9 percent. In his 2007 paper, Professor Coe compared what sixth-formers with a typical score in the ALIS baseline test would have gained in their A-levels over the same period. These pupils would have gained a low D-grade in 1996 but a low C-grade in 2006. It should be noted that this process was already underway during the previous years of Conservative government: from 1988 to 2006, pupils of roughly the same ability saw their average A-level grade rise from an E to a C.[8]

What was causing this grade inflation? Many different explanations were discussed, the most common being that exams had been dumbed down. Science seemed particularly badly hit by this trend, due in part to the introduction of a new 'Twenty-First Century Science' curriculum in 2006, which departed from the subject's fundamental academic base, and focused instead on 'scientific literacy', meaning understanding science in the 'real world'. Some questions from this period defied satire as if they had been written specifically for opposition politicians to include in our speeches. This was a multiple-choice question from an Edexcel 'Higher Tier' GCSE Science paper in 2006:

> Our moon seems to disappear during an eclipse. Some people say this is because an old lady covers the moon with her cloak. She does this so that thieves cannot steal the shiny coins on the surface. Which of these would help scientists to prove or disprove this idea?
>
> A) Collect evidence from people who believe the lady sees the thieves
> B) Shout to the lady that the thieves are coming
> C) Send a probe to the moon to search for coins
> D) Look for fingerprints[9]

For those unaccustomed to the English exam system, Edexcel is an exam board, and this leads to a second inflationary pressure. A peculiarity of the English exam system is that GCSEs and A-levels are set by independent boards. These boards have their origins in the days when British universities designed their own entry exams, largely out of the purview of central government. The name of one, Oxford, Cambridge, and RSA Examinations (OCR), still displays its origins. By 2010, there were four exam boards offering GCSEs: AQA, OCR, Edexcel, and the Welsh exam board, WJEC. Schools pay exam boards a per-pupil fee for their exams to be delivered, collected, and marked. Thus, the exam boards compete for their share of entries, creating a market for GCSE and A-level exams. This led to a widespread concern that the boards were incentivised to make their exams easier, creating a 'race to the bottom' in standards. Such concerns were exacerbated in 2011, when the *Daily Telegraph* sent undercover reporters to training seminars run by exam boards and found that tip-offs on what pupils should revise were rife. These seminars were held in hotels at a cost of between £120 and £230. At them, reporters heard chief examiners and subject managers from AQA, Edexcel and WJEC revealing to delegates what exams in their subjects would contain that year. According to the *Daily Telegraph*'s exposé, the WJEC chief examiner for history was recorded as saying, 'We're cheating. We're telling you the cycle. Probably the regulator will tell us off.'[10]

A further contribution to grade inflation was the modularisation of GCSE and A-level entries. Traditionally, English pupils had taken their exams all in one go, during a five-week period in May and June. Educationalists had long criticised this approach for giving pupils just one 'do-or-die' opportunity to do well. So, the QCA began modularising assessments, allowing pupils to take exams for their different modules across two years of study. In 2000, the AS-level was introduced, meaning that pupils studying for an A-level would take half of the modules at the end of Year 12 and the other half at the end of Year 13, along with resitting any modules from Year 12 to improve the grade awarded. At GCSE, modularisation was common in Science, Maths, and Foreign Languages. From 2009, all subjects were allowed to examine up to 60 percent of their content before the end of the course.

Modularisation meant the traditional May to June exam series was joined by another large exam series in January and a smaller exam series in November and March. Thus, pupils could take and retake their exams, banking their best grade. Between 2005 and 2010, the number of pupils being submitted for 'early entry' in English GCSE rose from 9,000 to 152,000, and in maths from 24,000 to 174,000.[11] There was a similar effect at A-level, with QCDA estimating that between two-thirds and three-quarters of students re-sat at least one of their A-level units in 2008.[12] This was good news for the exam boards: resits meant schools had to pay additional entry fees, and school expenditure on exams doubled from £153 million in 2003 to £328 million in 2011.[13] Needless to say, modularisation contributed to grade inflation. The biggest year-on-year rise in A-level pass rates occurred in 2002, when the first cohort who were entered for AS-levels finished Year 13, and the proportion of A-level passes jumped by 4.5 percentage points, from 89.9 percent to 94.3 percent.[14]

In 2008, concern over the state of our exam system led the Chief Executive of the Royal Society of Chemistry, Dr Richard Pike, to post an online petition to Prime Minister Gordon Brown. It called for urgent action and read:

> We, the undersigned, petition the Prime Minister to reverse the demonstrable decline in school science examination standards that is destroying our competitiveness. . . . The record-breaking results in school examination passes are illusory, with these deficiencies having to be remedied at enormous expense by universities and employers. This is compounded by key sections of the education community being in denial. Unless addressed, we will see a continuing decline in our international competitiveness, reduced prosperity for ourselves, and limited career prospects for our children.[15]

Within a month, the petition had been signed by more than 4,800 people.[16] What Dr Pike wrote of science could equally well have been written of any other subject in the curriculum.

False Equivalence

However, the greatest degradation to our exam system did not come from performance measures, modularisation, or grade inflation. It came from 'equivalencies'. During the 2000s, the government made what might have seemed at the time like a well-meaning policy change: passes in vocational qualifications began to be classified as 'equivalent' to GCSE grades and, therefore, count towards the 5*-C school performance measure. Some schools were already offering a small number of vocational qualifications at Key Stage 4 for select pupils to study alongside their GCSEs. Unlike academic qualifications at 16, where the GCSE is paramount, there is a wide array of vocational qualifications available in England. At Key Stage 4 (ages 14 to 16), the most popular were General National Vocational Qualifications (GNVQs) and—from 2004 onwards—Business and Technology Education Council qualifications (BTECs).

Both BTECs and GNVQs were originally designed for post-16 study before drifting down to Key Stage 4—often with the hope that they might re-engage disaffected pupils. Popular subjects included media, ICT, leisure and tourism, health and social care, applied science, and sport. The decision to make both BTEC Firsts and GNVQs qualifications equivalent to GCSEs was driven by a hope that this would achieve the long-desired 'parity of esteem' between academic and vocational study in English schools. With remarkable generosity, particular qualifications were made equivalent to multiple GCSEs: a BTEC First Certificate was worth two GCSEs, whilst a BTEC First Diploma, intermediate GNVQ, and OCR National Award were all worth four GCSEs. Schools began to realise that by entering pupils for vocational qualifications *en masse*—such as the highly popular Intermediate GNVQ in ICT—pupils only had to pass that, and one further GCSE, to meet the government's performance measure of 5 A*-C at GCSE. For many schools, the lure of playing the 'equivalencies game' proved too much, particularly those threatened by the Department with closure due to a poor 5 A* to C measure. In 2004, a *TES* reporter spoke to headteachers at the ten 'most improved' schools in England: six admitted their gains would have been significantly lower without using GNVQs.[17]

Headteachers who played this game saw their schools soar up the league tables. Even the most principled headteachers with an unwavering commitment to academic standards, seeing their colleagues garlanded with praise for 'improving' their school, would find it difficult to resist doing the same. The consequence was an explosion in pupils' entries into vocational courses, from 15,000 in 2004 to 575,000 by 2010, an increase of 3,800 percent.[18] In 2010, 40,000 pupils were entered for a BTEC First Certificate in Sport, 49,000 for a BTEC First Certificate in Applied Science, and 106,000 for an OCR National First Award in ICT—17 percent of England's entire Year 11 cohort.[19] More than anything else, it was these vocational qualifications which were driving the 'improvement' in pupil results at English secondary schools. If you strip them out of the headline figures from 2005 to 2010, the improvement almost disappears. Based on GCSEs alone, the increase in pupils gaining 5 A* to C was not 18.6 percent (56.3 percent in 2005 to 75.6 percent in 2010), but 4.8 percent (see Figure 6.2).[20]

The victims of this trend were the pupils. They left school to find that the vocational qualifications on their CVs had little, or even negative, labour market value.[21] Schools, headteachers, local authorities, and the government all colluded in the myth that these qualifications were 'equivalent' to GCSEs, as it allowed them to claim record improvements. Politicians and policy-makers could talk in pious

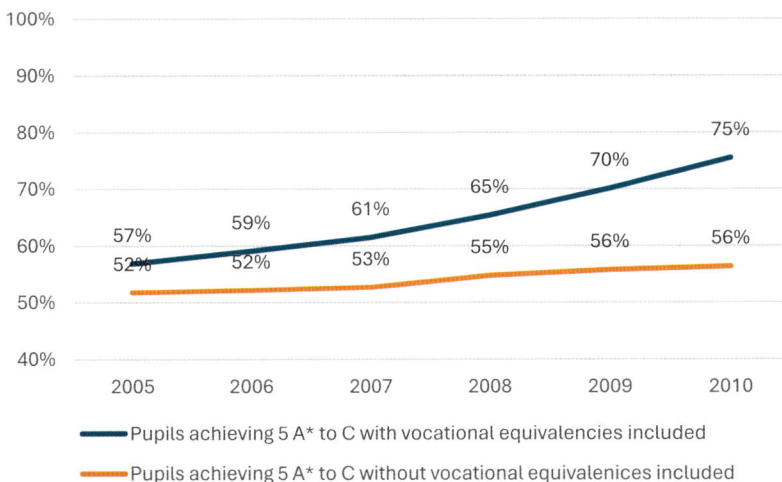

Figure 6.2 Percentage of pupils achieving 5 A*to C at GCSE in England with and without vocational equivalencies included.

tones about achieving 'parity of esteem' between vocational and academic study, but the great majority of vocational equivalencies carried no esteem whatsoever in further education or the workplace. The idea that one BTEC or GNVQ could be equivalent to four GCSEs was clearly nonsense. When Warwick Mansell from the *TES* investigated the average teaching time required for a GNVQ worth four GCSEs, he found it was just 1.2 times that of a single GCSE.[22] Of course, being largely coursework-based and often with low-grade boundaries, these qualifications were significantly easier to pass than GCSEs. In 2006, the proportion of pupils passing GNVQs in ICT and Science (the two most popular courses) were 80 and 86 percent, respectively, compared to a pass rate of 62 percent for all GCSEs.[23]

The ultimate irony was that these 'vocational' qualifications were not just of low value; they weren't even particularly vocational. The most popular was 'applied' versions of academic subjects which could just as easily be studied at GCSE, such as ICT, Science, and Physical Education. Even those with seemingly vocational focus, such as Travel and Tourism, rarely offered a 'hands on' experience of work, instead tending to be classroom-based, theoretical teaching *about* a job. For OCR's Level 2 National Certificate in Travel and Tourism, pupils might study a unit on 'Working as Airline Cabin Crew'.[24] However, knowing what an airline steward or stewardess does is unlikely to give pupils a competitive edge when applying for a job with British Airways. Arguably more helpful would be a solid grounding in English and maths, an understanding of world geography, and facility in a foreign language—all of which are offered by traditional GCSEs. Today, perhaps the greatest indictment of the equivalency policy is the enduring use of 'BTEC' amongst pupils in schools as a derogatory adjective. As the Urban Dictionary website records, 'Used to express something of lower grade, a downgrade of something, or a rubbish version of something.'

Clearing Out the Stables

Grade inflation had many factors, but its root cause was simple: the absence of safeguards. In the short term, everyone benefited from inflation: pupils were doing better, teachers were adding value, schools were celebrating rising results, and the government boasted of record improvements. It was pupils, who went into the real world to discover that the grades on their certificates were not worth what they thought, who paid the price. We used the 2011 Education Act to introduce safeguards which would put a once-and-for-all end to grade inflation in public examinations and qualifications. Part of achieving this would be to charge the qualifications regulator, Ofqual, with securing international comparability of qualification standards. As the 2010 White Paper, 'The Importance of Teaching', stated:

> The independent regulator of exam standards, Ofqual, plays a vital role, but until now has been asked to focus too narrowly on simply maintaining standards over time. This does not help us when other countries are improving

faster and making their education systems more rigorous. So, we have asked
Ofqual to widen its view to reflect the importance of keeping pace with—and
learning from—the rest of the world.[25]

In December 2011, we announced an end to modular GCSEs and A-levels, and
a return to exams being taken in the May and June of Years 11 and 13 at the end
of the two-year course. Modularisation was a case study in the tragedy of good
intentions: in trying to lessen the stress of summer exams, pupils were given the
even worse fate of continual exams. Schools developed a culture of rolling resits,
breeding a 'learn and forget' culture, where teachers were prevented from focusing
on deep understanding or love of a subject. Thanks to the changes we made, teachers can now teach their subject for the best part of two years before the tough but
necessary work of exam preparation begins prior to the summer.

Next to go were equivalent qualifications. Shortly after the election, Michael
Gove asked Professor Alison Wolf of Kings College London to carry out an independent review of vocational education. An economist specialising in labour mar-
kets, Alison was the ideal person to review this contested topic. She delivered the
Wolf Report in March 2011. It gave recommendations for how our education system
could deliver high-quality vocational education that is valued by employers and
exposed what Wolf later called the 'scandal' of low-quality vocational equivalencies.[26] Wolf never suggested the abolition of vocational study for pupils aged 14
to 16. However, she did suggest that we only allow qualifications of demonstrable
value to count towards performance measures. She also emphasised the importance
of schools teaching core academic subjects up to the age of 16—something that is
the norm in other developed nations. As a rule of thumb, Wolf suggested that most
pupils should spend all their time on academic subjects to the age of 16, but with a
maximum of 20 percent of a pupil's timetable aged 14 to 16 on vocational education
for a small minority of pupils disaffected with a pure diet of academic study.[27] If the
proportion is permitted to go higher, she argued, we create the risk that schools will
discourage some pupils who are capable of succeeding in those essential core academic subjects from doing so, thus curtailing the breadth of their post-16 options.

Alison Wolf's report was ground-breaking, and in January 2012, we implemented
her recommendations for schools in full. We took a scythe to the forest of vocational
qualifications, cutting the number approved for teaching at Key Stage 4 from 3,175
to 125—a 94 percent reduction. Of those 125 qualifications, we approved just 70
as of equivalent value to a single GCSE and, therefore, permitted to count towards
performance measures. Many have since accused us of denigrating vocational education.[28] However, this policy was not inspired by opposition to vocational study;
far from it. It was inspired by an opposition to low-value vocational qualifications.
As Professor Wolf told the press:

> Vocational studies can form a stimulating and demanding part of the curric-
> ulum. But pretending that all vocational qualifications are equally valuable

does not bring them respect. On the contrary, it devalues vocational education in people's eyes.[29]

Regulate

Responsible for implementing this swathe of changes to the exam system was
the newly created Office of Qualifications and Examinations Regulation (Ofqual),
which had taken over responsibility from the QCA. As well as being responsible for introducing the 2007 National Curriculum and overseeing the 2008 SATs
fiasco, the QCA pioneered a disastrous new alternative to the GCSE known as the
'Diploma'. This new qualification combined academic subjects with vocational
and workplace training, and at Foundation Level, was equivalent to five GCSEs,
and at Higher Level, seven GCSEs. As such, it took everything that was bad about
the GNVQ and BTEC equivalencies and made it worse. Approved for first teaching
in 2008, the Diploma's attempt to mesh vocational and academic courses of study
was impossibly convoluted, with one exam board chief executive calling it 'the
most complicated qualification that I have ever seen.' Labour Ministers and Civil
Servants predicted that somewhere between 50,000 and 160,000 pupils would take
the new Diploma, but in its first year, only 11,490 signed up. A colossal white ele-
phant, the Diploma was a final hurrah of muddled thinking on qualifications.[30] We
scrapped the Diploma as soon as we entered office, and as we had promised, we
abolished the QCDA (as the QCA had been renamed) soon after.

Ofqual, we hoped, would provide a much safer home for exam regulation, particularly when we appointed Glenys Stacey as its new Chief Executive in April
2012. A career regulator of formidable reputation, Glenys had previously been Chief
Executive of Animal Health and Chief Executive of the Standards Board for England,
which oversaw the functioning of Local Government. On arriving at Ofqual, Glenys
immersed herself in the education debate, simultaneously studying for a master's
degree in assessment at the University of Warwick, a short drive from Ofqual's head
office in Coventry. In her first summer as Chief Regulator, Glenys put in place measures to halt grade inflation, and 2012 was the first year in the 24-year history of the
qualification where GCSE grades went down: an important sign of intent.

However, controversy erupted over thousands of pupils who did not get the
C-grade they had expected in their English and English Language GCSEs. Being 60
percent examined through controlled assessment (formerly known as coursework),
these pupils entered their exams in June confident they were on track for at least
a C grade. However, an estimated 10,000 pupils were left angry and disappointed
when they received a grade lower than expected on results day in August that year.
An alliance of 150 schools, 42 councils, and six professional bodies, including
teaching unions, formed, taking Ofqual and two exam boards to the High Court for
a judicial review that autumn.[31] The alliance accused Ofqual of acting illegally in
moving the grade boundary between a C and a D to a higher position than it had
been for the January exam series, a 'statistical fix'—they claimed—to counter grade

inflation. In February 2013, Ofqual was found to have acted legally, and the case was dropped. The pupils and parents involved were understandably angry, but Glenys knew a greater good had to be served: shutting down once and for all the accusations of grade inflation in our system.

For Glenys Stacey, this bruising first year in office confirmed in her mind a final inflationary pressure that had to be curtailed: controlled assessment. This was work completed by pupils in non-examined conditions and marked by their class teacher, with some external moderation. It is notoriously difficult to ensure equity for such marks: pupils might gain help from their families and friends, and some teachers in some schools give pupils more assistance than others. There was an attempt to combat these issues in 2009 when the previous approach of 'course-work' was replaced with the tighter conditions of 'controlled assessment'. However, many of the same problems persisted. Ofqual's investigation into the 2012 English GCSE controversy exposed the level of positive teacher bias in controlled assessment. In the AQA English GCSE that year, 71 percent of foundation-tier students achieved a C-grade in their speaking and listening controlled assessment, 56 percent achieved a C-grade in their writing controlled assessment, but only 5 percent achieved a C-grade in the written exam.[32] Is it any surprise that teachers err on the side of generosity when marking the work of their own pupils? No, of course not. But it does not make for fair assessment policy.

In 2013, Ofqual suggested that we scale back the use of controlled assessment, which at the time constituted 25 percent of most GCSEs and 60 percent of English and Modern Languages. As a general principle, their report suggested that controlled assessment should only be used where there is no valid means of assessing the subject through an exam, such as the practical elements of Art, Music, and Physical Education. In all other areas, end-of-course examinations should be the default mode of assessment.[33] We agreed. And we made this a rule for all new GCSEs to be sat from 2015 onwards. As such, Glenys Stacey's most important achievement during her time at Ofqual from 2012 to 2016 was to restore the pre-eminence of the summer exam at GCSE and A-level. This was anathema to child-centred educators, who see such examinations as being anxiety-inducing and unfair. However, reams of academic literature have shown that it is underprivileged pupils who are negatively impacted when alternatives, such as teacher-assessed work, are used. If you want a level playing for every pupil in the country, external examination is your answer. Good assessment, like justice, is blind.

Of course, examinations are never going to be popular. They are stressful, frustrating, and often feel reductive. For this reason, education systems around the world have spent decades trying to devise alternatives, but to no avail. No alternative mode of assessment has ever been found which can offer the same validity and reliability as a standardised, timed, and externally marked examination. During our time working on assessment reform, I would often remind myself of this fact by misquoting Winston Churchill: 'examinations are the worst form of assessment, except for all of the others that have been tried.'

O no! Levels

The driver that led the then Secretary of State for Education, Sir Keith Joseph, to introduce the new GCSE in 1986 was to create one qualification that the whole ability range of pupils could enter at 16 years old. In a country beset by the class system, it was seen as iniquitous that there were two classes of school leaving qualification (the CSE and the O-Level). However, creating one qualification for what, by the age of 16, was and still is a wide range of educational attainment presented significant challenges.

The first challenge is the grading system that has to be sufficiently granular to reflect both performance for those at the very top of the attainment range as well as those who struggle to pass. Grades A to G were introduced, all of which were deemed as passes (technically, A to C was a 'Level 2' qualification, whilst D to G was a 'Level 1'). However, because the school league tables measured the proportion of pupils achieving grades A to C, public perception over time no longer saw a grade below a C as a pass. Students who, in the past, would have left school at 16 with valid academic qualifications (the CSE) could now be in a position of only having GCSEs at grades D to G, which most people—particularly employers—regarded as 'fails'. The other problem with the new GCSE qualification was that some of the more demanding content of the old O-Level had been moved out and transferred to the A-level qualification (generally taken by 16 to 18-year-olds). In reforming GCSEs, we knew there were a significant number of pupils who were capable of a much more demanding curriculum at Key Stage 4. We also wanted to cater to these pupils to remain competitive with the standards being achieved by young people in rival economies. One potential solution to these two challenges was to return to the previous two-qualification approach used before 1986, albeit using new names for the new qualifications.

The proposal was only one of many ideas being bounced around during our early months in government, and one I knew was fraught with risk. My own preference was to introduce more demanding content into the existing GCSEs and avoid any return to a 'two-tier' system. However, much to my surprise, on the morning of 21ˢᵗ June 2012, the *Daily Mail* ran the following headline, 'Return of the O-Level: Gove announces radical plan to scrap GCSEs'. On reading the article in full, I discovered that Michael Gove had also promised 'to tackle the culture of competitive dumbing-down' by having a single exam board deliver the new O-Level in each subject.[34] Neither of these decisions had been made in consultation with Ministers, nor had they been signed off by the Prime Minister or Deputy Prime Minister Nick Clegg (leader of our coalition partners, the Liberal Democrat Party). On hearing the news at a UN conference in Brazil, Clegg was furious, and he would prove much less forgiving than David Cameron.[35]

The proposal had been leaked to the *Daily Mail* (probably by Dominic Cummings) in order to blindside the government into accepting a *fait accompli*, even though the policy had not been through the approval process, Number 10 sign-off, or Cabinet. For the centre-left Liberal Democrats, moving back to the two-tier split of CSEs and O-Levels was anathema. The policy proposal never saw the light of day simply because it would never achieve the support of the Liberal Democrats, which in a coalition was essential for every policy. Although I had nothing to do with the proposal nor its leak to the press, I sensed that, in one way or another, I would pay the price, which I did. So spooked was Nick Clegg by this breach of protocol by Education ministers that he insisted that his key ally, David Laws, should return to government as an education minister to ensure proper Liberal Democrat oversight of education reform. The only position of sufficient seniority for a former Liberal Democrat Cabinet Minister (who had been forced to resign in the first weeks of the Coalition Government over an expenses issue) was my position as Schools Minister, and the summer reshuffle was only three months away.

New Look GCSEs

After a brief detour down the cul-de-sac of rebranding the core academic GCSEs as English Baccalaureate Certificates administered by a single exam board, Michael Gove finally announced his new plan for qualification reform to the House of Commons in June 2013. GCSEs would be retained but fundamentally reformed, extending the principles of our National Curriculum review to Key Stage 4 (pupils aged 14 to 16 years old). Thus, we would raise expectations with more challenging assessments for pupils, in line with those offered in the highest-performing jurisdictions around the world.

The challenge was how to achieve this when GCSEs are not set by the Department but by four independent exam boards. In line with the principles set out by David Cameron regarding greater ministerial oversight of quangos and arm's length bodies, the answer was that the Department for Education would devise 'Subject Content' criteria, with the new qualifications regulator Ofqual determining the assessment criteria, and this would be signed off by Ministers. These 'Subject Content' criteria documents would then drive the drafting of exam specifications by the four separate exam boards. All GCSE and A-level exam board specifications would then have to be submitted to Ofqual for approval, ensuring that exam boards were in compliance with both the DfE's Subject Content criteria and Ofqual's assessment objectives.

This was an important reform of the process, as it ensured ministers had the final say on the content of GCSEs and A levels, enabling us to give these qualifications a far greater grounding in knowledge and—in the words of our 2010 manifesto commitment—'ensure that our exam system is measured against the most rigorous systems in the world.'[36] Ofqual's remit—safely in the hands of Glenys Stacey—was to ensure that exam boards complied with the assessment criteria and did not allow any weakening of those criteria or lowering of grade boundaries to bring back the menace of grade inflation. We abandoned the move to one exam board for each qualification (rather than four) due to Ofqual's view that it involved too much risk at a time of significant reform to the entire exam and qualifications system. Instead, we invested Ofqual with responsibility to ensure consistency of standards between the four exam boards, ensuring that competition for market share no longer risked a race to the bottom in terms of the academic challenge of their exams.

In June 2013, Michael Gove set out a phased timeline by which this would be achieved. Unfortunately, for a minister who liked to quote the Silicon Valley motto 'move fast and break things', it was going to be a protracted process. The first wave of GCSE subjects to be reformed were English Literature, English Language, and Mathematics. Over the 2013 summer holidays, the Department shared drafts of the Subject Content criteria and Assessment Objectives for public consultation. They were then sent to the exam boards, who began developing new exam specifications and example materials to be submitted to Ofqual for accreditation. This was the most important stage, with new exams frequently requiring several iterations to ensure every board was following the Subject Content and Assessment Objectives correctly and establishing a comparable level of challenge. This process of design, review, and feedback took two years to complete, and Year 10 pupils began studying for the first new GCSEs in September 2015. It would then take a further two years before they sat their exams in the summer of 2017. And that was just phase one. After English and Mathematics, the next 20 most 'high volume' GCSEs (Science, History, Geography, Languages, and so on) were taught from 2016, and the remaining 25 'low volume' GCSEs (Ancient History to Urdu) were taught from 2017, with exams in those subjects finally being sat in August 2019.

By this time, Michael Gove had had three further jobs since being Education Secretary, there had been an election, a referendum, another election, and I had been reappointed as Schools Minister and had been in post for a further five years. For any politician hoping to pursue examination reform, be warned: it will take at the very least two Parliaments to complete.

Much like the national curriculum, the process of writing this Subject Content excited Michael's polymath mind. Being the best-read politician I know, he took great pleasure in overseeing the creation of the expert groups and dropping into their meetings to debate the relative merits of different Romantic poets or the latest research into the human genome. Some, however, would say he took too much pleasure. As could have been predicted, the National Curriculum in History was an area of significant controversy. Being a keen historian with a commitment to pupils learning 'our island story', Michael was heavily involved in the first draft, which was put out for consultation in February 2013. I thought Michael's intent—to ensure that pupils understand specific pivotal moments in British and world history—was right. However, the execution was a touch eccentric. In its first draft, the History National Curriculum would be taught chronologically through both primary and secondary school so that pupils aged 5 to 11 would learn from pre-history to 1707, and pupils from 11 to 14 would learn from 1707 to 1989. Some of the content chosen for specific mention was obscure, most infamously 'the Heptarchy'.* In addition, the phrase 'Britain and her empire' seemed designed to inflame tempers. Eminent historians assembled to pour scorn on Michael's curriculum in the national press, and a second draft was written for June 2013.[37] For those who accused Michael of stubbornness, it is worth remembering that on both the History curriculum, and on a return to O-Levels, he changed his mind. In most of the GCSE subjects, Michael was willing to let the expert groups thrash out the particulars of the new Subject Criteria, provided they remained within our fundamental parameters: more knowledge, more challenge, greater depth.

There was one exception. Michael's most significant legacy in GCSE reform is not in History but in English Literature. Rarely for a politician, Michael Gove studied English Literature at University. He set out his stall early, saying that the Subject Criteria for English Literature must require every pupil to study a nineteenth-century English novel, and did not back down. When David Laws questioned this requirement, he received the following note from Michael Gove's private secretary:

> The Secretary of State insists on this prescription because the nineteenth century represents the most important period for the novel as a cultural form. . . .
> A student of English Literature who hasn't studied a nineteenth-century novel is like a student of maths who hasn't studied multiplication.[38]

Michael prevailed. At the time of writing, eight Year 11 cohorts have now completed the new English Literature GCSE, all having studied a nineteenth-century novel.

As well as a nineteenth-century novel, the new English literature GCSE requires pupils to read a Shakespeare play, a poetry anthology, and a twentieth-century British text (fiction or drama). Crucially, the exam is now 'closed book': where pupils were previously permitted to bring the text into the exam, they now have to know the texts well enough to write about them from memory. English language, meanwhile, has 20 percent of the marks set aside for spelling, punctuation, and grammar—skills that—despite repeated predictions to the contrary—remain highly valued by employers. In Mathematics, the new GCSE incorporates content previously taught at A-level in areas such as ratio, proportion, and rates of change. Many responded by saying this would take more time to teach, and that was our intention. According to the 2011 TIMSS study, England ranked 39th out of 42 countries globally in terms of the number of hours spent teaching Maths to 14 to 16-year-olds, at 116 hours per year (around three hours per week).[39] If a beefed-up Maths GCSE meant more time spent on this subject in Years 10 and 11—which is so crucial to pupils' flourishing in later life—we were happy with that outcome.

In Science, we included new content covering the study of the human genome, gene technology, life cycle analysis, nanoparticles, and space physics. In History,

---

* These were seven early Anglo-Saxon kingdoms that existed until the eighth century, in case you are wondering.

we increased the proportion of British history in the exam from 25 percent to 40 percent and broadened its scope to cover medieval, early modern, and modern history. We introduced more Mathematics and statistical work into Geography, and required at least two examples of fieldwork outside of school. In Modern Languages, we placed a greater emphasis on communication through speaking and writing papers to ensure that pupils are learning how to *use* a language. Lastly, wherever possible, we asked boards to design examinations which could be sat by pupils of all abilities, stopping the use of tiered papers, where lower-attaining pupils are set 'foundation' papers with a maximum grade cut-off. Such papers remain necessary in subjects with a hierarchal curriculum: Maths, Science, and Modern Languages. But in other subjects, there is one exam for all, so no caps are placed on pupils' potential attainment.

A-levels went through their own process of reform, with four waves of subjects revised and accredited for teaching between 2015 and 2018. Once more, the focus was on broadening the range of content and increasing the level of challenge, with the overriding principle that A-levels should prepare students for university study. For that reason, we appointed the vice-chancellor of Lancaster University, Professor Mark E. Smith, to oversee the process and—as far as possible—engaged university academics to help create the new Subject Criteria.

Having been out of office from September 2012 to July 2014, I was unable to influence the first two phases of GCSE subject content reform. Nevertheless, I was pleased by most of the changes. I had followed the reforms from the outside and read the consultation documents as they were published and, as an MP, was able to give my views to ministers. The only area where, with hindsight, I would have sought significant changes was in the GCSE Subject Content in History. The periods covered in the statutory content are too broad and unspecific, requiring exam boards to include history from three eras: Mediaeval (500–1500), Early Modern (1450–1750) and Modern (1700-present day). It might as well have said 'study history'. And, as with elements of the primary history curriculum, the stated 'aims and learning outcomes' retain, in my view, too much of the skills-based conception of studying history. The GCSE subject content for History states that pupils should 'engage in historical enquiry to develop as independent learners and as critical and reflective thinkers.'[40] Laudable aims, but such language always carries the risk of perpetuating the misconception that such historical skills can be taught in isolation from specific knowledge. My view remains that a curriculum should focus more on the detail of precisely what needs to be taught instead of nebulous outcome statements.

It is for this reason that in 2021, following the success of the Model Music Curriculum, I commissioned Christine Counsell to draft a Model History Curriculum— a non-statutory but Department for Education-sponsored document setting out in detail the best history curriculum schools around the country have introduced. I first met Christine at a Policy Exchange event in June 2015, when she introduced herself as a university-based teacher trainer who had read Hirsch and believed wholeheartedly in the importance of a knowledge-based curriculum in schools. I remember answering with words to the effect, 'Who are you, and where have you been all my life?' She was then at the University of Cambridge Education Faculty, where for 19 years she ran the Secondary History PGCE and trained many teachers who would go on to work in many of the best schools created by our reforms. Though never willing to be associated with a particular 'camp' in the knowledge-skills debate, Christine had always held firm to the belief that a curriculum needs to be based on a core of what she terms 'substantive' content: clearly defined and carefully sequenced knowledge. Christine has since left Cambridge and founded 'Opening Worlds' with former history teacher Steve Mastin, supporting schools in introducing knowledge into their curriculum.

Keeping Accountable

The last feature of the old exam system to go was the 5 A* to C measure. School accountability measures may seem like an arcane area of policy making. However, they are fundamental to any system based on high autonomy and high accountability. A well-designed measure is perhaps a government's most powerful single lever for driving curriculum decisions in schools. However, a poorly-designed measure will drive all sorts of perverse incentives which harm pupils' education, and 5 A* to C was a very poorly designed measure. When a Conservative government introduced the measure in 1988, its intentions were good: a pupil with five or more C-grades at GCSE had significantly more opportunities to choose from post-16 than one without them. However, during the 20 years that followed, the measure was put under significant strain. In 1992, it became the headline figure in school performance tables, and later all schools were obliged to publish it on their website. In 2008, schools with 30 percent A*-C or lower were given notice to improve or risk closure.[41] The measure became totemic.

I have already explained how the Department modified this measure in 2006 to '5 A* to C *including English and Maths*', in an attempt to control the inflationary effect of 'equivalent' qualifications. However, this change did nothing to overcome a second corrupting influence the measure had on schools: the C/D borderline. Essentially, a threshold measure based around all pupils achieving a certain level, in this case, a grade-C, inevitably places a school's attention on a small subset of pupils. According to the '5 A* to C' measure, pupils improving from an E to a D or from a B to an A made no difference at all to the school's headline performance: it was only by changing the grades of pupils on the C/D borderline that schools could show they had improved. As a result, the so-called 'borderline kids' received a disproportionate amount of school resources. During the 2000s, school leadership teams became fixated on the achievement of these pupils, to the exclusion of others performing some way below or above a grade-C. Many school improvement services offered by consultants, local authorities, and—increasingly—academy chains focused on the C/D borderline. For example, guidance from one Local

Authority published in 2006 suggested the following strategy: 'Parents of C/D borderline pupils are invited in early during Year 10 to encourage high expectations and provide study support where necessary.'[42] To value the grades of these pupils over their peers was clearly unethical and created a lot of discomfort within the profession. But you could not blame schools for behaving in such a way. Ultimately, the fault lay with the Department for continuing to rely so heavily on a poorly designed measure.

During my 21-month break from the Department, David Laws set about creating its replacement. He assembled a brains trust, including his adviser Tim Leunig, a brilliant economist from the LSE, Hardip Begol, one of our best officials at the Department, and former Slaughter and May lawyer, Chris Paterson, who would go on to be one of our longest serving and most effective policy advisers. David Laws wanted a measure which averaged out the achievement of every pupil in every subject at a school, so the grade of every GCSE entry mattered equally. Secondly, he wanted a measure which took into account pupils' prior attainment, so schools with able intakes did not always outperform those with more challenging intakes. To create the formula, he enlisted two academics from outside the Department, Simon Burgess from the University of Bristol and David Thomson from the Fischer Family Trust (FFT), a move which reassured the profession that the measure would be fair and impartial. Together, they designed 'Progress 8'.

Announced in October 2013, Progress 8 measures how well pupils achieve across eight GCSE subjects based on their level of achievement at the end of primary school. The eight subjects which go into its calculation are from three categories: English and maths, which are double weighted; three GCSE subjects from the 'EBacc bucket'; and three subjects from an 'open bucket' of all GCSEs and approved technical qualifications. The score is scaled to zero, such that in schools with a Progress 8 score of 0.0, pupils are making average progress compared to pupils at the same starting point nationwide. In a school with a score of 1.0, pupils are achieving a whole grade better per GCSE compared to pupils at the same starting point nationwide. And in a school with a score of –1.0, pupils are achieving a whole grade worse. The complex process of calculating Progress 8 was made easier by our decision to change the grading system for all new GCSEs to 1 to 9 from 2016 onwards, replacing the previous scale of G to A*. During its design, officials gathered soft intelligence to ensure that Progress 8 'looked' right. In one trial of its validity, David Laws wrote a list of secondary schools in his Yeovil constituency, ranking them by reputation. The schools were then ranked by their provisional Progress 8 scores, and the two lists were compared. The correspondence was almost bang-on.

When it was used for the first time in 2016, the majority of schools—61 percent—had a score of between –0.3 and +0.3. However, it was the outliers that attracted the most attention. Out of 3,658 mainstream secondary schools, 37 achieved a Progress 8 of 0.7 or more, and seven achieved a Progress 8 of 1.0 or more.[43] This elite of schools was diverse: local authority schools, academies, grammar schools, faith schools, schools in areas of affluence, and schools in areas of deprivation. However, every one of them had a positive reputation, and we could state with confidence that they were amongst the best in the country for ensuring their pupils' academic progress. Progress 8 has allowed teachers to discuss the relative performance of schools with far more confidence than ever before. Prior to 2016, if someone told you of a rapidly improving school, your first question would be, 'How have they played the game?' This no longer happens. Progress 8 is such a robustly designed measure that nobody in English education can help but be impressed by a school with a high score, and many such schools—as later chapters will explain—have become beacons of excellence. Speaking to a teacher recently, he told me that whilst visiting another school, there are only two things he needs to look at to know its effectiveness: the Progress 8 score and the condition of the boys' toilets.

Stretch and Challenge

By stipulating that three GCSEs in each pupil's Progress 8 score had to come from the 'EBacc bucket' of Geography, History, Languages, and the Sciences, it helped in my drive to encourage more pupils to study a core academic curriculum up to the age of 16. In 2010, only 22 percent of pupils were entered for the EBacc, a figure I thought staggeringly low. This proportion almost doubled to 40 percent in 2016 and has since stabilised at around that level (see Figure 6.3).

Most of this increase has been driven by more pupils entering Geography and History, which—largely thanks to the combined effect of the EBacc and Progress 8 measures—are two of the fastest-growing subjects at GCSE over the past 13 years. The number of entries in Geography has increased by 112,000 pupils from 2010 to 2023, and the number of entries in History has increased by 97,000. The proportion

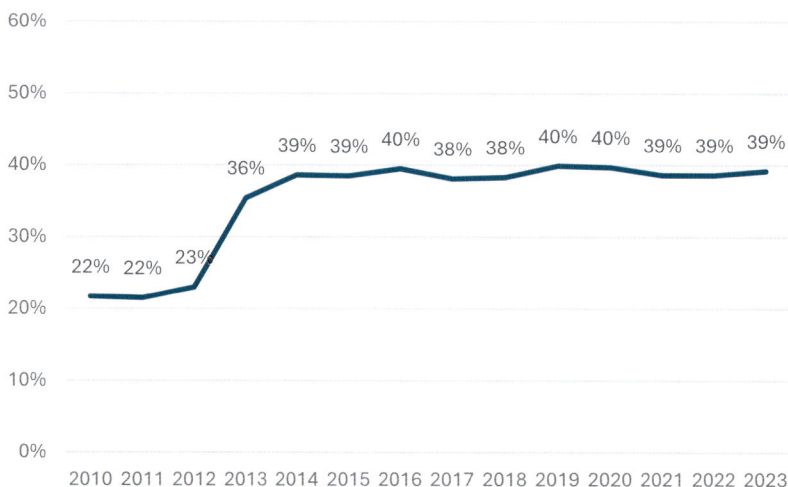

Figure 6.3 Proportion of pupils entered for the EBacc combination of subjects at GCSE, 2010 to 2023.

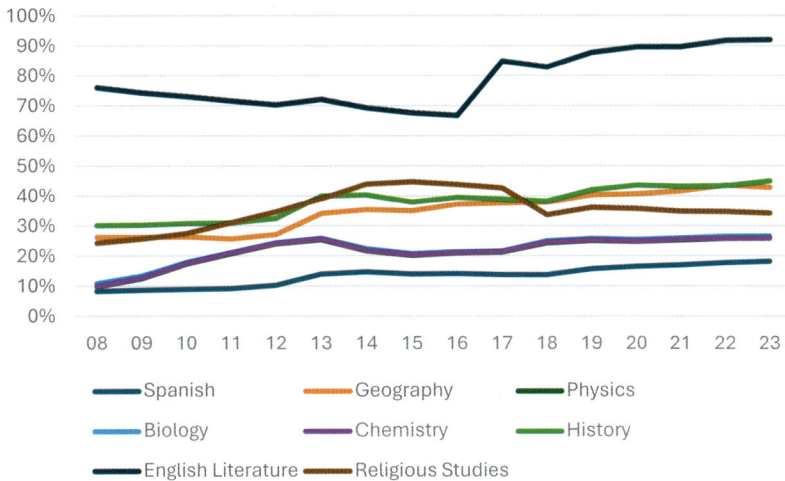

Figure 6.4 GCSE qualifications with the largest increase in entries as a proportion of the overall cohort, 2010 to 2023.

of pupils taking the academically challenging route of Triple Science (separate GCSEs in Biology, Chemistry, and Physics) has increased from 18 percent to 27 percent (see Figure 6.4).[44]

I do have regrets that the EBacc entry rate has never pushed much above 40 percent. Back in 2010, I envisaged that the EBacc would be a physical certificate posted to all pupils who achieve it following their results. In this way, I hoped it would achieve some cachet amongst the wider public. However, this plan was blocked by Dominic Cummings, whose jaundiced view of the Civil Service left him convinced they would fail to deliver on such a plan. He may have been right, but had this decision been different, I think the EBacc may well have gained more social currency than it has, commonly featuring—for example—in school leavers' CVs. A more important limiting factor on EBacc uptake has been modern foreign languages, which English pupils are infamously (and increasingly) reluctant to study. Spanish may be the fastest growing subject at GCSE over the last 13 years, but that has not made up for the precipitous fall in French and German entries, such that a lower proportion of pupils were entered for French, German, and Spanish at GCSE in 2023 compared to 2010. There remains a dire need for more language study in our secondary schools; for that reason alone, I believe the EBacc remains relevant.

In recent years, the EBacc has come under criticism from the arts lobby for undervaluing creative subjects at GCSE. Our government was always supportive of pupils studying creative subjects at GCSE, and taking the EBacc by no means precludes them from doing so. Entering the EBacc takes up seven or eight GCSE slots, leaving ample room for one, two, or even three additional qualifications. In truth, the decline in creative subjects is often exaggerated, and entries in Art and Design GCSEs have actually increased over the period 2010 to 2023. Entries in Music and Drama, it is true, have declined. However, they have always been small subjects, with only 8 and 14 percent of pupils entering for Music and Drama, respectively, in 2010. They are also unusual subjects in that many students enjoy them at school without studying for a GCSE, through—for example—instrumental lessons and school drama productions. In addition, as David Thomson from the FFT has observed, to blame their decline on Progress 8 (and, by extension, the EBacc) is questionable: the same phenomenon has been happening in Wales, where such measures do not exist, and much of the flight from Music and Drama GCSEs has not been to EBacc subjects, but to the uptake of non-GCSE qualifications in the same subject areas.[45]

The EBacc was always going to be controversial. In our pluralistic age, many think it plain wrong to value some subjects more than others, but I am unapologetic in doing so. A good curriculum requires a balance between academic, creative, and vocational subjects. However, in 2010 that balance was out, and we needed to reorientate schools towards offering pupils an academic common core. I do want to see pupils studying for creative GCSEs and high-quality technical qualifications. However, I want to see more pupils studying two or three sciences, History, Geography, and a foreign language. Today, many say the EBacc measure has gone too far. I would say it has not gone far enough.

Change We Can Believe

A final point on grade inflation. Having stopped this phenomenon in its tracks in 2012 (the Covid aberration notwithstanding), you might assume that GCSE grades in England will remain static forevermore. However, this is not the outcome we wanted, as we hope that—through the success of our reforms—pupils' academic attainment will actually start to rise. If this does come to be (and we very much believe it will), GCSE grades will have to improve accordingly—not through inflation, but due to genuine improvement. But how do we distinguish the difference? Thankfully, Ofqual devised a solution to this conundrum: the National Reference Test (NRT). First used in 2017, the NRT tests around 2 percent of Year 11 pupils each year, randomly selected from some 300 schools. It provides comparable, long-term data on the general Maths and English language ability of pupils in the months prior to their GCSE exams. Results in these tests are then benchmarked against the Grade-7, Grade-5, and Grade-4 boundaries at GCSE. If the NRT shows an overall improvement in the academic ability of Year 11 pupils, we will use that as a justification for Ofqual to raise the number of higher grades at GCSE. If it does not, we won't.[46]

In the Maths NRT, there was a steady improvement in pupil performance at all grade boundaries from 2017 until 2020. However, since Covid, pupil performance has returned to where we started in 2017. In English, there was no improvement up to 2020, and pupil performance is now below where it was in 2017.[47] Of course, such figures are challenging to interpret due to the disruption of Covid. However,

I take succour from the fact that continuity in results achieved pre and post-Covid may suggest real-term improvement. Year 11 pupils in 2024 entered lockdown half-way through Year 7, their first year of secondary school: for their general level of attainment to have held steady compared to their pre-Covid peers is—I hope—an indication of success. We cannot yet say for sure whether pupil attainment at GCSE has improved due to our reforms. However, I believe this moment is not far from arriving. If it does arrive, schools and pupils will be able to celebrate for the first time a rise in results that—because of the robust accountability system we have created—cannot be accused of inflation. This should be our legacy at the secondary level: not just improvement, but improvement in which the public can believe.

Notes

1 Figures calculated from Ofqual, 'Infographics for A level results', 15 August 2024.
2 Ruth Lupton and Polina Obolenskaya, 'Labour's record on education: Policy, spending and outcomes 1997–2010', *Social Policy in a Cold Climate Working Paper WP03*, 2013, 'Labour's record on education', p. 35.
3 'Focus on basics shakes up schools', *BBC News*, 20 October 2005.
4 E. Balls, 'Conservatives want to revive educational divide', *The Guardian*, 26 August 2009.
5 R. Coe, *Changes in Standards at GCSE and A-Level: Evidence from ALIS and YELLIS. Report for the Office of National Statistics*, 2007.
6 R. Coe, 'Improving education: A triumph of hope over experience', *Inaugural Lecture to Durham University*, 18 June 2013, p. vii.
7 Coe, 'Improving education: A triumph of hope over experience'.
8 Coe, *Changes in Standards at GCSE and A-Level*, p. 6.
9 T. Richmond and S. Freedman, *Rising Marks, Falling Standards: An Investigation into Literacy, Numeracy and Science in Primary and Secondary Schools*, London: Policy Exchange, 2009, p. 77.
10 H. Watt, 'Exam chief: "you don't have to teach a lot" for our tests', *The Telegraph*, 8 December 2011.
11 Department for Education, *Early Entry to GCSE Examinations*, 2011, p. 5.
12 Department for Education, *The Case for Change*, 2011, p. 18.
13 S. Coughlan, 'School spending on exams doubles to £328m in a decade', *BBC News*, 9 May 2012.
14 A. Smithers, *A-Levels, 1951–2014*, Centre for Education and Employment Research, University of Buckingham, 2014.
15 'Downing street petition demands reversal of catastrophic decline in school science exam standards', *Royal Society of Chemistry*, 27 November 2008.
16 G. Eason, 'Minister checks on science exams', *BBC News*, 5 December 2008.
17 'Easy way to top of league?', *TES Magazine*, 16 January 2004.
18 Department for Education, *The Wolf Report: Review of Vocational Education*, 2011, p. 48.
19 *The Wolf Report*, p. 145.
20 Figures available in *The Wolf Report*, p. 49.
21 *The Wolf Report*, pp. 31–32.
22 W. Mansell, *Education by Numbers: The Tyranny of Testing*, London: Politico Publishing, 2007, p. 125.
23 A. de Waal, *The Secrets of Academies' Success*, London: Civitas, 2009, p. 10.
24 de Waal, *The Secrets of Academies' Success*, p. 10.

25 Department for Education, *White Paper: The Importance of Teaching*, p. 47.

26 'Alison Wolf, professor of public sector management, King's College', *FE Week*, 14 October 2011.

27 *The Wolf Report*, p. 108.

28 Department for Education, 'Press release: Performance tables: only the highest quality qualifications to be included', 31 January 2012.

29 Department for Education, 'Press release: Performance tables', 31 January 2012.

30 The diploma policy is well covered in Richmond and Freedman, *Rising Marks, Falling Standards*, pp. 79–91.

31 R. Booth, 'GCSE English pupils "unfairly treated" by grade boundary changes', *The Guardian*, 28 August 2012; and 'GCSE English grades "statistical fix", High Court told', *BBC News*, 11 December 2012.

32 Ofqual, *GCSE English 2012*, November 2012, p. 51.

33 Ofqual, *Review of Controlled Assessment in GCSEs*, June 2013.

34 T. Shipman, 'Return of the O-level: Gove announces radical plan to scrap GCSEs', *Daily Mail*, 20 June 2012.

35 O. Bennett, *Michael Gove: A Man in a Hurry*, London: Biteback Publishing, 2019, p. 265.

36 *The Conservative Party Manifesto: Invitation to Join the Government of Britain*, London: Pureprint Group, 2010, p. 52.

37 R. J. Evans, 'Michael Gove's history curriculum is a pub quiz not an education', *New Statesman*, 21 March 2013; and W. Mansell, 'Michael Gove redrafts new history curriculum after outcry', *The* Guardian, 21 June 2013.

38 Quoted in D. Laws, *Coalition: The Inside Story of the Conservative-Liberal Democrat Coalition Government*, London: Biteback Publishing, 2016, p. 296.

39 Department for Education, 'Press release: Experts to visit Shanghai to raise UK maths standards', 18 February 2014.

40 Department for Education, *History GCSE Subject Content and Assessment Objectives*, June 2013, p. 3.

41 A. Lipsett, 'Schools threatened with closure "are not failing"', *The Guardian*, 20 June 2008.

42 Quoted in A. de Waal, *School Improvement—or the 'Equivalent'*, London: Civitas, 2008, p. 3.

43 K. Benyon, 'Changes in schools' Progress 8 scores over time', *FFT Education Datalab*, 23 April 2024, and figures compiled from Department for Education statistical releases.

44 Figures compiled from Department for Education statistical releases.

45 D. Thomson, 'What has progress 8 done for the creative subjects?', *FFT Education Datalab*, 5 July 2023.

46 See further explanation in Ofqual, *The National Reference Test in 2017*, December 2017.

47 National Foundation for Educational Research, *National Reference Test Results Digest 2024*, Slough: NFER, 2024, pp. 14, 19.

7 The Network Effect

So twitter and blogs are a lifeline; a way to access at least some unvarnished truth about what people really think. And while I don't want to overdo the impact of the blogosphere—policy is still primarily driven by the traditional internal processes—I do think its rise is having quite a profound effect.

Sam Freedman, 'When 140 Characters is Not Enough' blog,
April 2013

On 3 September 2012, my partner Michael and I went out for dinner to celebrate my 52nd birthday. I had survived my early brushes with the press, our curriculum reforms were underway, and the mystifying workings of a government department were starting to make sense. The following day, I was reshuffled out of Government. It was a sudden turn of events. On returning from dinner, I received a phone call from David Cameron's Private Secretary asking me to meet the Prime Minister in his House of Commons office the next morning. This was bad news: convention dictates that the Prime Minister uses his office in Downing Street to appoint ministers, but his office in Parliament to sack them. I experienced the one entirely sleepless night of my life, desperately unhappy that I would be leaving unfinished a job about which I had become so passionate. The next morning, I resolved to be good-natured, leave with grace, and work towards my return.

Whilst out of office, I continued to visit schools regularly, hopeful that I might one day reprise my role as Schools Minster. As I was no longer visiting as a minister in Her Majesty's Government, but just a backbench MP, I gained a valuable—and far more insightful—picture of English schools during those two years. Many things struck me. Firstly, how hardworking, conscientious, and energetic teachers are. This should go without saying, but amongst education reformers who focus too much on school accountability, there was sometimes an assumption that schools 'get away' with underachievement. If accountability structures were better designed and more strongly enforced, it was implied, teachers would work harder. I came to realise how misplaced such a diagnosis was. In many of the schools I visited where pupil underachievement was endemic, it was not due to a lack of effort on the teachers' part. Far from it: dedicated teachers were giving everything

DOI: 10.4324/9781003533474-8

they had to help their pupils. However, the conditions in which they worked made success impossible: out-of-control behaviour, misguided ideas about teaching and curriculum, and school initiatives that required teachers to work hard on all the wrong things. It also struck me how few—if any—of the ideas that we had been talking about in government had yet filtered through and into schools. Despite mentioning them in almost all our speeches, almost none of the teachers I met during my ministerial hiatus had heard of Hirsch or Willingham. And why should they have? They were all far too busy planning and teaching their lessons—often in very challenging circumstances—to listen to or read ministerial speeches, let alone follow our book recommendations.

Nothing that I saw over those two years dented my conviction that the progressivist ideology was the main impediment to improvement in our schools. It was humbling, though, to realise the limitations of centralised reform. A new national curriculum, better accountability measures, mass academisation, and ministerial speeches were only ever going to go so far. In terms of changing their practice, the only people the great majority of teachers were ever going to listen to were other teachers. If this thoughtworld was going to be challenged, the movement had to be grassroots. Politicians and officials might be able to provide the catalyst, but it was teachers who had to devise new behaviour policies, write new resources, and develop new approaches to teaching. What is more, these innovators would have to meet, organise, and share their ideas. Thankfully, that was precisely what was starting to happen.

The Knowledge Network

In early 2013, I established the Knowledge Network, a semi-formal social gathering of teachers, academics, and others who I had met in the years of Opposition and Government, who all shared a passion for a knowledge-rich curriculum and evidence-led teaching. Those initial meetings in a musty meeting room in the House of Commons or a nearby school brought together early luminaries of the reform movement. They included Katharine Birbalsingh, who was busy at the time trying to establish a free school with fellow Knowledge Network attendees Katie Ashford, Jonathan Porter, Joe Kirby and Barry Smith; Max Haimendorf, Kris Boulton and Bruno Reddy from King Solomon Academy; Daisy Christodoulou who was busy drafting *Seven Myths about Education*; Ed Clarke, a passionate Latin and classics teacher; and Mark Lehain head teacher and founder of one of the first free schools, Bedford Free School. Another early attendee was the Maths teacher and senior leader Stuart Lock, who would shortly become headteacher of Cottenham Village College. Politically, Stuart hails from the left, as do many of the most articulate proponents for knowledge-based teaching and stricter schools, for the principal reason that the children who most benefit from this approach are those from disadvantaged backgrounds. Political affiliation was no bar to attendance at the Knowledge Network events; quite the contrary: I welcomed with enthusiasm any teachers on the political left whose commitment to social justice had led them to reject the progressivist ideology in education.

Other attendees included my co-author and history teacher Robert Peal and the Religious Education teacher Robert Orme, both from the West London Free School (WLFS), which had recently been established by the journalist Toby Young. Together, they were working on a series of knowledge-based textbooks, which would later be published by Collins as 'Knowing History' and 'Knowing Religion'. Also from the WLFS was its Director of Music Ed Watkins, who would play a central role in the creation of the Model Music Curriculum in 2021. Other eminent teachers and policy-makers in attendance were James O'Shaughnessy, Tim Oates, and the think tanker Jonathan Simons. Old hands included Professor Anthony O'Hear and the long-serving head of the London Oratory School, John McIntosh. I mention these key figures because they all had made or would make significant contributions to the development of knowledge-based curriculum resources and evidence-led teaching methods. For such iconoclasts, challenging firmly established education orthodoxies was not easy work and meeting socially helped to strengthen the sinews of our movement, boosting its members' morale before they re-entered the fray.

At each meeting, we listened to a presentation on an area of policy or practice, such as how to design effective assessments or how to communicate a new behaviour system to your school community. However, the main event was always the socialising which followed the presentation, as fellow combatants from the front line of education reform shared their war stories over crisps and white wine. As Katharine Birbalsingh told me for this book, back when she decided to set up a free school in 2010, she was far more concerned about behaviour and school ethos than she was about curriculum. However, the ideas that our Knowledge Network meetings helped to foster turned her nascent free school—which would become Michaela—towards a knowledge-based curriculum. On my return to office in July 2014, Knowledge Network meetings were held in the Department, and I encouraged officials to attend so that they might learn from the passion and expertise of its members. The Network has continued to thrive and is now stronger than ever under the effervescent leadership of Loraine Lynch-Kelly, who first attended whilst Vice-Principal at St Martin's Catholic Academy, Leicestershire.

Another early Knowledge Network attendee was Tom Bennett, an RE teacher in East London and popular writer for *TES*, where his moniker was 'The Behaviour Guru'. He would go on to lead perhaps the most important grassroots movement for education reform of the past decade, both in England and abroad: researchED.

ResearchED

The researchED conferences can be traced back to a 2008 book by the *Guardian* columnist Ben Goldacre entitled *Bad Science*. In his book, Goldacre exposed a pseudoscientific fad that had become popular in English schools called 'Brain Gym'.

Brain Gym involves teachers leading pupils in physical exercises to stimulate their cognition, such as rubbing the 'brain buttons' on either side of their sternum to, allegedly, stimulate blood flow to the brain.[1] It would have been funny if schools, local authorities, and teacher training colleges had not been for years spending considerable public money on this snake oil.

There were many other pseudoscientific products being peddled to schools at the time, of which 'Brain Gym' became emblematic. Joining it was the concept of 'learning styles', which claimed that questionnaires could diagnose the different ways in which pupils learn, to which teachers should then tailor their lessons. Also popular was the theory of 'multiple intelligences', which claimed that intelligence is not singular, and instead, there are seven, or sometimes ten (the number often changed) different types of intelligence for which a school curriculum should be designed. Though these products were new, they were used to reinforce some decades-old progressivist principles, namely the opposition to whole-class, teacher-led teaching. If all pupils have different learning styles and different intelligences to nurture, then it stands to reason that their learning must take place independently or in groups, with teachers playing a facilitating role. Proponents of these theories were adept at co-opting scientific terminology to give a veneer of credibility to ideas which were—in fact—entirely devoid of evidence. Like many, Dominic Cummings was concerned by the readiness of schools to accept this pseudoscience and hoped to spur a conversation about the need to trial these educational interventions before they enjoyed widespread adoption. He asked Ben Goldacre—a doctor by trade—to write a report about what evidence-led practice might look like in schools. He delivered his report, *Building Evidence into Education*, in March 2013.[2]

The report was much discussed by teachers on Twitter, where reform-minded teachers had increasingly been gathering to share ideas during the early 2010s. On the evening of 18th March, a conversation took place on Twitter between Joe Kirby, Ben Goldacre, Sam Freedman, Tom Bennett, and Andrew Smith (see further on), about what next steps could be taken to help teaching become an evidence-led profession. Ben tweeted, 'set up an organisation, get a logo, a website, no money, organise an unconference.' Sam, who one month previously had left the Department to work for Teach First, replied, 'I nominate Tom to be in charge . . .'. As it turned out, Tom had been working on a book about the uses and abuses of education research entitled *Teacher Proof*, which would be published in July 2013.[3] A charismatic Glaswegian with a past life running nightclubs in London's West End, Tom is a popular and engaging speaker with a seemingly inexhaustible reserve of pop culture references to illustrate his points. As Sam recognised, he was an ideal candidate to lead the next phase in the movement.

Six months later, in September 2013, the first researchED conference was held at Dulwich College, South London. It was a DIY affair, run by Tom and his co-organiser Helene Galdin-O'Shea, along with an enthusiastic team of volunteers, mostly recruited from the Twittersphere. Around 40 speakers took part, a mixture of research-engaged teachers and classroom-engaged researchers. The coup was a presentation, via video link from Virginia, delivered by the emerging guru of the movement, Daniel Willingham. The headteacher Tom Sherrington, a speaker at the conference, wrote after the event: 'What a day!. . . a gathering of classroom and research practitioners meeting to exchange perspectives on the important work we all do. It was magnificent. It felt like the start of something. I hope that's true.'[4]

It certainly was. The next year, 700 delegates attended the second researchED conference held at Tom's own workplace, Raine's Foundation School in East London, on Saturday, 6 September 2014. Newly reappointed as Schools Minister, I attended the conference for the first time, and it was one of the most memorably exciting days of my entire time in office. I saw hundreds of teachers—on the first Saturday of the academic year—giving up their weekend to share ideas, meet like-minded peers, and learn more about education research. In my speech, I praised those assembled there for demanding much more evidence for the principles that they are asked to adopt in their classrooms.[5] For the first time, I saw a physically assembled group of hundreds of teachers with the courage to question the received wisdom of the education establishment and create new ways of working.

What was taking place was the confluence of a grassroots teacher-led movement and top-down government reforms, which would prove fundamental to the rejuvenation of English schools. Whether that confluence was coincidental or not is something that I have often pondered. Frustration amongst teachers with educational orthodoxies pre-dated our arrival in office, and it would be wrong to suggest that teachers involved in events such as researchED were universally supportive of our reforms. However, I would like to believe that our policies to give schools greater autonomy and our willingness to question received wisdom in our policies and speeches provoked debate and emboldened teachers. Perhaps that explains why this grassroots movement has—so far—been a very English phenomenon, with nothing of the same magnitude taking place in Scotland or Wales. Whatever the causal chain, we benefited immeasurably from our reforms taking place at a time when education blogging and Twitter were on the rise.

Where it's @

In November 2012, the *TES* reporter Richard Vaughan wrote an article on the rise of the teacher blogger, entitled 'Where it's @'.[6] It opened with an interview with Andrew Smith,* who was perhaps the most prolific of this new breed of commentator. Smith started blogging anonymously on his website 'Scenes from the Battleground' in 2006. I began reading it around 2012 and found Smith to be eloquent, acerbic, and frequently hilarious. When I finally met him at the 2013 researchED Conference, I was surprised to discover the man behind the blog was

---

* In the article, he was referred to by his online pseudonym 'Andrew Old'.

a quiet and mild-mannered maths teacher from the West Midlands. As the title of his blog implied, it was the state of behaviour in English schools which drove Smith to blogging. Over time, he widened his focus and began writing with great insight about the influence of the progressivist ideology on the schools in which he worked. In 2012, Smith wrote a 'summing up' of his thoughts, where he explained how the progressivist ideology 'still remains the orthodoxy in schools to the point where it is considered controversial, contrarian or provocative to actually challenge the basic doctrines.'[7]

Smith was a Labour Party activist. However, his diagnosis of the harm caused by progressive education led him to support many of our reforms. In the same interview with the *TES*, he said 'reforms around the curriculum are very positive', adding 'cracking down on grade inflation and removing the equivalencies between GCSEs and vocational subjects, that does strike a chord.' And Smith's writing, in turn, struck a chord with fellow teachers. By posting his blogs on various forums, he built up a small community of like-minded teachers. This community was greatly expanded by the arrival of Twitter, which Smith joined in 2009. In 2014, 'Scenes from the Battleground' received its millionth hit.[8]

Another early teacher blogger and Knowledge Network attendee was Katharine Birbalsingh, whose blog 'To Miss with Love' was compiled into a book of the same title published by Penguin in 2011.[9] As those familiar with English education will know, Katharine went on to become perhaps the best-known headteacher in the country after opening Michaela Community School in 2014 (see next chapter). However, in 2010, she was an assistant headteacher in South London, writing an anonymous blog and engaging in online discussions with fellow bloggers, including Andrew Smith, about who was to blame for the dismal state of the schools where they worked. In November 2010, Katharine gave evidence to the Education Select Committee in Parliament. There, she met an English teacher called Daisy Christodoulou, who had gained some recent attention for a policy report by a collection of Teach First alumni she had edited about school ethos and culture.[10] Daisy and Katharine talked about their experiences in London schools and found that they shared the same frustrations with entrenched low aspirations and the same ambition for thoroughgoing change. They would remain close friends.

Daisy duly set up her own teaching blog in 2011, entitled 'The Wing to Heaven'. Two of her first two posts were summaries of the work of E. D. Hirsch and Daniel Willingham, the latter of whom Daisy had been introduced to by the phonics advocate Tom Burkard in February 2011 and was up until then relatively unknown in the UK.[11] Like many who read her early blogs, Daisy expressed the sense of revelation that came from reading modern research into human cognition and realised that holding a different perspective on how pupils learnt was possible. She likened the experience to reaching the end of a well-constructed detective story and thinking, 'Ah! Of course! *That's* how it all fits together.'[12] Daisy's blog was an instant hit amongst the growing community of teacher bloggers, who were energised to discover that—in direct contradiction to the claims made during their training—there existed considerable academic research in *favour* of teaching knowledge.

Looking back, it is clear there was a 'moment' taking place between 2010 and 2014 for teacher-bloggers. In February 2014, Andrew Smith organised a curry at a restaurant in Brick Lane, in east London, for like-minded teacher bloggers to meet. Twenty-five showed up on the first occasion, and these meals became something of a half-term institution, another informal gathering boosting the movement. In 2015, Andrew counted 1,273 active education blogs in the UK.[13] Of course, these teacher-bloggers represented a wide range of opinion and not all were citing E. D. Hirsch and promoting teacher-led instruction, let alone supporting our policies. But, those that were had the energy that comes from being an insurgent movement, finding a collective voice to kick against the orthodoxy. This proliferation of teacher-bloggers was closely followed by our advisers at the Department. In particular, Sam Freedman was an inveterate tweeter and key vector for taking ideas from the blogosphere to ministerial offices. It was only recently that the government's IT infrastructure had even been updated to allow officials to use Twitter, and many teachers were taken aback when the Secretary of State's policy adviser—who was employed as a civil servant—started engaging with them from his personal account. However, it was important that he did, as teacher-bloggers would go on to play a significant role in our early reforms.

From 2013 onwards, many of their names began appearing in Michael Gove's speeches. That June, he gave a speech on the importance of teaching to the National College of Teaching and Leadership, where he name-checked Andrew Smith, Daisy Christodoulou, and Robert Peal (under his pseudonym Matthew Hunter).[14] He mentioned them and many others over the following year, as did I, having returned to office. Whether sympathetic to our policies or not, it was important for the profession to know that voices on the ground were making it to our offices. Importantly, as government ministers, we were able to engage in a mutual trading of legitimacy with teacher bloggers on the ground: their support bolstered our reforms, whilst mentions in our speeches amplified their voices.*

New media accelerated the spread of ideas. It seemed custom-made to empower insurgents to start new conversations about curriculum and teaching methods and challenge the education establishment's role as gate-keepers to those debates. Writing in 2015, Andrew Smith observed how social media had given frontline teachers a voice, allowing them to stand up to those who had previously spoken for them:

> educationalists can no longer claim a monopoly over educational thought. Opinions that might be orthodoxy in academic journals, conventional wisdom among those training teachers or articles of faith held by like-minded

---

* My thanks to Loic Menzies for this concept, which he introduced me to in his article '"Populism" and competing epistemic communities in English educational policy: A response to Craske and Watson Wiley' in the *British Educational Research Journal*.

professors of education, might be repeatedly revealed to be objects of derision among those who actually occupied classrooms. The most significant casualties of social media may turn out to be those who claimed expertise about the business of the classroom from positions which could not have been more insulated from the challenges and experiences of those actually in the classroom.[15]

Myth-busters

In a surprisingly short space of time, critiques of progressivist, child-centred teaching went from the fringes of the blogosphere to become a mainstream concern. An important milestone in this process was Daisy Christodoulou's first book, *Seven Myths About Education*. Having begun her blog in 2011, Daisy went on to work at Pimlico Academy (see Chapter 8). Here, the academy sponsor, Lady Caroline Nash, who was an early enthusiast for E. D. Hirsch, had established a 'Curriculum Centre', where teachers would work part-time whilst also developing knowledge-based resources for use in schools. Lady Nash encouraged Daisy to write *Seven Myths*, and the Curriculum Centre published it as an e-book in June 2013.

Daisy's book was an instant classic. In an interview with her in the *Guardian*, the journalist described it as 'one of the most talked-about [books] in education in the past 20 years.' Revealingly, the journalist—a veteran education correspondent—admitted that he had assumed her book would be 'Just another right wing moan . . . saying schools should get back to the 1950s.' However, he found her book to be forensically written, scrupulously footnoted, and argued with passion. What is more, he wrote—with evident surprise—that this critic of progressive education was raised by a Labour family living in a council block in London's East End and went to the local state primary until she won a scholarship to an independent girls' school.[16] *Seven Myths* was republished by Routledge the following year, with forewords from E. D. Hirsch and the assessment expert Dylan Wiliam. It received praise from within the teaching world and without, with Dominic Lawson describing it in the *Sunday Times* as a 'A heat-seeking missile aimed at the heart of the old educational establishment'.[17] In his foreword to the book, Wiliam wrote:

> In my view, this may well be the most important book of the decade on teaching . . . It should be required reading on every teacher training course, and schools that are genuinely interested in unleashing the power of education to transform the lives of young people should buy a copy for every teacher. I've never said that about a book before, but that's how good I think *Seven Myths About Education* is.[18]

What myths was Daisy Christodoulou slaying, to such rhapsodic reviews? They were simply the progressivist tropes that trainee teachers had heard for decades: teaching facts prevents understanding (Myth 1), teacher-led instruction is 'passive'

(Myth 2), and transferable skills are more valuable than traditional subjects (Myth 5). For each chapter, Christodoulou followed the same structure. She outlined the theory behind the myth, explained the evidence which showed it was misguided, and assembled evidence that these myths were indeed prevalent in schools. That last part was crucial. Opponents of the 'new traditionalists' (as Daisy and our allies were sometimes called) often accused them of setting up straw men in order to denigrate English schools. However, Daisy Christodoulou combed through documents published by the key institutions of the education establishment, which showed just how common these ideas were: the 1999 and 2007 National Curriculums; guidance produced by the ATL trade union; products for schools such as the RSA's 'Opening Minds' Curriculum and 'Building Learning Power'; and lesson guidance published by Ofsted, the schools' inspectorate.

If there was one thing I, as Schools Minister, took from reading *Seven Myths*, it was the extent to which Ofsted remained the single most powerful enforcer of the progressivist ideology in English schools. Back in the early 2010s, Ofsted would regularly publish guidance on 'good practice' for different subject areas, which featured descriptions of lessons, normally those that inspectors had rated 'good' or 'outstanding'. In total, Daisy Christodoulou compiled 228 such descriptions from reports published between 2010 and 2012. She showed how Ofsted inspectors systematically praised child-centred teaching methods such as group work, discovery learning, and projects whilst criticising teacher-led lessons and the explicit teaching of knowledge. Here, for example, is a 2011 Ofsted good practice resource for English entitled *Making English Real,* from which Christodoulou quoted the following passage:

> The English department aims to create and develop 'expert learners'. We are committed to establishing a learning environment that encourages students to feel confident about taking and acting on their own decisions. The primary focus will be on learning, rather than teaching, with students working in partnership with teachers, asking questions and reflecting on the learning strategies that work best for them.[19]

It is worth emphasising that these Ofsted guidance documents were immensely powerful in schools, as they were interpreted by head teachers as the best guide to what inspectors wanted to see in lessons. Until 2014, Ofsted inspectors still gave individual grades to lessons they observed, ranging from 'inadequate' to 'outstanding'. These judgements could swing a school's 'Quality of Teaching' grade from one category to another, so they carried significant pressure for teachers. What is more, their practice trickled down into schools' own internal observations, as senior leaders emulated Ofsted lesson judgements (or what they thought them to be) in their staff performance management policies. Meanwhile, private consultants charged schools four-figure sums to carry out 'mocksteds', and train staff to adopt—what came to be known as—the Ofsted teaching style. For classroom teachers, Ofsted had become the arbiter of what constitutes good teaching. Their judgements could make or break their career at a school, making the pressure to conform to the Ofsted style immense. It was with good reason that Andrew Smith labelled Ofsted the 'child-centred inquisition.'[20]

The Ofsted Teaching Style

Of all the areas in which teacher-bloggers influenced government policy, Ofsted was the most significant. In January 2012, Michael Gove persuaded Sir Michael Wilshaw to leave Mossbourne Academy, the school he had worked so hard to create, and become Her Majesty's Chief Inspector of Schools (HMCI). In a recent conversation I had with Michael Wilshaw, he recalled arriving at a 'disastrous' organisation, where delivery of inspections was seen as paramount, but very little thought went into their quality. For an organisation with such power, he knew this was unacceptable. Michael Wilshaw did a great deal to improve the quality of inspections during his first two years as HMCI. He brought all Ofsted inspectors in-house, ending the previous practice of contracting out inspections to private providers. In addition, he overhauled the training of inspectors and ensured that the quality of their work was more closely monitored through the appointment of eight regional directors.

In June 2012, Michael Wilshaw created a new Inspection Handbook for the coming academic year, which directly addressed the issue of an Ofsted teaching style. Its guidance to inspectors stated, 'The key objective of lesson observations is to evaluate the quality of teaching and its contribution to learning. . . . Inspectors will not look for a preferred methodology.'[21] Similarly, its guidance on how inspectors should reach their 'Quality of Teaching' judgement specified, 'Inspectors must not expect teaching staff to teach in any specific way or follow a prescribed methodology.'[22] Michael Wilshaw backed up this message in his public pronouncements. When interviewed by the RSA in May 2012 about what makes a good teacher, he explained that a 'very traditional teacher' teaching in 'a pretty didactic way' can still produce fantastic results. He concluded: 'We, and in that word "we" I include Ofsted, should be wary of trying to prescribe a particular style of teaching.'[23] Teachers around the country, exasperated by the Ofsted teaching style, breathed a sigh of relief and believed change was on its way.

However, government inspectorates are unwieldy beasts, and Ofsted is no different. The great majority of its inspectors are serving headteachers, paid on a daily rate to visit other schools. Ensuring that they all followed the new Handbook in every one of the roughly 7,000 inspections taking place each year was far harder than Michael Wilshaw could have anticipated. Once the new academic year was underway in September 2012, it transpired that many inspectors were ignoring the new Handbook, and continuing to promote child-centred approaches in their reports. On his blog, Andrew Smith set himself the mission of reading every new Ofsted report, which are all published online, to find examples of schools still being judged for conforming, or not, to an 'Ofsted teaching style'. He did not have to look hard. In September 2012, a primary school in Enfield's report stated, 'In good lessons . . . pupils are encouraged to work in groups and engage in independent learning activities.' In October, a primary school in Rochester's report stated that the quality of teaching 'is not good because. . . . Lessons are sometimes dominated by the teacher.' In November, a secondary school in Sussex was criticised because its teachers 'offer too few opportunities for students to work independently or in groups and too much of the "talk" comes from the teacher.'[24]

These are not just cherry-picked examples. In 2014, the think tank Civitas published a report—written by my co-author Robert Peal—which reviewed a sample of 130 secondary school Ofsted inspection reports from 2013. It found the following: 52 percent of reports favoured pupils learning independently from the teacher; 42 percent favoured group work, 18 percent criticised lessons where teachers talked too much; and the same proportion criticised lessons in which pupils were 'passive'. Within the entire sample of 130 reports, there was just one example of an inspector commending a more teacher-led approach.[25] This inconsistency between what Michael Wilshaw was saying, and what teachers were experiencing, caused great frustration. As Andrew Smith wrote at the start of 2013: 'There is definitely no excuse for Ofsted's chief inspector going around telling teachers that traditional teaching is fine while his organisation is using their unaccountable power to enforce the progressive consensus quite brutally at the school level.'[26]

Also frustrated were our advisers at the Department for Education, who were closely watching the discussions online. They were particularly concerned that free schools and academies, which were supposed to encourage innovation, might be stymied by the Ofsted orthodoxy. Blog posts by the likes of Andrew Smith provided valuable ammunition to Michael Gove and his advisers, who would cite such blogs in meetings with officials, demonstrating that this was no confected issue but a real and persistent problem. As the new academic year began in 2013, Michael Wilshaw reassured Michael Gove that the message was getting through to his inspectors. That September, Michael Gove gave a speech to Policy Exchange in which he reassured teachers that the 'personal prejudices and preferences' of inspectors had been addressed. He stated:

> as teacher bloggers like Andrew Smith have chronicled, time and again too much emphasis was given to particular practices like group work and discovery learning; while Ofsted inspectors marked teachers down for such heinous crimes as 'talking too much', 'telling pupils things' or 'dominating the discussion'. The good news is that Ofsted—under its inspirational new leadership— is moving to address all these weaknesses.[27]

However, Michael Gove's assurance was premature. As soon as reports from inspections were posted online from September 2013 onwards, the Ofsted teaching style was still very much in evidence. See this from a secondary school in Derbyshire, inspected that month:

> What does the school need to do to improve further? Make more teaching consistently good or better across the school by making sure that: teachers do not limit the time for students' active learning by talking at them for too long.[28]

Still out of office at the time, I followed the issue closely. I knew Michael Wilshaw had no attachment to child-centred or progressivist approaches. Therefore, it struck me as remarkable how difficult it was proving for him to stamp them out and a testament to the strength of the orthodoxy. A hard core of inspectors was clearly so habituated to this ideology that they seemed unable to express judgements on teaching in any other language than that of progressivism—even when explicitly told not to do so. In February 2014, BBC Radio 4 produced an episode of The Report entitled 'Ofsted's Ideological Battle', in which I tried to explain why this was: 'If you've got an inspector and they've spent 20, 25 years as a teacher, and they were trained themselves in a progressive approach to education, there's no reason why they even would have thought there's another approach to teaching.'

As the coverage of the debate on Radio 4 shows, by 2014, this issue had boiled over into the national press. In particular, they focused on the relations between Michael Wilshaw and Michael Gove's office, which had unfortunately deteriorated. There were other issues at stake, such as Michael Gove's decision not to extent the tenure of the Ofsted Chair, Labour peer Sally Morgan, with which Michael Wilshaw disagreed. In addition, Michael Wilshaw was infuriated by the abrasive treatment he was receiving from Michael Gove's office. This all flared up in January of 2014, with a leaked story in the *Times* about two reports on Ofsted soon to be published by think tanks close to the Conservative party. Entitled, 'Gove allies say "Sixties mired" Ofsted should be scrapped', the story explained:

> The two inquiries reflect growing frustration within the Department for Education (DfE) over complaints from heads and teachers about Ofsted reports that appear to contradict the thrust of government policy. Some protest that inspectors have criticised teachers for talking for too long in lessons.[29]

Michael Wilshaw was apoplectic with rage. He responded by giving an interview to the *Sunday Times*, published two days later, where he described himself as 'spitting blood'. He continued, 'I wanted to express my displeasure, my anger, my outrage at the stuff I read this morning.' Wilshaw refrained from attacking Michael Gove directly, stating that he still had 'a lot of time' for the Secretary of State, but expressed his displeasure at Michael Gove's advisers for briefing the press against him.[30] Few were left guessing to whom Michael Wilshaw was referring, particularly after a memo was leaked later that year showing that Dominic Cummings encouraged Michael Gove to fire Wilshaw in October 2013.[31] It was a regrettable affair and one in which Dominic did Michael Gove few favours. Michael Wilshaw was, by his own later admission in conversations for this book, too slow in addressing this issue of a progressivist bias amongst Ofsted inspectors. However, he was under immense pressure fighting battles on many fronts in his new role as HMCI and was hurt by what he saw as a betrayal of trust. Fundamentally, Michael Wilshaw and the Department were allies in a joint mission to root out ineffective practices from schools, and I was thankful he remained in post for another two years after this episode to see through his reforms.

Ironically, behind the surface froth of national press coverage, progress was actually being made on the question of Ofsted inspections. One month earlier, on 23rd December 2013, Ofsted published subsidiary guidance for their inspectors. It reinforced the point that inspectors should not judge schools on the basis of preferred teaching styles by, for the first time, making it unambiguously clear what 'styles' should not be shown preference:

> Do not expect to see 'independent learning' in all lessons and do not make the assumption that this is always necessary or desirable. On occasions, too, pupils are rightly passive rather than active recipients of learning. Do not criticise 'passivity' as a matter of course and certainly not unless it is evidently stopping pupils from learning new knowledge or gaining skills and understanding.[32]

Andrew Smith, whose tireless campaign had helped achieve this breakthrough, was delighted. In a post entitled 'A Christmas Miracle', he wrote, 'This is as good a protection as we've ever had. Don't let it be ignored. Merry Christmas.'[33] By Boxing Day, his post had received over 11,000 views—perhaps worrying over the Christmas period, but a testament to how much this issue mattered to teachers on the ground.[34] Michael Wilshaw went into overcommunication mode on this message, perhaps learning the political adage that what others call repeating yourself, we call message discipline. At the conference of England's main headteachers' union in March 2014, he told the assembled delegates (with a comparison that did not age too well):

> And let me repeat, more times than Boris Johnson has denied he wants David Cameron's job, Ofsted does not have a preferred teaching style. Inspectors are interested in the impact of teaching on learning, progress and outcomes. I accept that it's taken time to get this through to every one of our inspectors but I want to make this commitment to you this morning—I will personally take issue with any inspector who ignores our guidance and tries to tell teachers there is only one way to teach.[35]

Over the months that followed, Ofsted made a concerted effort to engage with their critics. In February 2014, the Director of Schools, Mike Cladingbowl, invited five teacher-bloggers to visit the Ofsted offices and speak directly about their concerns (a canny move, they all then blogged about it positively afterwards). In September, Cladingbowl and his colleague Sean Harford, Ofsted's National Director for Schools Policy, agreed to be interviewed by their tormentor in chief, Andrew Smith, on stage at researchED. In the background, Ofsted was speaking to many more members of the profession, and this engagement all fed into their newly produced Inspection Handbook for September 2014.

As well as reaffirming that inspectors should not favour any particular teaching style, the Handbook announced that Ofsted inspectors would no longer give individual grades to the lessons they observed. This was an evidence-led decision, informed by the increasingly influential Professor Rob Coe (he of exposing grade inflation fame—see Chapter 6). A seminal study called Measuring Effectiveness of Teachers (MET), funded by the Bill and Melinda Gates Foundation, found that lesson observation judgements for American teachers had little correlation to the future success of the pupils in their class. Essentially, it showed that external observers tend to be a poor judge of whether learning is taking place in a classroom. Rob Coe used the MET data to estimate the validity of observations carried out by Ofsted inspectors and suggested that English inspectors had only a 49 percent chance of choosing the correct category for the quality of a lesson—the same as flipping a coin.[36]

Teacher bloggers such as David Didau had been criticising the practice of graded lesson observation for years, arguing—it turned out correctly—that learning is essentially invisible, and good teaching is not always obvious to an external observer.[37] What is more, the practice of 'graded lesson observations' promoted a culture in schools where performative 'jazzy' lessons were seen as best practice, and demonstrating pupil progress became more important than ensuring learning was actually taking place. For years, teachers had traded horror stories of their lessons being graded 'inadequate' or 'requires improvement' on the basis of a short drop-in from an Ofsted inspector. This practice was now over, to the significant relief of the profession.

Today, Ofsted still faces considerable criticism. However, the positive legacy of Michael Wilshaw's tenure as HMCI should not be forgotten. He moved the focus of school inspection from judging the style of teaching to judging its impact. In doing so, he took on an organisation in which the progressivist ideology was embedded and turned it into one in which pragmatic, outcomes-focused judgements are the norm. It is notable that one of Michael Wilshaw's predecessors, Sir Chris Woodhead (HMCI from 1994 to 2000), tried to do the same. However, in 2002, he wrote that his attempts to turn the organisation around had been prevented by inspectors who could not forgo 'the flotsam and jetsam of progressive education'.[38] It is no small achievement that Michael Wilshaw succeeded where Chris Woodhead could not. Though his relationship with teacher-bloggers was at times adversarial, Wilshaw was ultimately aided by those who shone a light on the persistence of the progressivist ideology amongst his inspectors. Of all the citadels to the progressivist ideology to fall during our time in office, Ofsted was by far the most significant.

Notes

1 See B. Goldacre, *Bad Science*, London: Fourth Estate, 2008, Chapter 2.
2 B. Goldacre, *Building Evidence into Education,* London: Department for Education, 2013.
3 T. Bennett, *Teacher Proof: Why Research in Education Doesn't Always Mean What it Claims, and What You Can Do about it*, London: Routledge, 2013.
4 T. Sherrington, 'ResearchEd 2013: What a day!', *'teacherhead' blog*, 8 September 2013.
5 N. Gibb, 'The importance of teaching', *Speech to the researchED Conference*, 8 September 2014.
6 R. Vaughan, 'Where it's @', *TES Magazine*, 23 November 2012.
7 A. Old, 'A New Summing Up', *'Scenes From The Battleground' blog*, 16 September 2012.
8 A Smith, 'Now We Are Eight', *'Scenes From The Battleground' blog*, 24 October 2014.
9 K Birbalsingh, *To Miss With Love*, London: Penguin, 2011.
10 Policy First, *Ethos and Culture in Schools in Challenging Circumstances*, London: Teach First, 2010.
11 D. Christodoulou, 'Skills and Knowledge', *The Wing to Heaven blog*, 22 December 2011.
12 D. Christodoulou, 'Why you can't just Google it', *'The Wing to Heaven' blog*, 7 January 2012.
13 A. Old, 'Did blogs break the blob?', in R. Peal (ed.), *Changing Schools: Perspectives on Five Years of Education Reform*, Woodbridge: John Catt, 2015, p. 55.
14 M. Gove, *Speech to the National College for Teaching and Leadership*, 25 April 2013.
15 Old, 'Did blogs break the blob?', pp. 61–62.
16 P. Wilby, '"Britain's brightest student" taking aim at teaching's sacred cows', *The Guardian*, 24 November 2014.
17 D. Lawson, 'Seven myths about education by Daisy Christodoulou', *The Sunday Times*, 16 March 2014.
18 D. Wiliam, 'Foreword', in D. Christodoulou (ed.), *Seven Myths about Education*, London: Routledge, 2014, p. xii.
19 Quoted in Christodoulou, *Seven Myths about Education*, p. 92.
20 A. Old, 'What Ofsted Actually Want', *'Scenes From The Battleground' blog*, 16 February 2013.
21 Ofsted, *School Inspection Handbook*, June 2012, p. 9.
22 Ofsted, *School Inspection Handbook*, June 2012, p. 33.
23 Quoted in A. Old, 'What Ofsted Say They Want', *'Scenes From The Battleground' blog*, 13 October 2012.
24 All quoted in A. Old, 'What Ofsted Actually Want', *'Scenes From The Battleground' blog*, 16 February 2013.
25 R. Peal, *Playing the Game: The Enduring Influence of the Preferred Ofsted Teaching Style*, London: Civitas, 2014.
26 A. Old, 'Does sir michael wilshaw know what ofsted good practice looks like?', *'Scenes From The Battleground' blog*, 26 February 2013.
27 M. Gove, *Speech to the Policy Exchange Think Tank*, 5 September 2013.
28 Quoted in A. Old, 'New academic year. New inspection handbook. Same old Ofsted', *'Scenes From The Battleground' blog*, 6 October 2013.
29 'Gove Allies say "Sixties mired" Ofsted should be scrapped', *The Times*, 24 January 2014.
30 S. Griffiths, 'Schools watchdog Wilshaw "spitting blood"', *The Times*, 26 January 2014.
31 'Memo revealing DfE's fears over Ofsted chief—full text', *The Guardian*, 9 October 2014.

32 Ofsted, *Subsidiary Guidance: Supporting the Inspection of Maintained Schools and Academies*, January 2014, p. 19.

33 A. Old, 'A Christmas miracle—Ofsted get it right for once', *'Scenes From The Battleground' blog*, 23 December 2013.

34 A. Old, 'Why that Ofsted news is so important', *'Scenes From The Battleground' blog*, 26 December 2013.

35 M. Wilshaw, *Speech to the ASCL Conference*, 24 March 2014.

36 Rob Coe's research was covered at length in H. Waldegrave and J. Simons, *Watching the Watchmen: The Future of School Inspections in England*, London: Policy Exchange, 2014.

37 D. Didau, 'Where lesson observations go wrong', *'Learning Spy' blog*, 12 July 2013.

38 C. Woodhead, *Class War: The State of British Education*, London: Little, Brown, 2002, p. 21.

8 Academies and Free Schools

Now, an academy or free school that is trying to resurrect traditional forms of teaching. That really would be original.

Daisy Christodoulou, 'The Wing to Heaven' blog,
December 2012.

In the background of our first few years of curriculum and qualifications reform, the process of academisation was picking up speed. The Academies Act passed in July 2010 (see Chapter 4), extended the freedom to become an academy to all English schools. Over the first year, some claimed the number of schools converting to academies was below expectations, and we had exaggerated the demand amongst school leaders. However, by our second year in government, what had begun as a trickle was becoming a torrent. When we gained office, one of Prime Minister David Cameron's senior advisers made a bet with our policy adviser, Sam Freedman, that fewer than 2,000 schools would be academies by 2015.[1] As it transpired, we reached 2,000 academies by the summer of 2012 and 4,722 academies by January 2015, representing 14.6 percent of all primary schools and 61.4 percent of all secondaries.[2]

Today, we work in a system that is led by academies at the secondary level and approaching that point at the primary. As of the summer of 2024, there are 7,158 primary academies in England and 2,828 secondary academies, representing 43 percent of primary schools and 82 percent of secondaries. This represents 43.5 percent of schools overall, educating over half of all pupils in England. I can write with some confidence that the monopoly once held by local authorities as the organising principle for English state schools has been challenged to a point that is now irreversible. See Figure 8.1.

This process of academisation has followed different patterns amongst primary and secondary schools, with the majority of secondaries becoming academies as early as January 2013. This has much to do with size. The average primary school is three times smaller than the average secondary school (roughly 300 pupils compared to 1000). For this reason, primaries were generally more reliant on the central services provided by the Local Authority, whilst secondary schools could

DOI: 10.4324/9781003533474-9

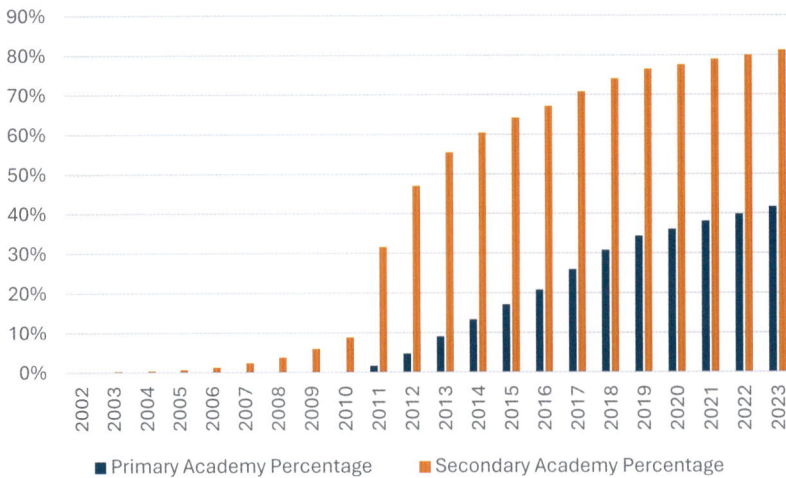

Figure 8.1 Percentage of Primary and Secondary schools in England that are Academies, 2010 to 2023.[3]

more easily bring in-house the expertise to become a stand-alone academy or—increasingly—group together to form a Multi Academy Trust (MAT).

A MAT is a charity regulated by the Department for Education with responsibility for operating two or more academies. As the administrator of multiple schools, one could argue a MAT is similar to a local authority. As with a local authority, a MAT keeps a top slice of a school's funding to pay for central services, though the proportion is typically less than that taken by a local authority, at around 5 percent. However, unlike a local authority, MATs have an organisational dynamism which makes them more likely to reach that holy grail of a 'self-improving' school system. They have no geographic constraints and can gain or lose schools according to the success they achieve for their pupils. In theory, good MATs will grow, under-performing MATs will shrink or disappear, and the school system will steadily improve. Perhaps more than any architects of the academies policy anticipated, MATs have come to dominate the landscape of English education. There were just 66 MATs in England in the summer of 2011, a figure which has grown to 1,180 today, administering around 90 percent of all academies.[4] The average MAT runs 8.5 academies, but there are 14 MATs with 40 schools or more, the largest at the time of writing being United Learning with 90 schools (See Chapter 12).[5] This is an extraordinary development: over the past 14 years; we have seen the creation of more institutions for administering schools than during any other period of English history.

Not all academies are part of a MAT. There are still around 1000 stand-alone academies with no layer of management between their governing body and the Department for Education, comprising about 11 percent of all academies. However, their number is falling, as the direction of government policy up until 2024 was to encourage such academies to join a MAT.[6] There are obvious benefits that come from conglomerations of schools, not just in terms of pooling central office functions. From the beginning, I have believed the most important advantage a group of schools can achieve is in developing a shared ethos and approach to education, which might challenge the progressivist ideology in English schools. This is particularly important for failing schools that become an academy with a MAT as their sponsor. For such schools, by far, the fastest and most effective route to improvement is through adopting the approaches to teaching, curriculum, and behaviour held within a successful MAT.

The speed of academisation does suggest there was little love lost between successful schools and their local authorities, many of which took the opportunity as soon as they could to gain more autonomy. Amongst failing schools forced to become academies under the sponsorship of another school or MAT, it was clear that the local authorities' monopoly on school improvement had been preventing change. This was a belief that pre-dated the coalition government, being a conclusion already reached by the architect of Labour's academies policy, Andrew Adonis. In his 2012 book *Education, Education, Education*, Andrew Adonis wrote: 'My ambition from the moment academies started to prove themselves successful after 2005 was to replace the entire bottom half of the comprehensive system with academies.' Of course, he never publicly explained this intention whilst in government, for fear of being burnt—he wrote—in effigy by a vocal pressure group called the Anti-Academies Alliance (more on whom later).[7]

Critics of the academies policy disagreed with the idea that academisation showed there was a latent demand for more autonomy amongst school leaders. Instead, they argued that schools were being bribed into academising by the promise of extra money. It is true that academies received more money, but only because funding that would have otherwise gone to the local authority for additional services—such as behaviour support, school improvement and central administration—instead went directly to the school. Though it varied from school to school, this figure could be up to 10 percent of a school's annual grant. In March 2011, the ASCL headteachers union surveyed 1,471 headteachers about their plans regarding academisation, and 58 percent cited greater autonomy and freedom as a reason. Granted, 72 percent cited financial gain.[8] However, that money was only attractive because school leaders believed they, or a MAT, would spend it better than the local authority. To claim that headteachers only pursued academisation to address short-term budgetary pressures at a time of austerity would be to accuse them of shortsightedness that I do not believe is fair. What is more, the gross per pupil funding for academies was the same as for local authority schools.

Most secondary academies have now been free from local authority control for ten years or more. Other than one secondary school on the Isle of Wight, I do not know of a single secondary (nor primary) academy that has needed to return to local authority control following its academisation. Academisation is a one-way street, and as such, it has brought a permanent change of status for almost 10,000

English schools. The only possible reason the policy gained such momentum was because the demand for greater autonomy from local authority control was there.

Although I agreed entirely with the principle of academisation, I watched the speed of academisation during our first five years in government closely. As an early enthusiast for the policy, I worked with the Labour government to help a struggling secondary school in my West Sussex constituency become an academy in 2009, one of the first 203 secondary schools to do so. Unfortunately, the change in designation brought little positive change to the school. Behaviour remained poor; the teaching approaches were not evidence-led, and the leadership team had little vision for how they would use their newfound freedoms. Mossbourne it was not. In 2012, only 51 percent of pupils at the academy gained five A*-C, including English and Maths. One year later, Ofsted placed the school in special measures, where it remained for the next three years. One member of a local anti-academy pressure group told a local newspaper, 'It's a tragedy for those kids and since it has become an academy in 2009 it has just gone downhill.'[9] Sadly, many of my constituents agreed.

This early involvement with an unsuccessful academy conversion robbed me of any *a priori* conviction that a school becoming an academy or joining a MAT will automatically lead to better outcomes for its pupils. Fundamentally, a school will only improve if what is happening in the classroom improves. All the changes to administrative responsibilities that academisation can bring—from site main-tenance to procurement—are of subsidiary importance to the classroom. If these changes do not, somewhere down the line, lead to more effective teaching and better pupil behaviour, then they are for nothing. The academy in my constituency was not unusual. In many schools, academisation proved to be a time-consuming and expensive process of rebadging, where the school received a new name and logo, but in all fundamental regards remained the same. If the school was already high-performing, there was little to lose from this process. But I feared that too many schools that were mediocre or worse were becoming academies only to carry on teaching in much the same way as before. If this were to remain the case, then the policy would fail to bring the transformation we promised. The structural changes of academisation would only make a difference in so far as they catalysed further change in the content and nature of classroom teaching.

Magical MATs

In some cases, this was happening. The Harris Federation has its origins in the Harris CTC in Crystal Palace, one of Kenneth Baker's original City Technology Col-leges, which was founded to replace the failing Sylvan High School in 1990. By 1999, Harris CTC was the most improved school in the area, with a 16 percent improvement in the number of pupils gaining 5 A* to C at GCSEs over the past six years.[10] As such, it was one of the dozen or so successful CTCs that pushed Andrew Adonis to design the academies programme during the early New Labour years (see Chapter 3). Much of its success was due to the vision of its sponsor, the businessman and founder of Carpetright Philip Harris, later to be ennobled as Lord Harris of Peckham. Born and brought up in South London, Lord Harris started his career running a market stall on Rye Lane in Peckham and went on to make a fortune in the carpet trade. He then committed more than 30 years of work to improving the life chances of children in London. Harris immediately saw in Andrew's plans the opportunity for his team at Harris CTC to replicate their success in schools across Southeast London, and from 2000 onwards, he became a key figure in the academies programme.

The first new school Harris took on was Warwick Park in Peckham, over the road from where Lord Harris grew up. It was a location of particular resonance for him, as it is where Damilola Taylor might have gone to secondary school. Taylor never did as, tragically, he was stabbed in the thigh with a broken bottle aged 10 years old and bled to death in the stairwell of a block of flats on 27 November, 2000. Along with the nationwide outrage at Damilola's death, Harris—whose own grandmother had once lived on the site where Damilola died—became involved in his commemoration. Turning the local secondary school into a Harris Academy became part of that mission.[11] Warwick Park reopened as Harris Academy Peckham in 2003, followed by Harris Academies Bermondsey, East Dulwich Girls and Merton in 2006, South Norwood in 2007, Falconwood in 2008, and East Dulwich Boys and Purley in 2009. These schools developed a reputation for high standards, particularly in terms of pupil behaviour. As Andrew Adonis told the *Financial Times*:

> Lord Harris now has an incredibly strong brand in south London, and I now have local authorities coming to me saying that they want a Harris academy. Not saying they want an academy—saying they want a *Harris* academy.[12]

Adonis was not wrong: I even enquired about having a Harris academy in my own constituency. In 2006, Lord Harris created the Harris Federation to oversee his growing number of schools and appointed as its Chief Executive Dan Moynihan, the successful headteacher of Harris Academy Crystal Palace (as Harris CTC became). Dan had been brought up in London (though north-west, rather than south-east), was educated in the inner-city during the 1970s, and learnt early—as he recalled in an interview with *Schools Week*—'how not to run a school'. Though he became head boy, it was not a happy experience, recalling 'the teaching was rubbish, the discipline was rubbish'.[13] As a youngster, Dan helped his dad run off-licences, where he witnessed the reality of social deprivation up close—alcoholism, drug taking, and violence. In an interview with the *TES*, he recalled, 'The area where I lived had all those challenges, too. That's why I understand the challenges for the kids in our schools: I was one of those kids.'[14]

Like all good headteachers, Dan Moynihan refuses to listen to those who say that you should not expect more from disadvantaged children. He created a central team at the Federation to codify what made Harris schools work and tasked them with spreading it to their new members. He developed systems of data-tracking between schools which are now commonplace but were then an innovation and fast-tracked promising colleagues to headship, ensuring a large proportion of Harris leaders are homegrown. In doing so, Dan and Lord Harris essentially created a prototype for the MAT. Since we began publishing MAT league tables in 2016, the Harris Federation has been consistently amongst the top-ranked trusts in the country for both primary and secondary schools. And almost 20 years later, Dan Moynihan remains its Chief Executive. In 2023, the Progress 8 score across all 26 Harris secondary schools was 0.32, meaning their pupils achieved, on average, GCSEs grades one-third higher than the average for their peers. The Harris Federation is one of only two large trusts in the country where disadvantaged pupils achieve a positive Progress 8 (+0.01 compared to −0.57 nationally). At the 22 Harris primary schools, 73 percent of pupils met the expected standard in reading, writing and maths, compared to 60 percent nationwide. Amongst disadvantaged pupils, this figure was 63 percent, compared to 44 percent nationwide.[15]

To sustain such strong results across so many schools is a remarkable feat, and something few other MATs can equal. The reason for their success is simple: they have a clear educational vision based on strong discipline and high academic expectations. Crucially, this vision has come from the top, as Lord Harris explained in his memoir *Magic Carpet Ride*:

> Dan worked really hard to keep improving results, developing standard systems for discipline, phonics, reading, numeracy and for tracking pupil progress in every school. Crystal Palace remained the template and we applied it to every school we took on, all the time improving and developing it. I think it was Dan who created the phrase 'Harris in a Box' to describe the formula we applied to new schools. It couldn't be too rigidly applied of course, because schools differed from area to area, but the principles—or 'Harris DNA' as Dan calls it—were applied universally.[16]

The Harris Federation's expansion was never plain sailing. From Warwick Park onwards, they would face opposition from some local residents, teaching unions, and an increasingly voluble pressure group called the Anti-Academies Alliance. These groups repeatedly speculated that academisation was the first step towards privatisation, something that has—despite vociferous predictions to the contrary—never come to pass. As wealthy academy sponsors such as Lord Harris have so often found, for those on the hard left, the possibility that sponsors could be acting out of genuinely philanthropic motives was difficult to conceive. At one primary school in Purley, Lord Harris recalls:

> We had demonstration after demonstration, which sometimes became really nasty and went on for years, long after we had turned the school around. I remember a protest where one of the parents was a senior member of a

public sector trade union and they had the kids, in their uniforms, parading outside wearing Michael Gove masks and shouting abuse at us.[17]

Despite their success, the Harris Federation has never been universally popular. It has been criticised for its high turnover of staff and its senior team's pay (Dan Moynihan is the best-paid person in English state education). However, any such criticism must be seen in the context of the schools that Harris Academies have superseded. They have replaced the likes of Sylvan High School and Warwick Park, where failure was entrenched, disorder was normalised, and nobody believed improvement was possible. In each school, and so many more, the Harris Academy is by orders of magnitude better for the pupils than its predecessor. We must ignore all of the jibes about 'cookie-cutter' schools. Replicating success is a virtue, and if we had multiple Harris Federations across the country, one can only imagine how much better the prospects of English children would be.

Runaway MATs

Unfortunately, we did not have multiple Harris Federations across the country. In fact, during the early development of the MAT model, there were some high-profile failures which ran the risk of discrediting the policy as a whole. Michael Gove and our advisers made no secret of their desire to expand the academies programme at speed in order to achieve sudden and radical change. As such, they were willing to tolerate the occasional misstep in order to serve the greater good of a wholesale transformation. Good MATs grow cautiously and deliberately, ensuring that expansion is not pursued at the expense of diluting their schools' 'DNA'. However, a high number of MATs seemed to be created simply to replicate the work of local authorities, with no clearly articulated vision for how their schools were going to transform, for the better, the education of their pupils. This gave birth to two troubling categories of MATs: 'mates' MATs', where schools grouped together with other friendly schools in the hope of avoiding too much oversight, and empire-building MATs, which pursued growth as a good in and of itself, with school improvement as a distant afterthought.

One soon came to recognise the tell-tale signs of an empire-building MAT: indiscriminate growth in geographically dispersed locations; no common template for how their schools would operate, instead praising the virtues of pluralism; and considerable money spent on external consultants—a clear sign that the people at the top lacked a strong vision of their own. Of course, in each case, this was a recipe for pupil results becoming stagnant or falling. The most infamous such MAT was the Academies Enterprise Trust (AET). Founded in Essex in 2008 as a group of three academies, it had expanded to 17 academies by 2011.[18] By September 2013, it ran 77 academies, spread across England—County Durham, Liverpool, Gloucestershire, Suffolk, Kent—and sharing little common identity.[19] As its Chief Executive rather concerningly told the *TES* in 2011, 'Each of our schools has a different ethos and culture. AET is not a clone; it is a committed governing body.' In September 2013, an investigation by the *Observer* revealed that AET—now the largest MAT in England—had purchased nearly £500,000 worth of services over three years from the private business interests of its trustees and executive, despite running a 'serious' deficit. None of the contracts had been put out to competitive tender.[20]

In addition, the AET was failing in its fundamental mission to improve the education of its pupils. The performance of schools which joined AET continued largely as before, or in some cases, got worse. In 2013, the Department barred the AET from expanding any further, and the following year eight schools were transferred from its control. A trust-wide Ofsted inspection took place in 2016, finding that results at eight schools had worsened after having joined AET.[21] That year, we published league tables for MATs for the first time, and amongst its secondary schools, the AET had the joint 34th Progress 8 score out of 48 large MATs.*,[22]

Unfortunately, AET was not alone in either the underperformance of its schools or its financial mismanagement. There was an unnerving line that could be drawn between charismatic headteachers we cited in speeches and financial mismanagement in newly created MATs. One such headteacher, who was awarded a knighthood in 2000 and was given nationwide responsibility for driving forward the academies programme as Schools Commissioner in 2006, became chief executive of an academy chain named E-Act in 2009. In 2011, he told *TES* of his ambition for E-ACT to reach 250 schools in five years.[23] By 2013, the Trust had reached 31 schools. However, that year, the Education Funding Agency (EFA) investigated reports of financial mismanagement. E-Act became the first MAT to be given financial 'notice to improve' by the EFA after they found a culture of 'extravagant' expenses, events at 'prestige' venues, business lunches, and first-class travel. The Trust had spent £351,000 on consultancy fees from 2008, £237,000 of which did not have proper order documentation. Around half of the 13 board members had contracts for services provided to the Trust, and there was a blurred boundary between the Trust and a money-making subsidiary called E-Act Enterprises Limited, which had some of its activities paid for by public funds. The once-feted Chief Executive resigned that year.[24]

Sadly, this was not unusual. The headteacher of an extremely impressive primary academy in South London, where Michael Gove delivered a speech in 2011, established a Trust which would convert the primary into an all through school as well as opening a satellite state-boarding school in Sussex. The whole enterprise collapsed around 2015 in a state of financial disarray, and it was revealed that the headteacher in question was earning £229,000 for his day job, as well as a further £161,000 as the director of a leisure centre built on the school site.[25] In Birmingham, the 'superhead' of Perry Beeches school was praised in speeches by Michael

---

* Though the AET came close to being broken up entirely, it is now—thankfully—stable under new leadership overseeing a more manageable number of 57 schools.

Gove and Nicky Morgan. From 2013 to 2015, he expanded from one academy to five, Perry Beeches II being opened by Michael and Perry Beeches III being opened by David Cameron. However, in March 2016, a damning report from the EFA found his MAT, Perry Beeches The Academy Trust, overclaimed on the number of its pupils eligible for free school meals and gave £1.3 million over two years to a company called 'Nexus', which in turn paid him a second salary of £160,000 a year, on top of his existing £120,000 salary. He resigned in May 2016, and the five academies were split between other MATs. The Trust was wound up in 2016 with a deficit of £1.5 million.[26]

I do not believe it was a coincidence that many politically lauded headteachers went on to lead scandal-beset trusts. Professional success is—to use a phrase Daniel Willingham is fond of—domain-specific. For us to expect successful heads to be successful administrators of large Trusts with considerable budgets without putting sufficient checks and regulations in place was naïve. The list of tawdry purchases by early academies' trusts was depressing: a jaguar car, a property in Normandy, an equestrian centre, satellite phones for foreign holidays, luxury flats, and so on. Some defended this as the 'creative destruction' necessary for sector transformation. What is more, such behaviour has never been exclusive to new school types. As Michael Gove observed in a 2014 speech, the Audit Commission had encountered at least 191 cases of fraud in local authority schools over the previous year.[27] Whether academies were more prone to mismanagement or not, there was a 'Wild West' atmosphere during these early days, and the level of oversight needed to improve. Thankfully, the academy programme had created its own sheriff who would arrive to bring some order to the town.

Future-proofing MATs

Lord Nash (as he would become) was one of Andrew Adonis's original academy sponsors in 2008. After 30 years working in private equity, during which time he was chairman of the British Venture Capital Association, he and his wife, Caroline Nash, established a children's charity named 'Future', which ran extra-curricular clubs in schools. However, the Nashes came to realise that for many of the children they were working with, school was the most stable institution in their lives. Clubs in music and sport might only ever make a difference at the margins—if they wanted to improve children's life prospects at scale, the Nashes realised they needed to improve those children's schools.

In March 2008, Westminster council voted to turn the underperforming Pimlico School into an academy, and the Nashes leapt at the opportunity to be its sponsor. A heavily unionised and politically high-profile school, Andrew Adonis tried to warn them off Pimlico as their first academy, but they insisted. As with Lord Harris before him, John Nash was beset with accusations of hidden financial motives from campaigners who supposed a successful venture capitalist supporting academisation must indicate the first step towards school privatisation. On arriving for his first consultation at Pimlico Academy, Lord Nash had to walk over pupils lying outside the school in cardboard coffins, no doubt intended to signify the death of state education. Once inside the room, he was confronted with the unnerving sight of a front row full of pupils wearing paper plate masks adorned with his face.

For Pimlico Academy's first headteacher, the Nashes took a gamble on a straight-talking Irishman called Jerry Collins, then Deputy Headteacher at a school in Camden. In two years and four months, Collins took the school from an Ofsted rating of 'Special Measures' to 'Outstanding', a record at the time. The enormous benefit that came to the wider community from this school turnaround gave the Nashes a taste for more. Having read Hirsch, Caroline Nash was moved to establish the Curriculum Centre to develop a knowledge-based curriculum and lesson resources for English schools (see Chapter 7). John and Caroline Nash became a power couple of the school reform movement, as John Nash later recalled in a speech to the Independent Academies Association: 'Nothing I have been involved in in my business life comes close to this experience of seeing the power of education in action, and there's certainly nothing else that would have attracted me to become a government minister.'[28]

In January 2013, Michael Gove asked John Nash to become a minister with responsibility for academies and free schools at the Department for Education. Thankfully, he agreed, and he was made a Peer, taking his seat in the House of Lords. Lord Nash's energy and humour made him a popular figure within the Department. He anticipated any criticism for being a transplant from the world of finance by leaning into the stereotype, frequently regretting—when faced with a difficult new problem from officials—that he hadn't chosen to spend his retirement on the golf course. In fact, John's background in private equity made him well suited to understanding the problems that emerged during the early days of MATs expansion. From 2013 to 2016, John set stricter controls on MAT growth and finances through the annually updated Academies Financial Handbook, published by the DfE's Education Funding Agency. As a statement of intent, John personally drove to the AET head offices in Essex soon after his appointment to deliver the news that their expansion was capped.

One of Lord Nash's most important interventions for ensuring a greater level of oversight in the academy-led system was the introduction of Regional Schools Commissioners (RSCs). During the early 2010s, there had been much discussion of the 'missing tier' between academies and the Department, particularly when it came to re-brokering failing academies from one trust to another. The days when Andrew Adonis could pick up the phone to any academy sponsors in the country were long gone. By 2014, with over 4,000 academies and growing, a greater level of local oversight and knowledge was needed. Appointed in September 2014, the Regional Schools Commissioners (now known as Regional DfE Directors) are eight civil servants, mostly former headteachers, who represent eight regions in England. It became their responsibility to oversee academies and free schools in their area, be it through re-brokering a struggling academy from one trust to another, approving new free schools applications, overseeing mergers between MATs, or encouraging MATs to act as sponsors for other academies. Their role is clearly confined to oversight, and—to distinguish them from Ofsted and local authorities—it was made clear from the start that RSCs would have no involvement in inspection or school improvement. One of the interesting innovations of the RSCs was to divide London between three separate regions, which cut into the capital like slices of a pizza: the South Central region oversaw North-West London, the Eastern region oversaw North East London, and the South Eastern Region oversaw South London. From the London Challenge onwards, London has been a leading source of successful school turnarounds, so this innovation meant the expertise that had been accumulated in the capital's schools might spread more quickly outside the city.

One MAT that did exactly that was Ark Schools. Ark, standing for Absolute Return for Kids, is a charity established by a group of hedge fund managers in 2002. It took on its first school, Burlington Danes Academy, in 2006, where the hedge fund manager and Ark donor Stanley Fink became its Chair of Governors, and Sally Coates was its turnaround headteacher (see Chapter 4). A professional and well-resourced outfit, Ark Schools has been at the vanguard of changes in English schools over the past two decades. They take on schools in areas of significant social deprivation and have achieved some outstanding successes. Ark Schools grew to three schools by 2007 and six by 2008. The Trust then spread outside London in 2009, taking over two secondary academies in Portsmouth and Birmingham. Following our expansion of the academies programme to primary schools, Ark opened three primary schools in 2011. Today, Ark runs 16 primary schools, 17 secondary schools, and seven 'all through' schools (both primary and secondary) across four regions—Hastings, Portsmouth, Birmingham, and London. At the primary level, they are the best achieving large MAT in the country, with 75 percent of pupils achieving the expected standard in reading, writing, and maths (compared to a national average of 60 percent).[29] And they have achieved this despite having twice the proportion of disadvantaged students across their schools than the national average.

Amongst all of the Ark schools, one of the most influential has undoubtedly been King Solomon Academy. Opened as a primary school in 2007 and a secondary in 2009, it is now an all-through school at the foot of the Edgware Road in central London. As a new academy with no predecessor institution, King Solomon had the then unusual opportunity to build a school culture from scratch. In doing so, it took its inspiration from American Charter Schools, which—like English academies—are free from local government control and have proven to be a wellspring of innovation. From the day that they opened, Ark King Solomon Academy (KSA) set a new benchmark for innovation. They took just 60 pupils for each year group and ran a longer school day, lasting from 7.50am to 5pm (longer still for pupils in detention). At lunchtime, pupils would sit six to a table and eat a 'family lunch' with pre-assigned roles such as laying the table, serving the food, clearing away plates, and wiping down the table for the next group. By far, the most important principle for its founding staff was school culture, which was upheld through a clear system of rewards and sanctions. The whole enterprise was underpinned by a combination of nurturing care and sky-high expectations of behaviour. Yes, there were detentions every night and pupils walked between lessons in silence, but there was also a school orchestra, drama productions, and frequent school trips in both the UK and abroad.[30]

Most remarkable of all, at the helm of this new venture was an Oxford science graduate called Max Haimendorf, who turned 30 a couple of months before the school opened. Max assembled a formidable team of founding staff, including Bruno Reddy as Head of Maths. Bruno's commitment to ensuring his pupils memorised their times tables led him to assign 'Times Table Rockstar' status to any pupil that did so particularly well. This turned into a classroom resource used in schools across the UK, and Bruno left KSA in 2014 to work on it full-time. His hugely popular brand of retrieval practice has since gone global and is currently used in 16,000 schools worldwide.

When I first visited KSA, the positive culture amongst pupils at KSA left me speechless, and I was delighted to see the innovation that policies of school autonomy had already unleashed. Here was a school with one of the toughest inner-city intakes imaginable, achieving behaviour so exemplary that I—habituated to the norm of low-level disruption in schools—could not quite believe it was real. Some aspects of pupil culture they had fostered were disarming. Instead of a round of applause, pupils would clap in unison, and to show appreciation or agreement in lessons, pupils would click their fingers, causing a ripple of 'audible nodding' to pass through a classroom. Some thought these innovations 'cultish'; I thought them inspired. Another early visitor was the former head of New York City schools and an influential figure in the American Charter School movement, Joel Klein. Michael Gove took Klein to visit KSA in 2011, where he observed:

> It reminded me of so many experiences I've had in the US where you see a school with traditionally highest-needs kids performing at such an exceptional level. Someone has to answer the question: if you can do it there, why can't you do it everywhere? . . . There should be a public outcry.[31]

Klein's question became all the more pertinent when King Solomon Academy gained its first set of GCSE results in 2014, and 93 percent of its pupils achieved at least five GCSEs at grades A* to C, including English and Maths. The following year, 95 percent of pupils at KSA achieved the A* to C, including English and Maths benchmark, making it the highest attaining comprehensive school in England. For Max and his team, who put their lives into building this school from scratch, the achievement was a vindication of their unorthodox and often criticised methods.

As Joel Klein had said previously, it was incumbent upon anyone who cared about transforming the lives of the least advantaged in society to take notice.*

Let a Thousand Flowers Bloom

The success of schools such as Ark King Solomon Academy helped build the case for our free school policy, introduced in 2010. Free schools are new state schools established with no predecessor institution, which operate outside of local government control with all the same freedoms enjoyed by academies. The policy was inspired by a similar policy in Sweden, as well as charter schools in the USA. Technically, KSA was not a Free School, as it was founded in 2007, and the terminology was only created after 2010. However, as a 'new academy', it was—along with Mossbourne and around 20 other Labour-era academies—indistinguishable in status from the free schools that followed.[32]

Of all the policies we introduced from 2010 to 2015, free schools were the most eye-catching and attracted the most media attention. We created the term 'free school' to help turbo-charge the existing power schools and trusts had to create new academies, but also to encourage other groups to do so—such as parents, teachers, charities, and faith groups. The policy was aided by a projected bulge in England's school-age population, as the total number of state-educated primary school children grew from 4.1 million in 2010 to 4.5 million in 2015. New schools would have to be created to accommodate this rise, and we did not want these new schools—as would previously have been the case—to be created by local authorities. We wanted them to be innovators, like KSA, and legislated in 2011 to require that any new school established in England must be a free school.

Free schools found an early proponent in the well-known journalist and political commentator Toby Young. A year before the new government even formed, he and a group of local parents began working towards the creation of a new secondary school in West London, to which Toby would send his four children. In an article in the *Observer* newspaper in August 2009, Toby wrote of the school he wanted to create in words that no doubt appalled the education establishment but filled me with confidence:

> My plan is to create a 'comprehensive grammar', that is, a school which is as close as possible to the grammar I went to—traditional curriculum, competitive atmosphere, zero tolerance of disruptive behaviour—but with a non-selective intake. It will be for 11–16s, with a total of 300 pupils. Assuming the Conservatives are in power by June 2010, I should be open for business in September 2011.[33]

---

* Max stepped down from his role as headteacher of King Solomon Academy secondary in July 2024 after 15 years in the job, during which the school has remained amongst the highest performing secondaries in England.

A man with no shortage of energy, Toby Young made good on his claim, and the West London Free School (WLFS) opened in September 2011, along with 23 other free schools. Of those schools, 17 were primary schools, five were secondary schools, and two were all through.

This first group of 24 free schools was an eclectic mix. Some were established by MATs, such as Ark and E-Act, and others by parent groups, such as the Stour Valley Community School and WLFS. Five were formerly independent schools which used the policy to move into the state sector, such as Batley Grammar School in Kirklees, which I visited in September 2011. On my train up to Yorkshire, I saw a pupil's tweet expressing disappointment to find out that the politician visiting her school was not Nick Clegg, as she had been led to believe, but instead 'some random' called Nick Gibb. It was a pleasure to visit the school regardless. Six of the first group of free schools had a religious basis: three Christian, two Jewish, and one Sikh. However, none could be exclusive to pupils from those faith groups, as we capped the proportion of faith-based admissions to a free school in their over-subscription criteria at 50 percent.

As anyone involved in their early foundation will testify, new state schools were not easy to create. Steering groups had to recruit pupils and parents to a school that did not exist, find a site (often temporary at first), build systems from scratch, and often fight off considerable animosity from unions and pressure groups such as the Anti-Academies Alliance. Despite this, the number of free schools created during our first five years in government defied all expectations. By way of comparison, in five years of fighting during the early 1990s, Kenneth Baker managed to open 15 CTCs. In ten years, Adonis opened 20 'new academies'. We opened 24 free schools in 2011, 45 in 2012, and 78 in 2013. By the end of the Parliament in 2015, we had opened 268. And by the time we left government in 2024, this number had risen to 650. This was a remarkable achievement by any measure and a testament to Michael Gove's ability to make a persuasive case for change and galvanise the Department for Education into action.

However, there was always a tension at the heart of the free schools policy and the academies policy as a whole. In his early speeches, Michael Gove sometimes extolled the virtues of pluralism that greater school autonomy would bring. At Haberdashers' Aske's Hatcham College in January 2012, he acknowledged that academy heads will 'come from a variety of different educational traditions' and said the academy programme is designed to let 'a thousand flowers bloom.'[34] However, three years previously, in a 2009 speech to the Royal Society of Arts, he was more specific about the type of flower he expected to thrive. When freed from bureaucratic control, Michael Gove predicted that the most successful schools will always be those that opt for traditional subject disciplines, rigour, and high academic expectations. Citing the Harris Academies, Mossbourne, and the KIPP Charter Schools in America as evidence, Michael continued: 'every group of schools which has made a triumphant success of freedom from bureaucratic control has done so by embracing an approach to education which has been—in the very best sense traditional.'[35]

The logic was sound. Local authorities were one of the main bastions of the progressivist ideology, so when academies and free schools were given the freedom to develop away from their oversight, they should—we hoped—feel, and an ineluctable gravitation towards more evidence-led and traditional approaches. I wanted this to be true, but the composition of the early free schools did not fill me with confidence. Many of the schools we approved showed no explicit desire to diverge from the progressivist ideology, and some were established with an explicit commitment to child-centred teaching methods. For example, one of the first primaries, named the Discovery New School, was a Montessori school with an educational vision that was even more child-centred than the mainstream. It was also, perhaps unsurprisingly, the first free school to be closed down in 2014, after Ofsted inspectors highlighted the risk that pupils would leave the school still unable to read and write.[36]

In retrospect, I should not have been surprised at the slow pace with which new, evidence-led approaches emerged. It is hard to emphasise how intellectually monocultural English schools were during the early 2010s, with similar approaches to every aspect of daily school life. Teachers at free schools and academies who wanted to do something radically different had to reinvent every aspect of school life, from lesson entry routines to homework quizzes, organisation of the lunch hall to running an effective centralised detention system. There were a growing number of teachers who were able to articulate the deficiencies with the orthodoxy of progressive education, but very few had yet been given the opportunity to develop alternative practices. The development of these alternatives in free schools and academies would have to be a slow and organic process. As we would find out, innovation takes much longer than emulation.

Of course, there were already some very good ideas out there. Schools such as Mossbourne and King Solomon Academy had shown what could be achieved in terms of pupil behaviour, and innovative teachers were starting to envisage what knowledge-rich teaching should look like through blogs and conferences like researchED. However, as an embryonic movement, it did not have the critical mass to influence the first few waves of new schools. In contrast, the progressivist ideas were so embedded within the sector that we approved a number of free schools in those first few years with a notably progressivist hue. I was frustrated that this grand structural reform was not yet going to have the impact on standards that we hoped. Thankfully, this frustration would not have to last for long.

Notes

1 S. Freedman, *The Gove Reforms a Decade on: What Worked, What Didn't, What Next?*, London: Institute for Government, 2022, p. 9.
2 Department for Education, *Academies Annual Report—Academic Year: 2014 to 2015*, November 2016, p. 15.

3 Thank you to Will Driscoll, publications editor at the Institute for Government, for providing these numbers.

4 'Multi-academy trusts by trust characteristics data', *Department for Education*, 1 February 2024 and M. Lucas et al., 'Transitioning to a multi-academy trust led system: what does the evidence tell us?', *National Foundation for Educational Research*, 2023, p. 5.

5 'MAT Tracker: mapping the country's multi-academy trusts', *TES Magazine*, 12 September 2024.

6 N. Plaister, 'The current state of play for MATs', *FFT Education Datalab*, 10 July 2024.

7 A. Adonis, *Education, Education, Education: Reforming England's Schools*, London: Biteback, 2012, p. 180.

8 V. Russell, 'Schools are converting to academies for financial reasons, survey shows', *Public Finance*, 14 March 2011.

9 'Ofsted publishes damning Littlehampton Academy report', *The Argus*, 26 February 2014.

10 'Below national average, but local state schools have improved exam results in the last six years', *Croydon Advertiser and East Surrey Reporter*, 19 November 1999.

11 P. Harris, *Magic Carpet Ride*, London: Biteback, 2017, p. 299.

12 Quoted in Harris, *Magic Carpet Ride*, p. 302.

13 'Profile: Dan Moynihan, chief executive, Harris Federation', *Schools Week*, 16 September 2016.

14 'Sir Dan Moynihan: "There is no point in blame—the buck stops with me"', *TES Magazine*, 3 October 2023.

15 Department for Education, Compare school and college performance in England.

16 Harris, *Magic Carpet Ride*, p. 301.

17 Harris, *Magic Carpet Ride*, p. 306.

18 'Academy chain aims to become biggest sponsor in the country', *TES Magazine*, 2 September 2011.

19 'Exclusive: Biggest academy trust, AET, set to give up more of its schools', *TES Magazine*, 9 March 2018.

20 D. Boffey, 'Academy chain under fire following revelation of payments made to bosses', *The Observer*, 20 July 2013.

21 Ofsted, 'Academies Enterprise Trust (AET) inspection outcome letter', February 2016.

22 Department for Education, 'Multi-academy trust performance measures: 2015 to 2016', 19 January 2017.

23 D Marley, 'Academy sponsor in talks over "super-chain"', *TES Magazine*, 18 March 2011.

24 'Culture of extravagant expenses' at academy group', *BBC News*, 17 May 2013.

25 'Durand Academy headteacher earning almost £400,000 a year, MPs told', *TES Magazine*, 26 January 2015.

26 F. Whittaker, 'Doomed Perry Beeches academy trust had a £1.5 million deficit', *Schools Week*, 6 June 2018.

27 M. Gove, 'The purpose of our school reforms', *Speech to Policy Exchange Think Tank*, 7 June 2014.

28 Lord Nash, *Speech to the Independent Academies Association National Conference*, 8 July 2013.

29 Department for Education, Compare school and college performance in England.

30 M. Haimendorf, 'How we achieved dramatically good GCSE results in the poorest ward in London', *TES Magazine*, 22 August 2014; D. Didau, 'What I learned in my visit to King Solomon Academy Part 1', 'Learning Spy' blog, 11 September 2014.

31 J. Grimston, 'Sack "lemon" teachers to save schools, says US guru', *The Times*, 30 January 2011.

32 This point is made in Adonis, *Education, Education, Education*, p. 184.

33 T. Young, 'Why I will set up a new school to give my children the best chance in life', *The Observer*, 23 August 2009.

34 M. Gove, *Speech on Academies at Haberdashers' Aske's Hatcham College*, 11 January 2012.

35 M. Gove, 'What is education for?', *Speech to the Royal Society of Arts*, 30 June 2009.

36 'Discovery new school in Crawley becomes first free school to shut', *BBC News*, 4 April 2014.

9 Phase Two

Okay. This is likely to be the bravest/stupidest post that I have ever written. I may upset people I like. I may anger people I respect. I may lose people I would rather keep. . . . So why am I defending Michael Gove?

Keven Bartle's Blog, January 2013

In February 2014, the *Economist* published a table of cabinet ministers ranked by the number of news stories each had generated over the past six months. At the top was the Prime Minister, obviously. Followed by the Deputy Prime Minister and Chancellor of the Exchequer. In fourth place was the Education Secretary, Michael Gove. With over 1,000 news stories generated, Michael's score was far ahead of his next closest rival, the Home Secretary, and almost triple that of the Foreign Secretary.[1]

Never had schools been so much at the forefront of national attention as during Michael's four years as Education Secretary, and never have been since. From his appointment in May 2010, Michael pushed education to the centre of national debate with a radical but intellectually coherent programme of reform. In his speeches, articles, and interviews, he advocated reform with the combative energy he learnt during his previous career as a newspaper columnist. This adversarial style would prove to be both his making and his Achilles Heel. Much like a driven chief executive of a large PLC, Michael was clear about what he was trying to achieve and determined in his convictions. He was willing to make enemies and thrived in an atmosphere of constant change. This allowed him to achieve more as Education Secretary than any of his predecessors but ultimately set a time limit on his tenure in the role.

Enemies of Promise

Michael Gove could never quite give up the working habits of a columnist. From 2013, his articles and speeches began to suggest—if I were to be uncharitable—that he was more concerned with winning arguments than winning support. In Michael's mind, there was a clear distinction between 'the profession': teachers who take a pragmatic approach to achieving what is best for their pupils; and the

DOI: 10.4324/9781003533474-10

'education establishment': unaccountable educationalists who promote a damaging ideology. However, this distinction was never so clear in the minds of the public, and Michael's attacks on the 'education establishment' increasingly missed the intended target and struck potential allies instead.

Following the letter from 100 university academics attacking our National Curriculum reforms in the *Independent* in March 2013 (see Chapter 5), Michael wrote a response in the *Daily Mail*, attacking its signatories as 'enemies of promise'. Famously, he went on to describe them as belonging to 'the Blob', an entity whose membership he extended to all branches of the education establishment, such as quango officials and union leaders.[2] 'The Blob' is the eponymous villain of a 1958 horror movie: an amoeba-like alien that crashes to earth, wreaking havoc in a small American town. First used by the American Education Secretary William Bennett during the late-1980s, the Blob is—in its defence—a more subtle analogy than it sounds. In the film, the Blob would subsume the townspeople who tried to stop it, thus growing larger and stronger with each attack. Bennett used the term to describe how, in a similar fashion, the American education establishment had the power to subsume government reforms and redirect them to their own ends, strengthening the very ideas such reforms were intended to challenge. As we had seen during the 1990s and 2000s, the same process had occurred in England, with reforms such as the National Curriculum and the creation of Ofsted.

This subtlety was lost on the general public, to whom the Blob sounded more like crass name-calling, creating a binary 'with us or against us' approach to reform. Michael never suggested that teachers were members of the Blob, but the belief that he did took root regardless. This mistake was easily made by those who conflated his attacks on trade union leaders with an attack on trade union members, constituting the vast majority of the profession. What is more, teachers who opposed our reforms perceived themselves to be the target, even if their main anger derived from issues far removed from the progressivist ideology of university academics, such as changes to the Teachers' Pension Scheme or cancelled school building projects. The trade unions and press encouraged this conflation: see the following headline from the *Times* in October 2013, 'Gove attacks striking teachers as he steps up war against "the Blob"'; or a trade union leader's statement from June 2014, 'Successful education systems value the views of the teaching profession, which Gove insulted when he called them "the Blob"'.[3]

In political communication, what you say and what audiences hear can be two very different things. Conservative politicians attacking state school teachers was a well-worn groove in public debates, so steering anywhere near such rhetoric risked slipping into its path. Michael belatedly realised this danger and tried to combat the impression that he was criticising teachers. In a speech delivered to a think tank in September 2013, entitled 'The Importance of Teaching', he stated:

> I am fortunate as Education Secretary because we have the best generation of
> teachers ever in our classrooms. . . . Whenever I can, I give thanks for their

work—not just privately, but on any public platform I'm given. Including this one.[4]

He was telling the truth. I don't believe there was a single speech Michael delivered as Education Secretary where he did not commend members of the profession, both generally and by name. However, it was not cutting through. Instead, by the summer of 2013, it had become a trope in the press and amongst the profession that Michael Gove hated teachers. Teachers, in turn, became increasingly vocal in expressing their anger with Michael. Facebook and Twitter pages dedicated to disliking Michael spread online; a pincushion displaying his face was put up for sale, as was a spoof book by 'Mr Michael Gove' entitled *Everything I know about teaching* (the joke being all 90 pages were blank). In June, Frank Furedi, a sociologist who was sympathetic to our reforms, wrote about the spread of 'Govephobia' for the website Spiked Online. This phenomenon, he wrote, 'now provides many teachers and educators with a kind of corporate identity. The very mention of Gove's name in a meeting is guaranteed to raise a collective smirk and the knowing shaking of heads.'[5]

Seemingly buoyed by negative press coverage, Michael became yet more adversarial in the New Year. In January 2014, the same month that his disagreements with Michael Wilshaw at Ofsted went public, he wrote a controversial opinion piece on the moral necessity of Britain's intervention in the First World War. This article reminded the public of his previous over-involvement in the History National Curriculum and was—Michael later admitted in conversation—an unforced error (particularly as he was seen to criticise the much-loved British sitcom 'Blackadder').[6] In May, Michael Gove initiated a high-profile investigation into the so-called 'Trojan Horse' plot amongst Islamists to infiltrate Birmingham schools, and in June, he publicly accused the Home Secretary Theresa May of not doing enough to prevent the spread of radical Islam in schools.[7] Simultaneously, his former adviser Dominic Cummings, who had left the Department for Education in January, was generating headlines with his long-read blogs, which included personal attacks on members of the government, and a 237-page manifesto on education reform which many found completely mystifying.[8] With an election only one year away, David Cameron was shown figures by his Australian polling guru Lynton Crosby showing that Michael was polling badly, not just amongst the teachers and teaching assistants, who make up nearly 600,000 members of the electorate, but also the general public.

On 15 June 2014, David Cameron removed Michael as Secretary of State for Education, replacing him with the much more conciliatory figure of Nicky Morgan. The previous day, a column in the *Economist* suggested an element of self-sabotage to Michael's downfall. Picking a fight with the Home Secretary showed that, after four years of non-stop reforming, he now had too much time on his hands. As the article suggested, 'Most of his reforms are done and the spadework of implementation, it is said, holds little delight for such a restless intellect.'[9] There was a paradox at the centre of Michael's move from Education. During his last year as Education Secretary, he was simultaneously hailed as the most disliked politician in Britain and the most successful. The best explanation for this contradiction is that both claims were true. The intense determination and willingness to expose failure, which allowed Michael to make so much progress in just four years, also led to his removal. Had Michael approached his reforms in a less polarising manner, he may have gained some more years as Education Secretary, but such a counter-factual is not worth considering: it would have required him to have been an entirely different person.

In our time working together, Michael was an inspiring colleague. He trusted me to lead the first stages of curriculum reform and gave me the courage and support to push for radical prescriptions. Though a conviction politician, he was not stubborn and often changed his mind when new information or better ideas came along. He drove a programme for education reform which involved neither the return of grammar schools nor profit-making schools via some sort of voucher system, building on the work David Cameron and I had begun in Opposition. I could see why David had made the decision to move Michael out of education, but I think it was wrong. I believe we would have made more progress more quickly had Michael remained in post. And I doubt his removal made any difference to the outcome of the 2015 General Election. But it was David Cameron's decision to make, and it brought with it one major consolation for me.

Common Ground

On the same day that David Cameron moved Michael Gove to the position of Chief Whip, he re-appointed me as Schools Minister—a post which I would retain for eight further years. I was told that Michael had requested my reinstatement as a condition of his departure, keen to ensure that there was a 'true believer' in place to protect the reforms. On the day of my re-appointment, David Cameron tweeted, 'Nick Gibb returns to Government as Minister of State for Schools—working with Nicky Morgan to ensure no letup in education reforms.' In his memoir *For the Record*, David Cameron wrote:

> Nick Gibb had enthusiastically backed my leadership campaign, and he'd been a brilliant junior education minister under Michael Gove. . . . But while I admired Nick's work, I had bought into the theory that if you are a minister and you are not destined for cabinet, at some stage you have to go. Good rule, but terrible example. I should never have moved him, and I made good on my mistake twenty-two months later when I gave him his old job back.[10]

I returned to the Department determined to vindicate the Prime Minister's decision and demonstrate the virtues of a subject-specialist minister driven by conviction in a specific cause rather than personal ambition. On the morning of Monday, 16

July, I was overjoyed once more to be taking the lift to the seventh floor of Sanctuary Buildings, where the Department for Education's ministers were then based. However, I returned to an atmosphere very different from the one I remembered. In September 2012, we had been at the peak of our reforms, fighting for radical change on every front. Two years later, most of these initial battles had been won, and it felt as if everyone in the Department was coming up for air. With most of our reforms to school structures and standards now in motion, we needed to take stock and prepare for the next phase. Such a gear shift was evident in the appointment of Nicky Morgan. 'Emollient' was the adjective most favoured by journalists at the time: a former city lawyer, committed Christian, and Sunday-school teacher, Nicky did not come to the Department with any great reforming agenda. Instead, she was seen as a pragmatic and likeable politician, well-chosen to contrast with Michael Gove's crusading zeal, and she brought in two first-class special advisers, Luke Tryl and Chris Wilkins. But with less than a year to go until the May 2015 election, the window for any new policies was narrow, particularly since Nicky had a marginal seat to defend.

I was comfortable with the objective of turning down the heat. During my two years out of office, I had come to realise the futility of reforming a sector without also trying to win its support. In 2012, I accepted an unpaid role on the board at the David Ross Education Trust (DRET), a group then of around 25 primary and secondary academies based in the East Midlands sponsored by the co-founder of Carphone Warehouse, David Ross. David is an impressive and principled individual who has put his wealth and experience from business towards philanthropic causes in education and the arts. With no ministerial red box to occupy my evenings and weekends, I spent all the spare time I could visiting DRET schools and speaking to their teachers. This provided a well-timed opportunity to see how our reforms were playing out on the ground. In my meetings with staff at the DRET schools, I was—in effect—one of their employers, and I did not always get those interactions right. When I challenged a teacher too hard on their resistance to using phonics or a school leader on why they were not combatting disruptive behaviour, I could see their indignation that a politician might question them about their craft face-to-face. It did not feel good.

The vast majority of teachers enter the profession because they want to do something they care about: nurturing young children and, particularly in secondary schools, teaching subjects for which they have a life-long passion. Compared to other professions, such as my own in accounting, questioning how teachers do their job is much more likely to feel like a personal attack. In my case, this would always be compounded by the fact that I was a Conservative politician, working in a sector which skews towards the political left. These interactions made me reflect on how I should approach being Schools Minister. On resuming the post, I set myself the following rules: always assume good intentions, praise good practice more than criticise bad, find common ground, and never talk about 'the Blob'.

Finding common ground was particularly important when it came to the trade unions. It is normal for a politician, Labour or Conservative, to see trade union leaders as the enemy, particularly when they oppose every decision you make in the most immoderate language possible, such as the Deputy General Secretary of NASUWT (and future General Secretary) who described our 2011 Education Act as a 'crime against humanity'.[11] However, I came to see much of this rhetoric as surface froth intended to keep happy the militant base who attend their conferences and vote in their elections. Once you learn to block out the noise, you discover that what union leaders care about above all else is pay and conditions for their members, something on which we could all find common ground. They also know the sector inside out and can easily spot a minister who is failing to keep on top of their brief.

Throughout my time in office, I held regular meetings with the main union leaders and established a working relationship with each of them. I always stressed my agreement with them that a well-rewarded teaching profession is vital for high-quality schools, and I worked hard to develop the arguments for the best pay settlement that was affordable to put to the Treasury. In addition, a small number of our policies—such as those on workload and the protection of teachers from the consequences of false allegations—were met by the union leaders with support. In one of our early meetings, Mary Bousted of the ATL union observed that my tone as Minister had become more constructive since returning from my hiatus, and, although she disagreed with almost all our education policies, she had never doubted, she said, my sincerity.

As a new Secretary of State, Nicky Morgan had less than a year until the election, but she did come to the department with some policies that she wanted to develop, in particular, reducing teacher workload, improving character education, and addressing concerns over mental health. I agreed with Nicky's concern with workload: teacher time is the most precious resource within our education system and anything that might take time away from planning, teaching, and marking should be introduced with caution. Nicky launched the Workload Challenge survey in October 2014 to help identify the drivers of unnecessary workload, with 44,000 teachers responding. It prompted a public debate about how everyone, from government ministers to middle leaders, could better protect teacher time. For us, it was a helpful reminder of the potential for accountability measures to drive low-impact work, with 53 percent of teachers reporting that the pressures of Ofsted, perceived or otherwise, caused unnecessary workload, particularly paperwork and the unnecessary collation of data.[12] In response, we continued to emphasise that the time-consuming accumulation of 'evidence' which had once been favoured by the inspectorate was no longer required.

In October 2014, Ofsted published the first of many 'myth-busting' documents, stating that inspectors no longer wanted to see individual lesson plans, specific types of data on pupil attainment, or extensive written feedback in books. I learnt as a minister that one of the greatest threats to teacher time is the collection of 'evidence' that interventions are being followed simply to please some form of external accountability.[13] In the past, both the Department and Ofsted had contributed towards a culture where 'evidencing' that you were doing a good job became more important than doing a good job, and we knew this needed to change. One example from the Reception class of a school was the Early Years Foundation Stage Profile—a vast scrapbook for each child with photos and examples of their work lovingly pasted into scores of its pages. It consumed hundreds of hours and was used to support the 'moderation' of teachers' assessment judgements of their young pupils. In time, we removed this requirement altogether, although this reform was opposed by the Early Years Lobby. More generally, we committed to offering a one-year lead in time to any further changes to the curriculum, qualifications, or accountability measures.

Caught Not Taught

However, I was more sceptical of Nicky's drive on character education in schools. Few would deny that schools—for better or for worse—can forge the moral bearings of young people. This occurs through the conduct of their staff as role models, the content of their assemblies, and the behaviour that they reward and sanction. However, the idea that schools can 'teach' character with anywhere near the same level of assurance that they 'teach' academic subjects is misguided. In my view, pupils mostly learn good character through their interactions within a school, not through timetabled lessons—placing me in the 'caught not taught' camp in this debate. A decent teacher in an effective school can guarantee the great majority of their class become good mathematicians. However, it is far less certain that she or he can guarantee they become 'good people'. What is more, the scope for 'teaching' or 'moulding' character is limited by time and resources. Those who have been educated at independent schools, where staff have the time and professional obligation to act *in loco parentis*, rarely understand the challenge of providing character education at a state school where the majority of pupils arrive at 08.30 and leave at 15.00. Like so many things in education, it is a question of opportunity cost. A discrete one-hour lesson on nebulous traits such as 'empathy' or 'grit' (a fashionable concept back in 2014) may seem relatively harmless, but not when you consider it is taking place at the expense of something we know can be taught, such as English or Maths.

Schools might help pupils 'catch' traits such as empathy through positive playground engagements with their peers or develop grit through working on their homework, taking part in sports fixtures, or having positions of responsibility within the school. However, even then, we should be realistic about how much can be achieved. Even in our most lauded schools, pupils will never learn character traits with the same level of assured success that they learn in academic subjects. Eton may have produced 20 Prime Ministers, but it has also produced a few crooks, frauds, and jailbirds.

When Nicky launched her drive on character education in December 2014, I was worried by the message—as per the Department press release—that we would now place 'character education on a par with academic learning'.[14] However, money was still scarce, and the drive remained small-scale, with Nicky allocating just £3.5 million for character education programmes delivered by external partners such as rugby clubs, St John Ambulance, and the PSHE Association. She also introduced the annual Department for Education 'Character Awards', where schools and organisations which showed innovation in this area could receive £15,000. Though effective at generating headlines, this push did not change the overall direction of our reforms, and the Department's Character Awards were quietly dropped after just two years.

Nevertheless, there was a risk that 'character education' would become a front by which the education establishment influenced the Department—once again—to promote the progressivist ideology in schools. I had to be vigilant in preventing this from happening, conscious as I was of David Cameron's instruction not to let up on our reforms. Nicky Morgan no doubt had a more 'muscular' interpretation of character development in mind (see all the money being given to rugby clubs), but many in the education establishment saw it as just another term for skills-based curriculum and child-centred learning. One of the first recipients of her Character Awards was School 21, a child-centred free school which taught much of its curriculum through 'project-based learning'—an approach for which there is no robust evidence of success. More recently, the school has achieved disappointing GCSE results and was graded 'Requires Improvement' by Ofsted. I could not blame Nicky for struggling to see this danger: she had been transferred to Education from the Treasury with no notice, so never had the luxury of time I had enjoyed to read up on education philosophies. Her antennae did not naturally turn towards this danger, and mine had to instead.

Culture Change

It was a pleasure to resume the day-to-day work of a government minister, which I always enjoyed. A large proportion of this work consists of reading 'submissions'. These are short explanations of policy decisions that ministers might want to take based on their instructions and public pronouncements, drafted by civil servants and ending with a menu of possible actions. With Michael Gove out of office, I received steadily more submissions promoting the child-centred ideology, often under the guise of character education. There were submissions suggesting that we add the teaching of character to the National Curriculum or that we develop new 'character' qualifications. As I saw all too clearly after Michael's departure, the language of the progressivist ideology was the default to which officials would inevitably return if not actively encouraged otherwise, a comfortable groove along which it felt easiest to travel. Civil servants would habitually avoid the use of the word 'pupil', as that implied a hierarchical relationship with teachers. Better 'students', even better, 'learners'. The term 'teaching' was avoided, with 'learning' used wherever possible instead. Supposedly elitist terms such as 'academic' were unwelcome, so 'school year' was habitually used over 'academic year'. Similarly, the word 'practice' implied drudgery, so 'activity' was always the preferred alternative. The word 'discipline' remained largely unmentionable in official documents, with 'behaviour for learning' seen as a far more palatable alternative. Pen at the ready, I would expunge all such language from policy papers, public documents, and draft legislation and tried—wherever possible—to explain to civil servants why it posed a threat to our reforms. I believe I gained something of a reputation for pedantry, but if there was one thing that I had learnt from reading Hirsch's critiques of the progressivist ideology, it was that language mattered. Words carry assumptions which, if allowed to go unchecked, could uphold a thoughtworld and stymie reform. One of the most important roles I could fulfil to combat this ideology within the Department was on a lexicological level, fighting it word by word, document by document.

Such work often felt like holding back a tide. Without a concerted effort to prevent it from doing so, I knew the progressivist ideology could flood back into our schools. From 2014 onwards, I took to describing myself as akin to the boy with his finger in the dam, unwilling to move for fear that the water would burst back through. As such, one of the most important jobs I had to do at the Department was to say 'no'—no to the demands we row back on terminal exams, no to suggestions that we add non-academic subjects to the National Curriculum, and no to initiatives that would distract teachers from their core mission, which should always remain, quite simply, to teach. On the question of adding non-academic subjects to the National Curriculum, calls in the media that 'schools really should teach [insert favoured issues here]' are the bane of the life of any school reformer interested in raising standards. For any media panic, it has become the semi-automatic response of interest groups—be they politicians, charities, faith groups, or celebrities—to demand that lessons on the issue in question be incorporated into the school curriculum. In 2018, Parents and Teachers for Excellence (a campaign group sympathetic to our reforms) decided to monitor this phenomenon, which they termed 'curriculum dumping'. That year, they identified 213 such calls for the school curriculum to incorporate new topics, including knife crime, obesity, gambling, litter picking, bushcraft, sadomasochism, Love Island, sign language, the 1819 Peterloo Massacre, revenge porn, tree climbing, trampolining, and, rather extraordinarily, 'how to swear'.[15] In individual cases, all of these issues (well, almost all) had merit in being known, but taken together, no school in the country has enough hours in the year to cover such a panoply of fleeting media fancies. What is more, none of these topics have the permanence and power of the content of an academic school curriculum. My response to these calls became increasingly automatic the longer I was in office—'no'.

We went into the 2015 election boasting in our manifesto of a track record of significant change in education: 4,000 more academies, 250 new free schools, a more challenging national curriculum, and qualifications, and more power for teachers to deal with disruptive behaviour. However, many were predicting that a Labour victory would stop our reform programme in its tracks. Leading up to the 2015 election, the Labour Party promised to end the free schools programme and introduce greater local accountability for academies. They proposed several policies which—I feared—would take power from schools and give it back to the education establishment, such as a new School Leadership Institute and local Directors of School Standards. Whilst our manifesto wrote of 'rigour in the curriculum' and 'discipline in the classroom', there was no such language in the Labour manifesto, which instead wrote of the importance of children's 'creativity, self-awareness and emotional skills.'

The 2015 election fell at a strange point of limbo in the journey of our reforms: we had made significant changes to school structures, but we had not yet won the argument on school standards. Winning this argument in any conclusive manner would, frustratingly, take more time than a five-year Parliament. Not only did we need the time for different teaching approaches to be introduced, we also needed time for these approaches to demonstrate improved pupil outcomes. At a school level, Year 7 pupils entering a secondary academy or free school in 2011 would only gain GCSE results in 2016. Year 1 pupils entering a primary academy or free school would only take their Year 6 national curriculum assessments in 2017. On a national level, the PISA, TIMSS, and PIRLS international surveys of pupil attainment take place at three to five-year intervals. The first indications as to the impact of our reforms might have shown up in surveys taken in 2015 (PISA and TIMSS) and 2016 (PIRLS), but a genuine reflection would be seen in surveys taken between 2018 and 2020. Fundamentally, school improvement is pegged to the education of young children and is, therefore, a process in which gains are slow to show. Thus, in the 2015 election, we could talk a lot about the radical actions we had taken but could not yet point to much evidence of positive impact.

So, I spent much of the early months of 2015 in a state of concern that a Labour victory would stop our reforms in their tracks, preventing them from fulfilling—in time—what I knew to be their promise. However, I should not have been so worried. On 7 May 2015, the Conservative Party won the election with a surprise majority of 12 seats. Having been returned as Prime Minister, David Cameron kept me in post as Schools Minister. Barring any mishaps, I now had at least five further years to see through our reforms. On returning to Sanctuary Buildings after the election, I knew that the next phase of our reforms needed to be different from the first. From 2010 to 2015, we had to blow up the concrete. The progressivist ideology was so embedded within the education establishment that we had to clear away its strongholds and lay foundations on which new ideas could be built. Our overriding theory had been that schools with the right accountability measures and sufficient autonomy would gravitate to new, evidence-led approaches. If our theory was correct, our second phase of reforms had to be the period when these approaches grew on a system-wide basis.

Our promise had been to build a school-led system, and from 2015 onwards, schools needed to take the lead. Where did that leave me as Schools Minister? In such a phase of the reforms, I saw myself as playing three important roles. Firstly, the finger in the dam: I was the Department's 'Dr No', spotting any policy proposal which might allow the progressivist ideology to reassert itself and stop it in its tracks. Fortunately, Theresa May—the new Prime Minister from 2016—was supportive of our reforms and aided in understanding them by her brilliant joint chief of staff, Nick Timothy (now the Conservative MP for West Suffolk), who had only the previous year been leading on the free schools movement as director of the New Schools Network. Secondly, I wanted to use my position in the Department to foster new, evidence-led approaches to teaching and encourage their spread to more schools. I wanted to help foster a 'culture change' in schools, and achieving this required me to exercise the soft power of making speeches, influencing appointments, introducing like-minded school leaders, using a more hard-edged approach to the accountability system, and—of course—convening my Knowledge Network meetings. Thirdly, in some very particular areas, I wanted to use the Department to incubate specific aspects of this culture change, such as the teaching of mathematics.

Spreading Best Practice

During my two-year hiatus from the Department for Education, Liz Truss was appointed as Parliamentary-under-Secretary of State for Education. When I moved back to the Department, she moved on to Environment, so our time never overlapped. However, she did leave the promising legacy of a Maths Mastery programme. East Asian jurisdictions such as Shanghai and Singapore influenced our primary and secondary curriculum reforms (see Chapters 5 and 6). However, in order to emulate East Asian outcomes, we knew teachers in England would also need to emulate their methods. With this purpose in mind, Liz launched the Maths Mastery programme in early 2014 to incubate a grassroots culture change amongst teachers towards a more rigorous approach to teaching mathematics. When I returned to the Department in July 2014, I asked officials to imagine the extent to which Liz Truss was obsessed by maths and multiply it by ten, determined as I was to continue and grow the programme.

To lead the Maths Mastery programme, we established 35 Maths Hubs based out of schools across the country. Overall coordination was provided by the National Centre for Excellence in the Teaching of Mathematics (NCETM), which we contracted with the education services company Tribal to run. Two individuals were key to its success: Debbie Morgan and Charlie Stripp. The Hubs became centres of expertise for the 'mastery' approach to teaching children mathematics. Crucially, the NCETM organised a teacher exchange, sending English teachers to Shanghai to observe lessons and Chinese teachers to England to teach model lessons. Over 700 English and Chinese teachers participated in the exchange from 2014 to 2019.

Seeing is believing, as one participant from a primary school in Leicestershire recorded:

> Seeing maths teaching in Shanghai and observing how lessons are planned and then discussed and refined by teachers there has been the most interesting and rewarding professional experience of my career. I've literally questioned everything I've done for the last eight years of teaching. It's really inspired me to be a better maths teacher.[16]

What was so different about the East Asian approach? Firstly, as the term 'mastery' implies, there is an emphasis on ensuring pupils work at a mathematical procedure or concept long enough for understanding to be assured. The expectation is not that pupils learn 'at their own pace' but instead that the great majority of pupils can attain proficiency if taught well. The convention in teaching in English schools had been to cycle through a number of topics over a term's work, so that topics are repeatedly visited, and pupils achieve understanding in time. However, mastery teaching approaches fewer topics but in greater depth, with the expectation that pupils only move on to the next topic once the previous one has been understood.

In March 2015, the Harris Federation showcased a lesson by a particularly effective teacher from Shanghai called Lin Lei at one of their primary academies in Essex. I went along to watch. It was a Year 4 class, I recall, and in a 35-minute lesson, with all pupils facing the teacher and engaged throughout, Lin taught them to carry out complex types of long multiplication through a clear explanation of calculation methods. The whole lesson was devoted to how to multiply a pair of two-digit numbers ending in a zero. She used the example of 70 × 30.

'Step One', she said. 'Throw away the zeroes. How many zeroes have we thrown away? Two.'

'Step Two: multiply 7 × 3. What is 7 × 3? 21.'

'Step Three: Pick up the zeroes. How many zeroes did we throw away? Two. How many zeroes do we pick up? Two. So, 21 plus two zeroes equals 2100.'

The class then performed many more similar examples individually. I went around the class and could see that every pupil understood what they were doing and were performing the calculations correctly.

As I saw in that primary school in Essex, mastery teaching also has a greater emphasis on interactive whole-class teaching, where the teacher guides pupils through problems in a clear and deliberate fashion. In 2014, Professor David Reynolds of Southampton University and his Chinese postgraduate research student Zhenzhen Miao published some important research. They videoed lessons in both countries to find out what teaching methods were being used, and the difference was clear: in Chinese classrooms, whole-class interactive teaching made up 72 percent of lesson time, compared with only 24 percent of lesson time in England. In England, almost half of the time—47 percent—was used up on pupils working individually or in groups, compared with only 28 percent of the time in China.[17]

Thirdly, Mastery teaching is very deliberate, with thought going into the most granular of details, such as the variation in difficulty within a sequence of exercise questions (something teachers term 'minimal differences'). In East Asia, this thought is embodied in professionally produced resources, such as textbooks. In England, one of the most baleful consequences of the child-centred orthodoxy has been a prejudice against textbooks, long caricatured as representing boring, unimaginative teaching. The legacy of this prejudice is evident in international comparative data. According to the 2011 TIMSS survey, 70 percent of Singaporean pupils in Year 5 were taught by teachers using textbooks as a basis for instruction in lessons. In Finland, the figure was 95 percent. But in England, the figure was 10 percent.[18] To help rehabilitate the use of textbooks in English schools, we arranged for adaptations of two Singaporean mathematics textbooks, entitled 'Maths No Problem' and 'Inspire Maths', for use within the Maths Hubs.

The Maths Hubs offer free or low-cost professional development to neighbouring schools and have spurred a culture change in our teaching of mathematics. What is more, through their model of cascading expertise, they offer significant value for money. The initial cost of establishing the Maths Hubs programme was £11 million, and in 2016 we pledged a further £41 million to the programme for four further years, allowing us to train a cadre of 700 specialist mastery teachers and reach 8,000 English primary schools—half the total number in England.[19] The impact has been enormous. Since we introduced the Maths Hubs programme, the ranking of English pupils in the international PISA tests has moved from 27th in 2009 to 16th in 2018 to 11th in 2022. English pupils are coming closer to achieving the outcomes of pupils in Shanghai and Singapore, and it should be of little surprise that we have East Asian teaching methods to thank—at least in part—for their progress.

We took the principles of the Maths Hubs programme and applied them to other areas of the curriculum and school organisation. The approach involved identifying 30 to 40 schools across the country that were exceptional in their delivery of the relevant area of education. As well as being high-performing schools, to qualify as a Hub, the school had to adhere to the principles set out in a recent report which would reflect the government's evidence-led approach to policy. We would also appoint a 'centre of excellence' to provide the Hub schools with expert advice and to administer the scheme. The Hub schools would be funded to spread best practice to other schools which felt they could benefit from such support.

The Behaviour Hubs programme was announced in 2019, with the first 22 schools and two multi-academy trusts appointed as Behaviour Hubs in April 2021, rising to 50 schools and ten MATs by April 2023. Leading this programme was our newly appointed Behaviour Tsar Tom Bennett, whose researchED conferences had been leading the evidence revolution in English schools since their inauguration in 2013 (see Chapter 7). The Behaviour Hubs were required to follow the principles set out in Tom Bennett's seminal paper on school behaviour, *Creating a Culture*.[20] Tom's review was published in 2017 and set out in detail how schools can create the ethos and environment conducive to the exemplary behaviour of students. It included the importance of visible leadership, consistent practices, high levels of commitment by teachers and parents, staff training, and high expectations of students. We commissioned Tom to write the report because we knew his approach worked and was evidence-led.

We took a similar approach to the teaching of foreign languages. Since the previous government ended the compulsion to study a foreign language to age 16 (reducing it to age 14), the numbers taking a GCSE in French or German plummeted. Prior to 2004, over 80 percent of pupils were entered for a GCSE in a modern foreign language. By 2010, that had reduced to just 39 percent.[21] As a proud trading nation, I felt this was an indictment of our education system. I also believe that foreign languages are an indication of a high-quality curriculum that brings with them wider cognitive advantages for pupils. But when I saw foreign language teaching in our schools, I was appalled by what I perceived as poor practice. No wonder so many were put off. Gone was the systematic teaching of vocabulary and grammar, and in its place, an almost 'Berlitz guide' to learning common phrases. Ian Bauckham, headteacher of the Bennett Memorial Diocesan School in Kent, was a French teacher by background, and he shared my concerns. In November 2016, I asked Ian if he would write a paper setting out the optimal and evidence-based approach to teaching languages. We decided it would carry more weight if it were published by the Teaching Schools Council, a grouping of the leaders of the teaching schools.

Ian's paper, the '*Modern Foreign Languages Pedagogy Review*', was clear that pupils need to be taught in a systematic way, vocabulary, grammar, and how words and sounds are pronounced. It advocated the practice of the spoken tongue and memorisation of vocabulary and grammar. It emphasised the importance of including an introduction to the culture, history, and literature of the language and the use of high-quality textbooks.[22] Once these key principles had been established, we needed to spread that best practice, which, again, we did through the Hubs approach. We identified a small number of exemplary schools supported by an expert centre, which in this case was the languages department of York University.

One particular language that I was keen to promote was Mandarin, given the growing economic and strategic importance of China. A chance discussion with Oliver Letwin in 2015 in the anteroom of the Chief Whip's office in Number 9 Downing Street gave me the impetus to create the Mandarin Excellence Programme. I had read that it takes 3,200 hours of study to be competent in Mandarin. At two hours per week and assuming no break for holidays, this would mean 30 years of study! The idea of the Mandarin Excellence Programme was to require eight hours of study per week, four hours in the classroom, and four hours of homework each week. The approach to teaching would be based on the successful methodology of Katharine Carruthers of the Institute of Education. Officials and I had seen her textbooks and concluded they were in tune with the systematic teaching of vocabulary, grammar, and writing, the latter being notably challenging.

The programme was launched in 2016 with the aim of having 5,000 pupils taught Mandarin from scratch to reach competency or fluency by 2020. The programme was funded with £10 million annually and was administered jointly with the Institute of Education and the British Council. Originally in 76 secondary schools that we carefully selected on the basis of their proficiency in teaching languages and their willingness to conform to Katharine Curruthers's pedagogical approach. The Mandarin Excellence Programme has been hugely successful, with cohorts of committed students taught by passionate and accomplished teachers, overseen and trained by Katharine and her team. There are now 13,000 students on the programme and nearly 100 schools delivering it. It is unapologetically elitist, with pupils having to commit to eight hours of study per week and with an annual 'hurdle test' to ensure both students and school remain on track. My ambition was and remains to ensure that pupils be proficient on the international standard HSK Level 4 and 5 as well as achieve high grades at GCSE and A level (originally the Pre-U exam).

Phonics teaching was another area where I believed the hub model had something to offer. Although schools had achieved an 82 percent pass rate in the Phonics Screening Check by 2019, a figure that reached 92 percent when the Year 2 retakes were included, I was still not happy with those figures nor the consistency of phonics teaching in our primary schools. I was particularly concerned that the pass rate for those children eligible for free school meals was just 72 percent. Given that phonics is very much a mechanical exercise, like learning the scales for those being taught to play the piano, there was no reason for there to be an attainment gap. The only explanation for the gap was poor teaching in too many schools, particularly in more prosperous areas where weak phonics teaching was camouflaged by children having learned to read at home. I knew, therefore, that we had to do more to improve the teaching of phonics in schools. Every year, I wrote to several hundred primary schools, congratulating them on achieving a 100 percent pass rate in their Phonics Screening Check, many of which were in areas of significant deprivation. Harnessing the expertise of these schools through the principles of another Hubs programme was, to me, the answer. And so the English Hubs programme was born.

Established in 2018, the approach was the same as for the other Hubs. We identified 34 primary schools that were high achieving in the Phonics Screening Check as well as in the Key Stage 2 assessments in reading, writing, and maths. We funded these schools to support weaker schools in their region. Through that programme we have seen early signs of success, but changing and improving practice in 17,000 primary schools is a long process, delivered school by school.

In leading this culture change from 2015, I was permitted for the first time to recruit some assistance. At a government department, the Secretary of State is permitted to employ two to three Special Advisers, who are 'Special' because, unlike all other civil servants, they can be politically partial. They can then employ many more 'policy advisers', who fulfil a similar role, but must be politically impartial, so they cannot work on anything related to their minister's political party. Following the election in May 2015, I argued hard for my own policy adviser and was permitted in August to appoint the co-author of this book, Robert Peal, to the role. Having trained as a history teacher in 2011, Robert joined the think tank Civitas in 2013, and it was there that he caught my eye, writing a history of teaching methods in English schools from the 1960s to today entitled *Progressively Worse* in 2014. I encouraged everyone working in education whom I met as minister to read Robert's book. Through its historical narrative, it demonstrated two vital justifications for our reforms: that child-centred teaching had become an orthodoxy in English schools from the 1960s to today, and this approach had failed to fulfil its promise to improve the education of young people.

Following the publication of *Progressively Worse*, Robert spent a year working at the West London Free School, one of the first 24 free schools to be established during the previous Parliament. As such, he was well-placed to help keep me connected to the changes that were happening in our most innovative schools (see Chapter 8). It was in these grassroots, teacher-led changes that I saw a genuine reform movement, with a momentum of its own, now growing out of English schools.

Notes

1 'The Goveometer', *The Economist*, 15 February 2014.
2 M. Gove, 'I refuse to surrender to the Marxist teachers hell-bent on destroying our schools', *Daily Mail*, 23 March 2013.
3 'Viewpoints: Michael Gove's exit as education secretary', *BBC News*, 15 July 2014.
4 M. Gove, 'On the importance of teaching', *Speech to the Policy Exchange Think Tank*, 13 September 2013.
5 F. Furedi, 'Govephobia: The malady sweeping right-on Britain', *Spiked Online*, 10 June 2013.
6 M. Gove, 'Why does the left insist on belittling true British heroes?', *Daily Mail*, 2 January 2014.
7 M. Gove, 'May and Gove in row over extremism in schools', *BBC News*, 4 June 2014.
8 B. Quinn, 'Michael Gove ally Dominic Cummings in personal attack on David Cameron', *The Guardian*, 16 June 2014.
9 'Michael Gove, school swot', *The Economist*, 14 June 2014.
10 D. Cameron, *For the Record*, London: William Collins, 2019, pp. 391–392.
11 G. Paton, 'NASUWT: new education law a 'crime against humanity'', *The Telegraph*, 20 November 2011.
12 Department for Education, *Government Response to the Workload Challenge*, February 2015.
13 R. Adams, 'Ofsted tells teachers what not to do in effort to dispel inspection myths', *The Guardian*, 17 October 2014.
14 Department for Education, 'Press release: England to become a global leader of teaching character', 16 December 2014.

15 M. Burke and M. Lehain, *Clogging up the classroom: The jostle for curriculum content*, London: Parents and Teachers for Excellence, 2018.

16 Department for Education, 'Press release: Shanghai maths exchange shows power of international partnership', 25 January 2019.

17 D. Reynolds and Z. Miao, 'How China teaches children maths so well', *The Conversation*, 26 September 2014.

18 TIMSS, *TIMSS 2011 International Results in Mathematics*, Boston: TIMSS and PIRLS International Study Centre, 2011, p. 392.

19 Department for Education, 'South Asian method of teaching maths to be rolled out in schools', 12 July 2016.

20 T. Bennett, *Creating a culture: How school leaders can optimise behaviour*, London: Department for Education, 2017.

21 N. Woolcock, 'GCSE pupils shun languages amid fears they won't help career', *The Times*, 3 December 2023.

22 I. Bauckham, *Modern Foreign Languages Pedagogy Review*, Teaching Schools Council, 2016.

10 The Reform Movement

Michaela have assembled a fiercely passionate team committed to making a difference in the lives of the children they teach. It's not perfect, but never have I visited a school where the vision so closely aligns with the reality. The amount of thought, care and, yes, love, put into their school will surely make it a success.

David Didau, Michaela School: Route One Schooling,
'The Learning Spy' blog, 12 May 2015

In my mind, the progress of the public debate regarding English schools can be tracked by which school held the mantle of 'most talked about' in the country. When the academies programme began during the 2000s, this was Mossbourne Community Academy (see Chapter 3). During the early 2010s, it was King Solomon Academy (see Chapter 8). By 2016, by far and away, the most talked about school in England was—and to some extent it still is—Michaela Community School, along with its headteacher, Katharine Birbalsingh.

Katharine Birbalsingh

I first became aware of the force of nature that is Katharine in 2010. Having started her blog about life as a senior leader at an inner London school in 2007 (see Chapter 7), Katharine Birbalsingh was invited to speak at the Conservative Party Conference in October of that year. In just under eight minutes, Katharine summarised the burden of bad ideas in English schools, and her impassioned call for change raised the roof of Birmingham's International Conference Centre. Drawing on a ten-year career teaching across five different London schools, Katharine excoriated the low expectations and culture of excuses she had experienced, explaining how well-meaning sympathy for the disadvantaged in society had led teachers to lower their expectations and keep poor children poor. She described the pupil who attributes his misbehaviour to 'anger management', and black boys whose indiscretions go unpunished by teachers for fear of being called racist. Katharine, who is herself of mixed Indian and Afro-Caribbean descent, observed, 'black children underachieve because of what the well-meaning liberal does to him.' It was heady

DOI: 10.4324/9781003533474-11

stuff. Katharine described how, as a state-educated pupil who got into Oxford University, she had always been a 'serious lefty' who once read Marxism Today. But towards the end of her speech, she admitted to 'the shame that I have felt, literally shame, because in the last election I voted Conservative'. A vigorous applause and a prolonged standing ovation ensued.[1]

One month earlier, Katharine had been appointed Vice Principal at an academy in South London. However, so intense was the media attention caused by her speech at the Conservative Party Conference it was agreed that her new role was no longer tenable, and she left her job. In any other period of recent English history, Katharine Birbalsingh would most probably have faced eternal banishment from the state sector. However, thanks to the free school policy, she could instead set about founding her own school. It took time for Katharine's proposed free school to find a home. At first, it would be based in Lambeth, then Wandsworth, but unconstructive local councillors and the challenge of finding a suitable site pushed her north of the river. Eventually, she was given a site to open a school in Wembley Park in September 2014.

The four years between making her speech at the Conservative Party Conference and opening a new school were very difficult for Katharine. She stopped using social media after suffering racist and sexist abuse online and struggled to find work in schools. Once she started to recruit families from the local area in Wembley for the school, meetings were disrupted, not by local parents, but by councillors, teaching unions, and members of the Anti-Academies Alliance bussed into the area. She faced taunts of 'Tory Teacher', as if the two designations were by definition incompatible. Even prospective pupils were targeted with flyers, discouraging them from attending the school. As Katharine recalled, 'I used to joke that perhaps our detractors thought we were setting up a factory to build nuclear arms but in reality we were establishing a school in the inner city to serve deprived children.'[2] Speaking with her today, Katharine still keeps copies of these flyers within easy reach on a shelf behind her office desk so that she can show uncomprehending visitors just how intense the opposition to her school once was.

However, that four-year wait, though painful for Katharine, may have been the making of her school. During that period, she was able to recruit a steering group of teachers who had drunk deep from the growing number of critiques of the progressivist ideology and thought hard about how to devise alternative approaches. Many were prolific contributors to the teacher blogosphere, in particular her deputy headteacher Joe Kirby, whose weekly posts on his blog 'Pragmatic Reform' had done much to popularise the ideas of Hirsch, Willingham, and others. Katharine and her steering group were the first free school founders to diagnose in its entirety the limitations of the progressivist ideology and build an alternative educational philosophy from scratch. Over the months prior to September 2014, they would meet every few weeks in a flat in Islington owned by one of the school's governors. During these meetings, they reimagined every aspect of a school's functioning from first principles. All classroom practices would serve a knowledge-rich curriculum, from lesson resourcing to assessment, pupil equipment to homework. Similarly, everything to do with school culture would deliver exemplary behaviour, from uniform to lunchtime, movement around the building to pupil rewards. I was invited along to one of the meetings and was struck by and in awe of the ambition of their plan. I left the meeting daring to imagine what could be possible if this school fulfilled its promise.

Katharine dedicated the school to her friend, an 'old school' teacher of Caribbean heritage who was the best she had ever worked with. The teacher in question had died in 2011, but she would live on in the name of Katharine's new establishment—Michaela Community School.

Whilst previous academies had innovated in areas such as behaviour or curriculum, the staff at Michaela innovated in every way conceivable. As many of them had been recruited from the teacher blogosphere, they kept writing online about what they were doing once employed at Michaela, evangelising from the very beginning for a new paradigm in education. In addition to Joe, there was the deputy headteacher Katie Ashford's blog 'Tabula Rasa'; the founding head of humanities Jonny Porter's blog 'to learn is to follow'; and the head of science Olivia Dyer's blog 'Edu Dyertribe'. Michaela teachers were regular attendees at our Knowledge Network meetings at the Department. Katharine has always encouraged an open-door policy at Michaela, welcoming visitors from the UK and abroad, many of whom—in turn—wrote about what they saw. Today, Michaela hosts about 800 visitors a year, mostly teachers and headteachers, and Katharine estimates that around 7,000 people have come to see the school since it opened in 2014.

One blog, written a year and a half into the school's existence, listed 42 blogs already written about the school, with titles such as 'A pilgrimage to Jerusalem', 'Sympathy for the Devil', and 'The obligatory Michaela post'.[3] The praise that visitors recorded was fulsome, often describing the 'through the looking glass' sensation of seeing standards of teaching and behaviour that they had never previously imagined possible, particularly in a converted Further Education college block in Brent, northwest London, where half of the pupils were from disadvantaged backgrounds, and one in four had special educational needs. One visitor, Jo Facer (who went on to work at the school), wrote in July 2015, 'Michaela have stripped away every educational gimmick and are just teaching very well. . . . Lessons are the simplest I have ever seen, and without doubt the most effective.' She concluded, 'If the school can keep its focus on these simple things as it grows, it will be the making of a revolution in education.'[4]

Michaela is well-known for being strict. However, this does not result in an unpleasant school, but one where pupils are happy and know where they stand. Visiting schools, I often reflect on the paradox that it is in schools with permissive discipline where you see pupils who are visibly stressed and teachers who have to shout to gain compliance. However, in schools with a warm-strict behaviour policy, pupils and teachers are at ease, and a sense of calm prevails. Nowhere is this truer than at Michaela. As a visiting secondary school teacher from Ireland, recorded in 2017:

> Michaela has been called 'the strictest school in Britain' but the atmosphere is not oppressive. Michaela teachers are tough: they are strict and firm, but they are not cross. . . . Very many of [the pupils] were brimming with enthusiasm.[5]

Other visitors commented on the joyful atmosphere amongst the school's pupils. I first visited Michaela soon after it opened in 2014 and was, like so many others, in awe. Having returned home, with a chance to gather my thoughts, I wrote to Katharine, telling her that Michaela was 'everything we dreamed of from the free school movement.'

In December 2016, the *Guardian* published an extended and largely favourable interview with Katharine, entitled 'Inside Britain's strictest school'. Her interviewer observed of the school, 'Every detail, and the silent corridor routine, has a single purpose: to maximise the pupils' time in front of a teacher so that learning takes centre stage.'[6] This followed a piece in the *Sunday Times* the previous month. In the *Sunday Times* piece, Katharine told her interviewer, 'We are more than just a school. We are also about helping to question the prevailing orthodoxies of our British education system.'[7] She was right: at that point, Michaela was a school, think tank, publishing house and social justice movement all rolled into one. Both interviews were written to coincide with the first Michaela book, entitled *Battle Hymn of the Tiger Teachers*. It contained 30 essays written by its teachers, as well as testimonials from Michaela's parents and pupils. The book was launched with a conference at the school on Saturday, 21st November 2015, to which hundreds attended and thousands more watched online. I could not attend, as Michael and I were married that day. After 29 years together, the 2013 Marriage (Same Sex Couples) Act finally allowed us to marry. Despite the pressures of her book launch and conference during the day, Katharine—who by then had become a close friend—still came to our wedding and reception that afternoon.

These three paradigm-shifting schools—Mossbourne, KSA, and Michaela—were all founded in London. The question many were asking was whether their approach could work in other parts of the country. It was not long before that question was being answered with a resounding yes. Children are children, be they from Brent or from Bradford, and Bradford was where another remarkable free school was attracting visitors. Founded in 2012, Dixons Trinity Academy (DTA) was the first secondary free school to be awarded an Ofsted 'Outstanding' judgement in 2014. Its founding headteacher, a charismatic young Liverpudlian named Luke Sparkes, had been part of the Future Leaders programme, part-run by Ark, which in 2008 sent him and a group of other aspiring headteachers to visit charter schools in the USA, such as KIPP, Uncommon Schools and Achievement First.

Sparkes returned to Bradford determined to establish a school along the same 'no excuses' philosophy he had seen in America. The term 'no excuses' was becoming popular in England as a response to once-widespread use of pupils' socio-economic background to explain low attainment in schools. It is easy to see how making excuses on behalf of pupils can appear sympathetic; 'deprivation is destiny' went the old saying. However, such an outlook is the first step towards the soft bigotry of low expectations, where pupils from deprived backgrounds or certain ethnic groups are expected to fail. It was this outlook that Sparkes and his founding team sought to challenge at DTA, where half of the pupils derived from the city's five poorest wards, and many from Pakistani or Indian heritage did not speak English at home. As Sparkes wrote in a piece for the *TES* in 2014:

> We believe that students will rise to the level of expectations placed on them. . . . Some people have labelled our same day detentions as draconian and the fact we 'sweat the small stuff' as petty; however, those that have visited the school have quickly recognised that our structures liberate teachers to teach and students to learn.[8]

They certainly did. The Department's former policy adviser, Sam Freedman, who visited the school early in its second year, claimed it to be the best school he had ever seen. Others who made the journey to Bradford wrote similarly effusive blogs to those being written about Michaela. The regular Knowledge Network attendee Stuart Lock, who had recently taken on his first headship at a secondary school in rural Cambridgeshire, blogged about how visiting DTA pushed him to expect more from his own school. As he wrote, 'Most of all, I came away with a feeling of reasonable aspiration for my school. CVC [Cottenham Village College] is a very good school indeed . . . But I felt that I'd been challenged to be even better.'[9]

In Lock's reflection, you can see the power of the free schools and academies policy, which is—more than anything else—emulation. Critics would often argue that free schools, being set up from scratch, were *sui generis*, offering few lessons for established schools. I disagree. It would, of course, be very difficult for a mainstream school to emulate the model at Michaela or DTA in a wholesale fashion. In terms of creating a positive school culture, it is easier to start a school than to fix one. However, any visitor to a high-attaining free school can see aspects of what they are doing and bring it back to their setting—be it approaches to teaching, lesson planning, or behaviour management. My favourite analogy for this process was provided by Clive Wright, headteacher of Saint Martin's Catholic Academy in Leicestershire. A regular visitor to Michaela, he described himself as akin to a fashion designer from a high-street store watching the catwalk at Paris Fashion Week. As he told me, 'I think to myself, "I could never pull off that whole outfit, but I can certainly take this or that aspect back to my store."' Thus, exemplary free schools can act as haute couture to our high-street schools, pushing them to be more ambitious, more inventive, and more daring.

Cambrian Explosion

By 2015, a grassroots reform movement was firmly underway in English schools. I have profiled particular schools to illustrate what was taking place, but there were dozens more making important innovations about which I could write and hundreds more being influenced by what they were doing. Watching on from the Department, the most thrilling aspect of this movement was to see that the battle between different educational philosophies, which for decades had been waged on paper, had leapt off the page and was now being waged on the ground in classrooms throughout England.

This process was captured by the writer Ian Leslie in a feature he wrote for *The Guardian* in March 2015, entitled 'The revolution that could change the way your child is taught'. Through a visit to Dixons Trinity Academy in Bradford and an interview with the American teacher trainer Doug Lemov (see further on), Leslie captured the interplay between the loosening of school structures we were pursuing in government and the grassroots movement emerging on the ground in schools. He wrote:

> The rise of charter schools and academies has precipitated a Cambrian explosion of new ideas and innovations, stimulating a debate about methodology led by teachers themselves. The internet has provided platforms for teachers to talk to other teachers, beyond their own schools and outside official oversight. On social media, teachers are sharing ideas, evidence and techniques, organising conferences on education research, and arguing about the most effective way to teach reading or maths. After years of debate among academics and politicians over how to raise teacher standards, the problem is being solved by the practitioners.[10]

During our early years at the Department, when we tried to build a case for an alternative to the child-centred progressivist orthodoxy, we always came up against the problem that there were so few schools one could point to that were doing anything radically different. There was no shortage of academic evidence that we could cite suggesting progressivist ideas were misguided, quoting material from the likes of E. D. Hirsch and Daniel Willingham. More recently, the Australian educationist John Hattie synthesised hundreds of meta-analyses of education research in his 2009 book *Visible Learning* to show that interventions where the teacher is an 'activator' (more teacher-led) were consistently more effective than those where the teacher is a 'facilitator' (child-centred), a finding—Hattie observed—that ran counter to what trainee teachers were 'indoctrinated' to believe.[11] However, it took an unusual type of teacher to base their practice around research papers, effect sizes, and randomised controlled trials. The evidence that most teachers care about is what other schools are doing. Such was the power of the progressivist orthodoxy; there was very little that anyone could point to as an alternative. Academies and free schools transformed this situation. In October 2014, the *TES* reported on the beliefs that were driving the reform movement in England:

> These centre on a zealous desire to transform the educational chances of society's most disadvantaged and the conviction that, to do so, more academic 'rigour' in schools is essential. There is an insistence on the teaching of facts, as opposed to isolated skills, and an emphasis on the importance of direct, didactic, teacher-led instruction and strict 'no excuses' discipline. . . . The new guard may be relatively small in number, but they hold powerful positions, share a philosophy and many are members of the same tightknit, overlapping networks. Collectively they could exert a huge influence over what happens in schools.[12]

The article singled out Daisy Christodoulou as the movement's intellectual leader, quite an accolade for someone still aged only 29. It claimed her book *Seven Myths About Education* had become 'a bible for the growing band of neo-traditionalists' as it 'crystallises their misgivings about "so-called progressive" education'. This traditionalist versus progressive dichotomy had become a popular way of framing the debate, particularly amongst those online, as they assigned themselves (or, more likely, each other) into these two opposing camps.* In September 2016, *TES* published a '30-second briefing' for its readers entitled, 'What is the traditional versus progressive education debate?'.[13] As with the labels generated by any philosophical difference, such dichotomies can prove a useful entry point to an issue and shorthand in conversation thereafter. But as the debate matured, I increasingly came to think the terms 'progressive' and 'traditionalist' obscure more than they reveal in education.

When I consider the work of teachers at our most innovative schools, the 'traditionalist' label does not serve them well. Yes, they were devising an alternative to the child-centred progressivist orthodoxy, but 'traditionalism' implied a desire to move backwards, perhaps to a mythical period known as 'the 1950s', where uniforms were smart, teachers were respected, and pupils were translating English to Latin by the lower fifth. This was often the caricature of my position in the press, with a leading educationist describing me in the *Guardian* in 2010 as pursuing 'an unreconstructed 1950s grammar school agenda'.[14] However, this did not capture the new types of teaching our reforms had unleashed. Firstly, a 'traditionalist' or '1950s' approach suggests many features that leading academies and free schools are not, such as exclusively single-sex, academically selective, and permitted to use corporal punishment. Secondly, far from being backward-looking, these schools were pioneering, basing their decisions on high-quality evidence from cognitive

---

* Interestingly, the progressive/traditional dichotomy was one that Christodoulou sought to distance herself from in the introduction to *Seven Myths about Education*, preferring to characterise the ideas she critiqued as 'romanticism'.

science, controlled trials, and exemplar schools. For this reason, I prefer to use the term 'evidence-led' instead of 'traditionalist'

As has become a popular refrain amongst teachers interested in research, teaching is a craft not a science, so it will never be evidence-*based*, but it can be evidence-*led*. For a school with a genuine desire to provide the best possible education for their pupils, the evidence does not provide a set template on how to do so, but it does provide useful indicators of what might and might not work, offering 'best bets' for ensuring success. During the early 2010s, the dominant narrative in evidence-led teaching was negative, calling out the child-centred shibboleths such as 'learning styles', 'project work', or 'thematic curricula' for lacking sufficient evidence of success. However, as the reform movement developed, the narrative in evidence-led teaching became much more positive, using research to trial, adapt, and share new approaches to teaching.

Teachers in England are now at the forefront of an evidence revolution, redefining what good teaching looks like from inside our schools. They have drilled down into the minutiae of what teachers do with a remarkable level of precision and—through blogs, conferences, and a growing number of books—created a shared understanding of what makes good teaching. Watching this process take place has been one of the most rewarding experiences of my time in office and the quality of ideas now on offer to teachers is by orders of magnitude better than just ten years ago. Then, there were only a handful of books I could recommend on what evidence-led teaching might look like in schools. Now, there are so many that it's hard to keep up.

You will find far better guides than this regarding the new approaches produced by the evidence revolution. However, for the uninitiated, allow me to summarise what I believe to be four of the most significant areas where teachers in English schools have been translating research findings into classroom craft.

Feature 1—Knowledge-rich Curriculum and Resourcing: Hirsch and Willingham established the importance of knowledge as a precursor to complex thought. The next step has been for teachers to develop resources which ensure that knowledge is presented in an optimal way to their pupils in both the short term (a single lesson) and the long term (a scheme of work). Limitations in pupils' cognitive load mean that new information needs to be introduced steadily and in a sequence which ensures—as far as possible—that requisite prior knowledge is in place before new ideas are introduced. To ensure this sequencing takes place consistently throughout a school or academy trust, booklets have become pervasive, and textbooks increasingly popular, having long been derided as emblematic of 'bad practice'. In addition, visualisers which project a teacher's or a pupil's work directly onto the whiteboard now rival PowerPoint as the favoured mode of disseminating knowledge, as teachers can direct pupils' attention to the content that needs to be learnt, and model procedures such as mathematical working or the structuring of a paragraph much more effectively.

Feature 2—Direct Instruction: A seminal paper for the reform movement was written in 2006 by three academics—Paul A. Kirschner, John Sweller, and Richard E. Clark, entitled 'Why Minimal Guidance During Instruction Does Not Work'. It gathers decades of research to show that a teacher-led approach, often termed 'direct instruction', results in better outcomes for pupils than the alternative, which they group together as 'constructivist, problem-based, experiential and inquiry-based teaching'.[15] The term 'direct instruction' was popularised by an American educationist named Zig Engelmann. His work during the 1960s and 1970s to create carefully scripted and sequenced lessons was repeatedly shown in empirical studies to achieve better results for students than the child-centred approaches, which were so much more popular at the time, and he has latterly come to be seen as something of a prophet of the evidence-led teaching movement. As Englemann's resources showed, there is a world of difference between good direct instruction and poor. For this reason, teachers have developed extensive taxonomies explaining what high-quality teacher instruction involves. These include features such as reviewing prior knowledge, anticipating misconceptions, and guiding pupil practice. Two of the most popular guides to effective 'teacher-led' instruction are from America but have achieved as much—perhaps even more—prominence in England. One is 'The Science of Learning' produced in 2015 by an organisation called Deans for Impact founded by the inspiring Texas-based policy-maker Ben Riley.[16] The other is Barak Rosenshine's 'Principles of Instruction', which, since its 2012 publication in *American Educator*, has been used for training purposes throughout English schools.[17] The author and headteacher Tom Sherrington wrote *Rosenshine's Principles in Action* for publication in 2019, giving specific examples of how to apply the principles in classrooms.[18] By Spring 2024, it had sold 60,000 copies.[19]

Feature 3—Checking for Understanding: The popular caricature of direct instruction is that of a teacher at the front of the classroom, waffling on about their subject, with no concern for their pupils looking on in boredom and incomprehension. Of course, such teaching has and does take place, and the pain of experiencing it is—I am sure—what accounts for much of the intuitive appeal of child-centred methods. However, the best alternative to bad teacher-talk is not less teacher-talk but better teacher-talk. Central to this is checking for understanding, whereby teachers intersperse their lessons with regular questioning to ensure pupils have understood what has been taught before moving on. Working out whether a class of 30 pupils has understood a concept or idea is one of those perennial challenges for any teacher. As a consequence, strategies for whole-class questioning have become increasingly refined in recent years. Approaches such as choral response, short multiple-choice quizzes, and mini-whiteboards can help ensure that no pupil's struggle to understand an idea goes unnoticed. Such approaches also help pupil motivation, creating a sense of collective accountability and making it harder for pupils to coast through lessons below the radar.

Feature 4—Retrieval Practice: Amongst teachers, one of the most powerful findings of cognitive science is the 'retrieval effect'. Popularised by psychologists such as Henry Roediger, this is the finding that the frequent recall of information, termed 'retrieval practice', strengthens its place in our long-term memory. This implication of the retrieval effect for teachers is that testing should not be seen as a burden, used only for the purposes of formal assessment, but a crucial aspect of learning to be deployed in most, if not all, of the lessons they teach.[20] Teachers in England have taken this idea and worked on finding the most effective way of designing retrieval practice for pupils in and out of the classroom. During the early days of Michaela, Joe Kirby popularised the concept of a knowledge organiser, where the most impactful knowledge in any topic—be it geography keywords, French vocabulary, or chemical equations—is synthesised into a single document from which teachers can create quizzes and pupils can revise. In doing so, he did much to rehabilitate the use of quizzing as a teaching tool: not drill and kill but, as Kirby put it, 'drill and thrill'.[21] More recently, science teacher Adam Boxer has created a hugely popular platform called Carousel to which teachers can upload quizzes and on which pupils can repeatedly test themselves and assess their answers online.

Teach Like Lemov

The four preceding features give, I hope, an indication of the granularity with which reform-minded teachers have been refining their craft in English schools. In doing so, one American educator has been a standout inspiration: Doug Lemov. The godfather of the modern trend towards codifying classroom practice, Doug Lemov has achieved a cult-like status on this side of the Atlantic. Back in 1997, Doug co-founded a charter school in Boston, where he became principal one year later at the age of 28. He went on to become a regional director at a network of charter schools based in and around Boston and New York called Uncommon Schools, which helped inspire early English-free schools such as King Solomon Academy and Dixons Trinity Academy. Whilst at Uncommon Schools, where Doug would ultimately become Managing Director, he began cross-referencing data on test scores and pupil demographics to find the teachers who were achieving the strongest results with the most disadvantaged pupils. He visited those teachers' classrooms and observed the techniques they used to bring out the best in their pupils. These techniques he compiled into a document known as 'The Taxonomy', which became an underground hit amongst American teachers, with copies being photocopied and passed from school to school like samizdat literature in the old Soviet Union. Encouraged by his colleagues, Doug Lemov published 'The Taxonomy' in 2010 under the title *Teach Like a Champion: 49 Techniques that Put Students on the Path to College.*[22]

Now in its third edition, *Teach Like a Champion* is one of those books that has been so successful it is hard to believe nobody had written it before. Perhaps it is because, historically, teaching had been seen as an art, not a craft, and thought to be too intuitive to distil into readily shareable techniques. Doug did not agree. His genius was to give catchy names to the common techniques of good teaching such as 'no opt-out' and 'begin with the end'. In doing so, he has created a shared vocabulary to describe what effective teachers repeatedly do. His term for the optimal school behaviour culture, 'warm-strict', has become particularly popular in England's best schools. It encapsulates a culture where teachers combine high expectations of pupil conduct with compassion, always being clear that it is care for pupils' wellbeing that drives their decisions: strictness, without any trace of malice. For example, effective teachers don't wait for pupils to put their hands up to answer questions, allowing high-attaining pupils to crowd out their struggling peers. They target particular questions to particular pupils, something Doug called 'cold call'. Effective teachers find the optimal place to stand in any classroom from which they can best monitor pupils and their work, something Doug called the 'pastor's perch'. Effective teachers never talk over pupil misbehaviour, stopping for a moment to correct a pupil before continuing once full attention has been achieved, something Doug called 'self-interrupting'. Not only did he name these techniques, Doug worked with videographers to film them occurring 'in the wild', building up an extensive library—first on DVD and now online—for schools to use in their training.

In September 2014, Doug Lemov visited England as a guest of the Ark Academy network. The think tank Policy Exchange duly invited him to deliver their first annual education lecture, hosted at King Solomon Academy. Doug has since made repeated visits to England and often writes about how our schools are using the *Teach Like a Champion* techniques in his 'Field Notes' blog. In a 2021 interview with *Schools Week*, he suggested that teachers in England have been more responsive to his ideas than back home in America. Though the American charter school programme inspired our academies policy, he suggested 'the quality of schools and trusts that were founded in the UK' may have 'actually surpassed the US.' Pointing to the engagement that English teachers have made with the ideas of cognitive science, Doug observed, 'I feel really optimistic for your country, and less so for mine.'[23]

The following year, Policy Exchange hosted its second annual education lecture, delivered by none other than E. D. Hirsch. At the age of 87, he delivered a spirited overview of his life's work to an audience of teachers and policy-makers assembled in Pimlico Academy, London. I was given the honour of introducing Hirsch, and following my remarks, he kindly quipped that he was gratified to hear my praise, as 'it's so rare for people in the USA in high political office to read books.' I was more than a little star-struck: Jonathan Simons of Policy Exchange later described my meeting with Hirsch 'backstage' in an empty classroom as the closest education policy might come to a rockstar moment (with myself, I hasten to add, as the adoring fan).[24] I made sure that Edward Hardman, my former Parliamentary researcher who had first suggested I read Hirsch, was also invited to the event.

Like Doug Lemov, E. D. Hirsch reflected on the curious experience of finding his ideas achieving more popularity in England than his native America. During the 2010s, something akin to the 'British invasion' of the American music scene during the 1960s seemed to be happening in teaching. Like the Beatles and Rolling Stones selling rock and roll music back to an American audience, English teachers were embracing E. D. Hirsch's and Doug Lemov's ideas and putting them into practice with more fidelity—perhaps—than teachers back in America.

I am certain that the fertile ground for such ideas in England is a direct result of giving schools and teachers the freedom to innovate out of the grip of local authority control and the progressivist ideology. E D Hirsch and Doug Lemov are often criticised by the education establishment both at home and abroad: Hirsch for promoting the memorisation of inert facts at the expense of understanding and creativity, and Lemov for making children 'robotically' comply with teachers' demands (both criticisms are, I would contend, wrong). There was a time in English schools when barriers would have been put in place to prevent their ideas from being tried, but no longer. Instead, teachers have been able to apply these ideas, achieve success, and pass them on to others. In England, we have created a school system where teachers can gravitate towards what works in the classroom, as opposed to what is approved.

Teach First

It would be wrong of me to attribute England's education reform movement entirely to government policy, as it has—like any movement—involved the fortuitous alignment of many different factors. One of the most important has been the runaway success of a teacher training programme called Teach First. What do Max Haimendorf, Daisy Christodoulou, most of the founding team of Michaela Community School, and my co-author all have in common? They entered the profession through Teach First. Founded in 2003 by Brett Wigdortz with the support of Andrew Adonis, there is very little reason why his idea should have been a success. When he began working on the project in 2001, Brett Wigdortz was a 28-year-old American management consultant with no experience in schools or education policy and next to no experience of Britain, having only arrived in the country that year. However, this inexperience allowed Brett to see something that his British contemporaries had missed: that a younger generation of British university graduates could be attracted to careers which offered less in terms of money but more in terms of social impact.

Brett worked for McKinsey and Co, a leading consultancy firm which had written a report on what they might contribute towards improving London's struggling schools. One of their ideas was to design a programme which would recruit top university graduates and train them to work in underperforming schools. In February 2002, Brett began working full-time on the idea. A theme of his 2012 book *Success Against the Odds* is how naivety about the English education system worked to his advantage, particularly when coupled with his very American spirit of positivity. He was frequently told his idea would fail due to bureaucratic challenges, graduates' fear of teaching in disadvantaged schools, and the innate cynicism of the British mindset. As one colleague told him early on, '[W]e don't do revolutions in this country mate'.[25] However, in September 2003, Teach First was launched with its first group of 186 participants working in 45 secondary schools around London. This cohort would prove to be a vintage crop: 20 years later, at least six members of that initial cohort have become headteachers, and two are Multi Academy Trust CEOs. Teach First grew larger in every subsequent year, having found an untapped demand not only amongst schools struggling to recruit staff but also amongst graduates looking for more meaningful careers. In 2012, it placed 996 teachers in disadvantaged schools covering six different regions across England, making it—nine years after its inception—the largest graduate recruiter in the country.

From the start, Teach First sold teaching to graduates as a social mission. Through its distinctive style of training, with a six-week residential 'boot camp' over the summer and an unapologetic focus on achieving positions of leadership in education, it bred amongst a new generation of 'activist' teachers intent on revolutionising the quality of English schooling and changing the life chances of millions of young people. Over 17,000 teachers have now been trained through Teach First, of which around 100 are currently working as school headteachers. These 'activist' teachers will continue to be some of the most important players in England's education reform movement for many decades to come. Teach First has received a fair amount of criticism over the years, particularly for the expense of its training and the requirement for its participants only to teach for two years. By Brett's own admission, the name of his organisation was unfortunately chosen, implying—as a common quip states—that its participants will 'teach first, bank later'. However, Brett's genius was to create an aura of social prestige around teaching in disadvantaged schools which—for decades—England had lacked. In doing so, he has recruited into the system a calibre of teachers with a drive for social justice which is impossible to quantify; he has, in the words of Andrew Adonis in *Education, Education, Education*, 'reconnect[ed] the top universities with state teaching.'[26] As Wigdortz wrote of Teach First in 2012:

> The idea that British students aren't idealistic has been discredited. They do not want to live lives of quiet desperation. They want to make a difference. They want to change young people's lives. They are interested in more than themselves and getting as high a salary as possible. These days when they have a real choice about the paths they could take, they are choosing to work in some of the most challenging roles in the country.[27]

What Works

The burgeoning evidence revolution was another development with which our policies were fortunate to align. However, the Department did help 'nudge' the teaching profession towards this development through our establishment of the Education Endowment Foundation (EEF) in 2011. In opposition, we had concerns about the quality of education research in England. Very few policies or initiatives were based on high-quality scientific research methods, such as that involving Randomised Controlled Trials (RCTs). Common practices seemed to be advocated through the collation of teacher opinion rather than the effectiveness in achieving outcomes. We considered establishing an organisation similar to the National Center for Education Research in America. Tasked with evaluating evidence and conducting research, it would be independent of the Department for Education and, crucially, independent of the education sector; in other words, a 'What Works' clearing house. The opportunity to implement such a policy came about, however, by chance.

In the summer of 2010, we reversed a Labour policy to extend free school meals to a greater proportion of pupils, thus saving £137 million. However, we only belatedly realised that we had to spend this money within the 2010–11 financial year to avoid paying it back to the Treasury. £137 million was not an insignificant sum, and we wanted to find a more lasting way to use this windfall than simply sharing it amongst all schools. Instead, the Director General for Schools in the Department, Jon Coles, came up with the idea of using the money as an endowment to establish our own 'What Works' clearing house. This organisation would spend the endowment over ten years gathering and presenting research findings for the easy consumption of teachers as well as commissioning and overseeing its own trials. We called the new organisation the Education Endowment Foundation (EEF). The EEF was formally established in March 2011 in partnership with the Sutton Trust, one of the UK's leading education charities. Its mission was to help teachers use evidence to improve pupil outcomes, particularly those who are disadvantaged. Its first step was to synthesise evidence from thousands of education trials into an easily accessible 'teaching and learning toolkit', hosted online and continually updated as new evidence is found. As of 2018, 13,000 trials had been included. The toolkit assesses different interventions according to three criteria: impact, cost, and strength of evidence.[28] Some of the toolkit's findings have been unsurprising—homework, for example, has a higher impact at secondary than at primary. Some findings were controversial, such as the research that found that teaching assistants—whose numbers had ballooned during the New Labour years from 73,000 in 1997 to 169,000 in 2010[29]—have little impact on pupil outcomes for a very high cost unless more effectively deployed.

In addition to synthesising existing research, the EEF began commissioning its own, and in doing so, it has become the largest commissioner of education research in England. As of August 2020, the EEF had funded over 190 projects at a cost of more than £110 million in 13,000 English schools, thus reaching some 1.3 million young people.[30] From its inception, the EEF has championed RCTs, seen by the scientific community as the gold standard for measuring the impact of any intervention. In 2018, the EEF estimated that 10 percent of all RCTs ever carried out in education research had been commissioned by the EEF.[31] Under the leadership of Kevan Collins until 2020 and Becky Francis thereafter, the EEF's impact on teachers in England has been profound. According to independent surveys by the NFER, the proportion of teachers using the EEF Toolkit when deciding how to improve pupils' education has risen from 4 percent in 2012 to 41 percent in 2022. Amongst school leaders, the rise was from 11 percent in 2012 to 70 percent in 2022.[32] As of August 2023, their regular digital newsletter has 47,000 subscribers.[33] In just over a decade, the EEF has become a mainstay in teachers' decision-making process, contributing to the professionalisation of the sector. No longer are teachers powerless in the face of consultants and advisers selling the latest fads with the infamous phrase 'research shows that . . .'. Instead, they are active participants in the evidence debate.

The EEF is as important in showing teachers what *not* to do as what to do. Amongst teachers, there is a growing expectation that interventions should be backed up with evidence. This has empowered them to resist wasting time and money on low-impact interventions. The era of 'faddism', which so burdened our schools during the 1990s and 2000s, is now over. During the early years of researchED, speakers and delegates often debated what it would take for teaching to become a 'mature profession', with a commonly accepted and evidence-led model of what makes good teaching. Taken together, movements such as researchED, organisations such as the EEF, and the grassroots efforts of classroom teachers mean the profession is well on the way to making this vision a reality. At the Department, we have tried to be a handmaiden to this development through our open-source approach to school data. This was part of a wider government drive from Prime Minister David Cameron to make government Departments more transparent and merge some 1,700 government-related websites into the gov.uk domain. In education, this has greatly aided the evidence revolution. In a high autonomy, high accountability system, school information has to be made accessible in a user-friendly format. There is no point in holding schools to account and then burying accountability data in complicated spreadsheets on hidden corners of the internet. So, from 2010, our default position has been that all non-sensitive school data should be made freely available for the public to consume—be it researchers, schools, or just interested amateurs.

As soon as we entered office, we consolidated all league table information into one easy-to-access online location. According to the National Audit Office's 2012 report 'Implementing Transparency', this resulted in an 84 percent increase in the use of our online school data in the space of a year.[34] In addition, the Department implemented a consistent calendar of statistical releases in areas such as exam results, attendance, pupil demographics, and the school workforce. Then, in November 2012, Michael Gove announced that we would open up the Department's

National Pupil Database (NPD) to a greater range of third parties whilst—of course—ensuring pupil-level confidentiality. The NPD is one of the richest educational datasets in the world, containing longitudinal information on pupils such as characteristics, schools, prior attainment, and exam results—a goldmine for education research.

When Michael Gove stepped down in 2014, the *Guardian*'s education editor, Richard Adams, suggested that—in 20 years' time—his greatest legacy may be two relatively unknown policies, one of which was the opening up of the National Pupil Database.*,[35] Time will tell, but the decision has already led to a proliferation of research. It also inspired the academic and researchED regular Dr Rebecca Allen to found Education Datalab in February 2015, in association with the Fischer Family Trust education charity. Education Datalab has generated findings on topics as diverse as the growth of MATs, the changing popularity of different GCSE and A-level subjects, and the impact of Covid on pupil attendance. Sometimes, their findings made tough reading for me as a minister, but I would welcome them regardless, as the ready availability of such research has greatly enhanced the quality of education debate in England.

In the panoply of evidence now being generated, one type still—in my mind—overrides all others. In a self-improving school system, the performance of individual schools is the most important indicator of what is and is not working. What Doug Lemov likes to call 'existence proof'. Following the 2015 election, we set about redesigning the school performance tables website for a second time round, making it even easier for users to compare how schools perform. We involved 250 trial users in its design, and I gave extensive feedback. The design of a government website may seem like a meddlesome level of detail for a minister to become involved in, but it really mattered: readily available school performance data is crucial to system-wide improvement, and we had to get it right. Launched in March 2016, the 'Compare School Performance' website was up and running in time for the first-ever set of Progress 8 results that summer.

In the following years, this website has played a key role in disseminating the quite astonishing achievements made by pupils at our best schools. It is the results achieved by these exemplary schools which have truly started to turn the tide in England's education debate.

Notes

1 K. Birbalsingh, *Speech to the Conservative Party Conference*, October 2010.
2 K. Birbalsingh (ed.), *Battle Hymn of the Tiger Teachers: The Michaela Way*, Woodbridge: John Catt, 2016, p.11.
3 'Blogs about Michaela by people who've visited the school', *'A Roller in the Ocean' blog*, 7 December 2015.

---

* The other, rather gratifyingly, was the phonics screening check.

4 J. Facer, 'Keep it simple', *'Reading All the Books' blog*, 18 July 2015.

5 K. Barry, 'Visit to Michaela', *'Kate Barry' blog*, 22 June 2017.

6 R. Adams, '"No excuses": inside Britain's strictest school', *The Guardian*, 30 December 2016.

7 S. Griffiths, 'Is this the strictest teacher in Britain?', *The Sunday Times*, 13 November 2016.

8 L. Sparkes, 'Our free school has shown that the US charter model can flourish in the UK', *TES Magazine*, 28 May 2014.

9 S. Lock, 'A visit to Dixons Trinity Academy, Bradford', *'Mr Lock's Weblog' blog*, 6 December 2016.

10 I. Leslie, 'The revolution that could change the way your child is taught', *The Guardian*, 11 March 2015.

11 J. Hattie and G. Yates, *Visible Learning and the Science of How We Learn*, Abingdon: Routledge, 2014, p. 182.

12 W. Stewart, 'The Blob 2: this time it's personal', *TES Magazine*, 17 October 2014.

13 S. Wright, 'The 30-second briefing: What is the traditional versus progressive education debate?', *TES Magazine*, 14 September 2016.

14 R. Williams, 'So, who is Nick Gibb?', *The Guardian*, 17 May 2010.

15 P. Kirschner, J. Sweller, and R. Clark, 'Why minimal guidance during instruction does not work: An analysis of the failure of constructivist, discovery, problem-based, experiential, and inquiry-based teaching', *Educational Psychologist*, vol. 41, no. 2, 2006, pp. 75–86.

16 Deans for Impact, *The Science of Learning*, Austin: Deans for Impact, 2015.

17 B. Rosenshine, 'Principles of instruction: Research-based strategies that all teachers should know', *American Educator*, Spring 2012.

18 T. Sherrington, *Rosenshine's Principles in Action*, Woodbridge: John Catt, 2019.

19 J. Powell, 'Should Rosenshine really be teachers' definitive guide?', *TES Magazine*, 9 April 2024.

20 H. Roediger et al., *Make It Stick: The Science of Successful Learning*, Harvard: Harvard University Press, 2014.

21 J. Kirby, 'Drill and thrill', *'Pragmatic Reform' blog*, 9 October 2016.

22 D. Lemov, *Teach Like a Champion: 49 Techniques that Put Students on the Path to College (K–12)*, San Francisco: Jossey Bass, 2010.

23 J. Staufenberg, 'The big interview: Doug Lemov', *Schools Week*, 13 December 2021.

24 J. Simons, 'Sunday thoughts: Will the education system miss Nick Gibb?', Substack, 19 November 2023.

25 B. Wigdortz, *Success Against the Odds: Five Lessons in How to Achieve the Impossible: the Story of Teach First*, London: Short Books Ltd, 2012, Chapter 1.

26 A. Adonis, *Education, Education, Education: Reforming England's Schools*, London: Biteback, 2012, p. 42.

27 Wigdortz, *Success Against the Odds*, Chapter 3.

28 'England has become one of the world's biggest education laboratories', *The Economist*, 31 March 2018.

29 Ruth Lupton and Polina Obolenskaya, 'Labour's record on education: Policy, spending and outcomes 1997–2010', *Social Policy in a Cold Climate Working Paper WP03*, 2013, p. 28.

30 Education Endowment Foundation, *EEF Annual Report 2020*, p. 8.

31 *The Economist*, 31 March 2018.

32 *EEF Annual Report 2022*, p. 10.

33 *EEF Annual Report 2023*, p. 36.

34 National Audit Office, *Implementing Transparency*, 18 August 2012, p. 9.

35 R. Adams, 'Michael Gove: a controversial but influential education secretary', *The Guardian*, 15 July 2014.

Schools with traditional education methods dominated the top of last month's league tables, prompting a piece in *The Times* declaring that 'stricter schools get better results'. So has Nick Gibb, a staunch proponent of such approaches, won the education war?

Samantha Booth, *Schools Week*, 10th November 2023

In 2012, Michael Gove promised that the academies and free schools programme would let 'a thousand flowers bloom.'[1] Over the years that followed, an unprecedented period of education experimentation took place, and now—13 years later—we are in the privileged position of seeing which flowers are blooming the brightest. Much attention in the education debate is often paid to London, so let's look instead at two schools which have grown up side-by-side in South Yorkshire.

A Tale of Two Schools

School A was established as a free school in 2014 by a former computer science teacher and edtech start-up founder, based on a philosophy called 'expeditionary learning'. The curriculum would be designed around half-termly projects called 'expeditions', which culminate in pupils creating some form of a product, be it a book, art exhibition, or documentary film. When doing their own research, pupils would be allowed to work independently outside of the classroom on laptops in open-plan rooms. Only a small number of subjects, such as Spanish, would be taught more traditionally rather than through cross-curricular projects. At School A, there would be 50 pupils per year group, they would not have to wear uniforms, and the behaviour system would be based around weekly community meetings where students challenge or apologise for poor behaviour.[2]

School B, another free school, was established a 30-minute drive from School A in 2018 with a very different philosophy. It would teach an academic curriculum based around traditional subjects and built, first and foremost, on the acquisition of knowledge. They would configure their classrooms in rows, promote didactic teaching, and encourage their teachers to pride themselves on being subject

DOI: 10.4324/9781003533474-12

experts. On behaviour, they would have sky-high expectations and clear sanctions. As they stated on the staff recruitment page of their website, 'if you think it is too harsh to give a child a detention if they do not have their pen, [this] is not the school for you.' They knew this might seem demanding but promised such an approach would foster a safe and inspiring culture in which pupils could thrive.

School A gained its first GCSE results in 2019, with a respectable Progress 8 score of 0.2 (0.0 being average). Over the following two years, it earned much positive media coverage in newspapers such as *The Times*, the *TES*, and *The Guardian*, in the latter of which a columnist noted their 'excellent GCSE results'.[3] However, School A has been unable to sustain its early success. When exams resumed after Covid in 2022, its Progress 8 score dropped to −0.77, placing it in the 93rd percentile for comprehensive secondary schools in the country.

School B, with its knowledge-based curriculum and warm-strict approach to pupil behaviour, fared considerably better. Pupils took their GCSEs for the first time in 2023 and achieved a Progress 8 score of 2.24, which meant pupils at School B outperformed their peers of similar ability levels in other schools by more than two whole grades in each subject—an astonishing score. Out of the 3,091 comprehensive schools entering pupils for GCSEs that summer, School B was the third-best school in England for pupil progress. Meanwhile, its child-centred Yorkshire neighbour, School A, continued to struggle, achieving a Progress 8 score of −0.59 in 2023, placing it as joint 2,774th in the country. In terms of progress made from primary to secondary school by disadvantaged pupils, School B was the best school in the country in 2023 and second best in the country in 2024. At the warm-strict School B, disadvantaged pupils achieved an average GCSE grade across eight subjects of 6.3 in 2024, compared to an average grade achieved by disadvantaged pupils at the progressive School A of 3.2.

The contrast between School A and School B was particularly striking: both free schools, both located in post-industrial Yorkshire towns, both with a comparable proportion of pupils eligible for free school meals. However, at School B, disadvantaged pupils achieved GCSE grades almost twice as high as those at School A. Across the country, a similar—if less stark—contrast has played out between thousands of schools. It can be said in no fewer words: pupils at schools which follow a teacher-led, knowledge-rich approach do consistently better than pupils at schools which do not, particularly the most disadvantaged students. Those who advocate child-centred teaching can continue to talk up the merits of their approach. However, helping underprivileged pupils fulfil their academic potential is not one of them.

Best in Show

School B is Mercia School in Sheffield. Since its foundation in 2018, it has been led by Headteacher Dean Webster, a no-nonsense former PE teacher from the nearby town of Bolsover, who was inspired by visiting schools such as Michaela to establish something similar in the north. Like many exceptional school leaders I have met, he is personable but does not let this conceal his ambition for his school. The competitiveness for which Webster is famed in his local football league he brings to his drive for success at Mercia School. Dean has not sought the limelight as much as other free school leaders (although one of his unorthodox job adverts went viral in February 2023 for stating that only candidates prepared to work 'ridiculously hard' need apply).[4] So, when Mercia School achieved its first set of GCSE results in 2023, teachers and policy-makers around the country were keen to know more. Dean showed me around Mercia School in 2023, and I was astonished by the academic standards reached by the pupils. However, I was not astonished by the approaches to achieving it. Amongst the schools which dominate the Progress 8 league tables, the common features are becoming clearer each year: knowledge-based curriculum, teacher-led lessons, and a warm-strict approach to behaviour (see Table 11.1).

As a measure, Progress 8 is not perfect. Schools where a large proportion of pupils speak English as an additional language are advantaged; as such, pupils consistently make faster progress from primary school than their peers.[5] Nor can Progress 8 tell you everything about a school: important features such as sports fixtures, drama productions and educational trips are hidden from the data. In addition, I always urge people to look at a school's Progress 8 score in conjunction with its EBacc entry rate, to check whether pupils are doing well in the most valued subjects. However, with all this in mind, Progress 8 remains—by a margin—the best measure ever devised for summarising schools' efficacy when it comes to their core mission: teaching.

Looking at the top ten schools for Progress 8 in each year since 2016, three categories of schools have dominated. The first is established, stable schools, which outperform their peers due to exceptional consistency in vision and leadership. Secondly are faith schools, with Catholic, Church of England, Jewish, and Muslim schools all represented. This is due, in part, no doubt, to their strong moral vision and school culture, which is generally stricter than the national norm. A number of Muslim faith schools run by the Star Academies Trust consistently feature amongst our highest-performing schools, thanks to the remarkable leadership of former headteacher and Trust CEO Hamid Patel (see Chapter 12). The third category is those innovative free schools and academies which have ridden the wave of the evidence-led revolution in English teaching, many of which—such as Harris Academies, Ark King Solomon Academy, Dixons Trinity Academy, Michaela Community School, and Mercia School—have featured on these pages. As for schools with an explicitly child-centred progressivist approach, none have ever come close to troubling the top of the Progress 8 league tables.*

* There is one exception to this claim: the Steiner Academy in Hereford has a distinctly child-centred ethos. However, as a school for pupils aged 3 to 16, its very high Progress 8 score is a statistical quirk. This is because, as an all through school, many of its Year

Table 11.1 Top Ten non-selective secondary schools in England by Progress 8, 2016 to 2024

	2015–16		
	School	Pro. 8	Att. 8
1.	Tauheedul Islam Girls' High School	1.37	64.8
2.	The Steiner Academy Hereford	1.31	47
3.	Tauheedul Islam Boys' High School	1.15	61.8
4.	Harris Academy Battersea	1.14	59
5.	Ark King Solomon Academy	1.08	60.2
6.	St Andrew's Catholic School	1.08	62.7
7.	The City Academy, Hackney	1.02	59.1
8.	Harris Girls' Academy East Dulwich	0.93	58.3
9.	Outwood Academy Portland	0.93	58.4
10.	Sheffield Park Academy	0.93	52.3

	2016–17		
	School	Pro. 8	Att. 8
1.	Tauheedul Islam Girls' High School	1.81	64.5
2.	Wembley High Technology College	1.65	64.4
3.	Tauheedul Islam Boys' High School	1.55	62
4.	Harris Academy Battersea	1.47	59.8
5.	The Steiner Academy Hereford	1.37	48.7
6.	Forest Gate Community School	1.3	57.6
7.	Dixons Trinity Academy	1.22	58.1
8.	Brampton Manor Academy	1.18	57.4
9.	Chesterton Community College	1.12	64.9
10.	Preston Muslim Girls High School	1.11	59.4

	2017–18		
	School	Pro. 8	Att. 8
1.	Tauheedul Islam Girls' High School	1.9	67.5
2.	Wembley High Technology College	1.9	67.1
3.	Dixons Trinity Academy	1.55	63.2
4.	The Steiner Academy Hereford	1.41	47.7
5.	Bolton Muslim Girls School	1.39	61.6

	2018–19		
	School	Pro. 8	Att. 8
1.	Tauheedul Islam Girls' High School	2.16	69.9
2.	Eden Boys' School, Birmingham	1.69	64.4
3.	Eden Girls' School Coventry	1.61	58.3
4.	Wembley High Technology College	1.58	66.8
5.	Michaela Community School	1.53	61.4

(Continued)

Table 11.1 (Continued)

2017–18

	School	Pro. 8	Att. 8
6.	Eden Girls' School Coventry	1.36	57.4
7.	Tauheedul Islam Boys' High School	1.35	62.1
8.	William Perkin C of E High School	1.34	60.1
9.	St Anne's Catholic High Sch. for Girls	1.3	57.2
10.	Eden Girls' School Waltham Forest	1.29	59.8

2018–19

	School	Pro. 8	Att. 8
6.	Heartlands Academy	1.47	60
7.	Bishop Douglass School Finchley	1.39	53.4
8.	William Perkin C of E High School	1.31	60.9
9.	Preston Muslim Girls High School	1.24	61.7
10.	Dixons Trinity Academy	1.21	59.4

2021–22

	School	Pro. 8	Att. 8
1.	Michaela Community School	2.27	74
2.	The Steiner Academy Hereford	2.15	54.3
3.	Tauheedul Islam Girls' High School	1.73	69.6
4.	Eden Girls' Leadership Academy B'ham	1.67	63.7
5.	St Andrew's Catholic School	1.38	68.1
6.	St Peter's Catholic School	1.38	68.1
7.	Bentley Wood High School	1.34	62.9
8.	Ealing Fields High School	1.32	65.1
9.	Preston Muslim Girls High School	1.3	60.3
10.	The Hurlingham Academy	1.3	66.2

2022–23

	School	Pro. 8	Att. 8
1.	Michaela Community School	2.37	72.6
2.	Tauheedul Islam Girls' High School	2.30	73.1
3.	Mercia School	2.24	70.1
4.	The Steiner Academy Hereford	2.18	46.8
5.	Eden Girls' Leadership Academy B'ham	1.98	70.5
6.	Eden Boys' School, Birmingham	1.83	63.7
7.	Yesodey Hatorah Senior Girls School	1.65	59.5
8.	Eden Girls' School Coventry	1.49	59.9
9.	Tauheedul Islam Boys' High School	1.47	62.1
10.	St Peter's Catholic School	1.45	66.6

(Continued)

Table 11.1 (Continued)

	2023–24		
	School	Pro. 8	Att. 8
1.	Michaela Community School	2.55	79.1
2.	Mercia School	2.09	69.4
3.	Tauheedul Islam Girls' High School	2.05	70.8
4.	Eden Boys' School, Birmingham	1.59	63.7
5.	Menorah High School for Girls	1.57	69
6.	The Steiner Academy Hereford	1.57	46.6
7.	Mossbourne Victoria Park Academy	1.54	65.2
8.	Eden Girls' School, Coventry	1.52	61.2
9.	Mossbourne Community Academy	1.47	64
10.	The St Thomas the Apostle College	1.45	60.5

In 2019, England's most controversial free school—Michaela Community School—gained its first set of GCSE results. From its establishment in 2014, the thousands of visitors who came through its doors inevitably speculated about how the school would perform at GCSE. Sceptics predicted pupils would kick against the school's 'oppressive' atmosphere as they got older or underperform due to a teaching style that prioritised memory over understanding. Supporters, meanwhile, predicted exceptional results. The latter were not disappointed. For the past three years, Michaela has been the best secondary school in England for pupil progress. In each of those years, it has achieved Progress 8 scores of over 2.0, an achievement which would have been thought scarcely possible when the measure was designed back in 2013. In the summer of 2024, pupils at Michaela gained an average GCSE grade of 7.9 across their eight best subjects, better than over 90 percent of the selective grammar schools in England. Bearing in mind this is a comprehensive school in an underprivileged corner of northwest London, the achievement of pupils at Michaela is, quite simply, extraordinary. For the head-teacher Katharine Birbalsingh, it has been quite a journey: from starting a teaching blog in 2007 to speaking at the Conservative party Conference in 2010 and losing her job thereafter, to establishing a free school in 2014, to—finally—making that school the single most successful in the country by 2022. On GCSE results day that August, she tweeted: 'High expectations. No excuses. Discipline. Teacher as the authority leading. Traditional teaching methods. Belief in small c conservative values. Let's do this all around the country!'

As that tweet demonstrates, Katharine is a headteacher with strong convictions who relishes public debate. This landed her and the school in hot water, most notably in early 2024 when a Michaela pupil challenged the school in the High Court for not providing a space where Muslim pupils could pray at break time (the High Court, it should be added, found in favour of the school). Michaela has weathered other controversies, such as publicity surrounding Katherine's views on 'white privilege' and girls studying physics. However, these temporary flare-ups pale in significance compared to the real contribution Michaela Community School has made to the education debate in England and abroad. It has demonstrated something that—until the past five years—most teachers in England would have dismissed as impossible. Underprivileged pupils, if placed in an all-ability school with a warm-strict behaviour policy and evidence-led teaching methods, can comprehensively outperform grammar school pupils in some of the most prosperous

---

11 pupils will have been at the school in Year 6, where pupils regularly gain amongst the worst scores in the country—in 2011, for example, not a single pupil achieved a Level 4 or above in English and Maths. Because pupils at the Steiner Academy Hereford are working from such a low baseline, they are shown to have made remarkable progress by Year 11, despite attaining GCSE grades roughly in line with the national average, with an Attainment 8 score of 46.6 in 2024.

parts of the country. Establishing that proof point is, above and beyond anything else, Michaela's legacy to the English education system.

Ofsted Revisited

By the second half of my tenure as Schools Minster, the argument against the progressivist ideology was being won not just on paper but also on the ground. In June 2019, Andrew Smith wrote about how much had changed in the education debate on his blog, reflecting that many of the experiences he had as a teacher during the child-centred heydays of the 2000s are now 'bizarre tales that newer teachers might struggle to believe.'[6] He was right. By 2019, it was possible for teachers—if enrolled in the correct course—to enter the profession and receive sensible training in evidence-led methods, with scant exposure to the child-centred ideology. One headteacher recently told me that he would struggle today to employ a newly trained teacher who *had not* heard of cognitive load theory, a key component of the defence for knowledge-based teaching which was almost unknown amongst English teachers just ten years ago. Bad ideas are still present in the system, and their superficial appeal remains strong, but they are no longer an orthodoxy. As Andrew Smith wrote in the same piece, 'The collapse of the progressive hegemony is now a historical fact.'[7]

In few places was this more evident than the schools' inspectorate, Ofsted. Ofsted was once the chief enforcer of the progressivist ideology in English schools, routinely handing out negative judgements to schools which did not conform to the so-called 'Ofsted teaching style'. As explained in Chapter 7, Sir Michael Wilshaw spent his five-year term fighting this in-house ideology and gained many battle scars in the process. When his term of office ended in December 2016, Michael was succeeded as Her Majesty's Chief Inspector of Schools by Amanda Spielman. Amanda's entry into education began when she joined the management team of the fledgling Ark Schools network in 2005, where she played a central role in the Trust's success. This led to her appointment as Chair of Ofqual in 2011, where she skilfully steered the exams regulator through our curriculum and assessment reforms. Amanda is a formidable intellect, and as an early adopter of Daniel Willingham's work, she was an enthusiast for the evidence revolution in English schools.

Amanda's appointment mirrored the maturing of England's education debate, from the adversarial years of early change to a more sober, evidence-led period of reform. In one of her first major speeches as Chief Inspector at the Wellington College Festival of Education in June 2017, she signalled her intention to bring a greater focus in school inspections to the 'substance of education . . . the real meat of what is taught in our schools and colleges: the curriculum.' By curriculum, Amanda did not mean qualifications and the school timetable, as the word had so often been used to imply. Instead, she meant the educational vision held by a school for its pupils. Illustrating this view, Amanda quoted Professor Michael Young of the Institute of Education, an apostate from the world of progressive education who had latterly come to preach the knowledge gospel: 'Schools enable young people to acquire the knowledge that, for most of them, cannot be acquired at home or in the community.'[8] Only a few years previously, to hear the Chief Inspector speak so openly about the importance of knowledge to a curriculum would have caused an uproar. But, the profession's reception of Amanda's new focus on school curriculum was largely positive.

Part of the reason for this was that Amanda took a scrupulously evidence-based approach to her work as Chief Inspector. She understood that there was a gulf between what the government had asked schools to teach and what schools were actually teaching. So, she spent her first two years at Ofsted working on an evidence-gathering programme, publishing a series of research reviews and subject-specific reports. These, in turn, helped inform a thoroughly revised Ofsted Framework, published for first use in September 2019. The most significant change brought about by this Framework was to combine two of the previous four 'headline' Ofsted judgements—'Teaching, learning and assessment' and 'Outcomes'—into just one, known as 'Quality of education'. This judgement would combine pupil outcomes with an evaluation of the quality and ambition of a school's curriculum. Crucially, teachers were saved hours of workload in gathering, presenting, and explaining internal data for inspectors to scrutinise. As was made clear in the 2019 Framework, Ofsted inspections would no longer be concerned with internal data—all they would look at would be external data and the quality of the school curriculum. Their inspection of a school's curriculum was broken down into three easy-to-remember categories:

● Intent—what the school curriculum hoped to achieve;

● Implementation—how the school curriculum was taught and assessed;

● Impact—the subsequent outcomes for pupils.

As Amanda liked to explain, she wanted to connect the engine of the national curriculum to the wheels of what was happening in schools, and the 2019 Ofsted Framework did this brilliantly.[9]

For better or for worse, Ofsted is a significant driver of teacher behaviour in English schools. By making the school curriculum a central focus of her time as Chief Inspector, Amanda spurred an effervescence of curriculum discussions on the ground amongst teachers in England. Many teachers responded to these changes positively—partly because it spared them much of the burdensome and soul-destroying need to present internal data for external scrutiny. In addition, Amanda's training for Ofsted inspectors encouraged them to take a more collaborative approach whilst visiting schools, as could be seen in the new 90-minute phone call, which—from 2019 onwards—would proceed the first inspection day and establish a working dialogue between headteachers and the lead inspector. But also because most teachers have a fundamental passion for the subject or age range they have chosen to teach. After an excessive focus on data and paper-collecting exercises, the inspectorate was finally focusing on the substance of schooling.

There is a truism, often attributed to Arthur Schopenhauer, about the process through which a novel idea must pass: first, it is mocked, then it is resisted, and finally, it is considered as self-evident. By around 2019, this had become my experience. Occasionally, it would stick in my craw to meet a member of the education establishment who had once railed against our reforms, only for them—ten years later—to say something along the lines of: 'Teaching should, of course, be knowledge-based, nobody has ever disagreed with that.' However, in politics, one must take victories in whatever form they come, and hearing former opponents come round to the merits of knowledge-based teaching as 'self-evident' is surely one of them. What is more, by the late 2010s, this changing consensus in favour of evidence-led approaches was making it significantly easier for us to bed in our reforms, particularly when it came to teacher training.

Who Teaches the Teachers?

Until we entered office in 2010, the majority of graduates trained to be a teacher through a university, most commonly on a Postgraduate Certificate of Education (PGCE) course. Lasting one year, PGCEs are run by university education faculties and typically involve two placements at nearby schools, each lasting 12 weeks. Aspiring teachers who have just completed a three-year degree will often transfer to the education faculty at the same university and complete their PGCE in a fourth year. Others might change university to complete their PGCE in a part of the country where they hope to start their career.

For those who enter teaching later in life, returning to university to train can be less appealing: older trainees might not live close to a university; they could feel out of place studying alongside recent graduates, and they are less prepared to lose a year of earnings. For this reason, from the 1980s onwards, governments made various attempts to introduce 'school-based' training schemes, predominantly aimed at career changers. By 2010, two well-established routes were in place. Firstly, the Graduate Teacher Programme (GTP), where trainees learnt on the job whilst working within a school for a year as a salaried, unqualified teacher. Secondly, School-Centred Initial Teacher Training (SCITT) courses, where a consortium of local schools group together and offer teacher training. On both programmes, teachers could become qualified with little or even no university involvement. Contrary to popular myth, a PGCE is not necessary to become a qualified teacher, though it does have market value, particularly for those wanting to teach abroad. Schools offering GTP or SCITT courses would sometimes buy in the services of a university to provide extra training or a PGCE qualification. However, school-based routes are fundamentally different because schools design and lead the training, bringing in universities' services at their discretion, not—as was traditionally the case—the other way round.[10]

In a 2006 Department survey, GTP and SCITT routes achieved higher approval ratings than conventional university courses.[11] However, these school-based alternatives remained relatively small. There was a lot of demand for the GTP, but places were difficult to find, often reserved for trainees—such as teaching assistants—who had an existing relationship with a school. SCITT courses, meanwhile, proved popular amongst those in the know but struggled to gain market recognition. As a consequence, university-based courses continued to dominate the sector: in 2008, the proportion of trainees entering the profession through school-based routes was 18 percent.[12]

When we entered office in 2010, we promised to expand the proportion of trainees on school-based courses to over 50 percent by 2015. This was not just for the sake of encouraging more career changers to enter teaching. Much more important, in my view, was to challenge the intellectual monopoly that university education faculties held over the 'thoughtworld' of teacher training. With around 70 such faculties, there was, of course, some variation and notable exceptions, such as Christine Counsel at the University of Cambridge (see Chapter 6). However, almost all university education faculties remained steeped in the progressivist ideology. In many regards, they were its wellspring. Every year, tens of thousands of teachers had to imbibe the mantras that teacher-led approaches are bad, child-centred alternatives such as discovery learning are good, behaviour management should not be based on sanction, and systematic synthetic phonics is unmentionable. Following its publication in 2014, the evidence gathered in my co-author Robert Peal's book *Progressively Worse* only confirmed such impressions.[13]

Amongst teachers, it was a common refrain that you were taught pie-in-the-sky theories about education at your university seminars but actually learnt how to teach at your school placements. At best, universities' child-centred theorising was irrelevant to a teacher's future career; at worst, it was actively harmful. In either case, the opportunity cost was enormous: teaching is an extremely challenging job, and a training year should be pragmatic, evidence-based, and give those entering the profession the greatest possible chance of success. In 2010, I suspected that very few trainee teachers were receiving such preparation. Of all the different sectors of the education establishment, university education faculties were—by a stretch—the most difficult with which to work. Visits and meetings were hard to get, particularly as a shadow minister. When they were arranged, the atmosphere would be frosty, as the teacher trainers used academic jargon and obfuscation to prevent any fruitful discussion. There were, I hasten to add, some exceptions. A small number of those working at universities have proven to be a joy to work with and a constructive source of challenge as we designed our reforms. However, the main message I received whenever I visited university education faculties was, as Jim Callaghan had been told 40 years previously, 'keep off the grass'. Meetings I had usually consisted of being talked at for 90 minutes in a boardroom with no appetite or opportunity for discussion. If I, as a minister, showed any interest in what they taught, they would mistily invoke the virtues of 'academic independence', and insist the government had no place stepping on their hallowed turf.

I was not so convinced. Universities trained most of the future staff in our schools, which are the second largest public sector employers after the NHS. University education faculties should, therefore, be viewed—first and foremost—as a public service provider. However, that is not how they perceived their role. So, if we could not work with the universities, we would have to work around them. Hence, our ambition to make school-based routes the majority providers of teacher training, an ambition we achieved within five years. The first way we did this was by rapidly expanding the number of SCITTs in England, giving them much more market prominence. New SCITTs were established by Teaching Schools, a designation modelled on Teaching Hospitals, which we gave to high-achieving schools, and increasingly to MATs. The number of SCITTs grew accordingly from 56 in 2012 to 71 in 2014 to 155 in 2016.[14] By that date, it had become more or less expected for any large MAT to provide teacher training, something that proved highly popular amongst both them and their trainees. Particularly for MATs such as Ark or Harris, which from their inception promoted a shared education ethos across their schools, having a SCITT allowed them to train teachers in their routines, policies, and philosophy. For those trainees who stayed on at a trust's schools, the transition from trainee to teacher was much smoother.

Future Academies, the MAT which grew out of Lord Nash's sponsorship of Pimlico Academy, is a good example. It established a SCITT in 2014, and by 2017, it was named the third best teacher training provider in England by the *Good Teacher Training Guide*.[15] The Future Academies SCITT was an early adopter of the evidence revolution and became well known for its pragmatic, evidence-based training, twice being rated Outstanding in all categories by Ofsted. It has expanded to around 50 trainees a year and helps the MAT staff some of its most challenging schools. When, in 2016, Future Academies took over the chronically failing Phoenix Academy in West London, their SCITT provided a lifeline of well-trained, philosophically aligned new teachers (whom Lord and Lady Nash took to calling 'scittles'). By 2024, 60 percent of the Phoenix Academy teaching staff were graduates of the SCITT, and it was the best secondary school in the trust with a Progress 8 of +0.07.

The second way in which we expanded school-based training was by introducing a new route called School Direct. As the name suggests, School Direct allows prospective teachers to apply directly to a school for their training, often with the expectation that they remain working there having gained their qualification. School Direct placements could be paid or unpaid, with the former replacing the GTP from 2012. Schools recruiting trainees through School Direct would still have to work with an accredited ITT provider, either a university or a SCITT, through which the trainee would gain their qualification. However, the recruitment, administration, and training would all be provided by the school. School Direct has proven to be very popular: since 2017, around one-third of postgraduate entries to the profession each year have taken this route. By 2015, the monopoly universities once held over teacher training was no more. That year, the number of postgraduate

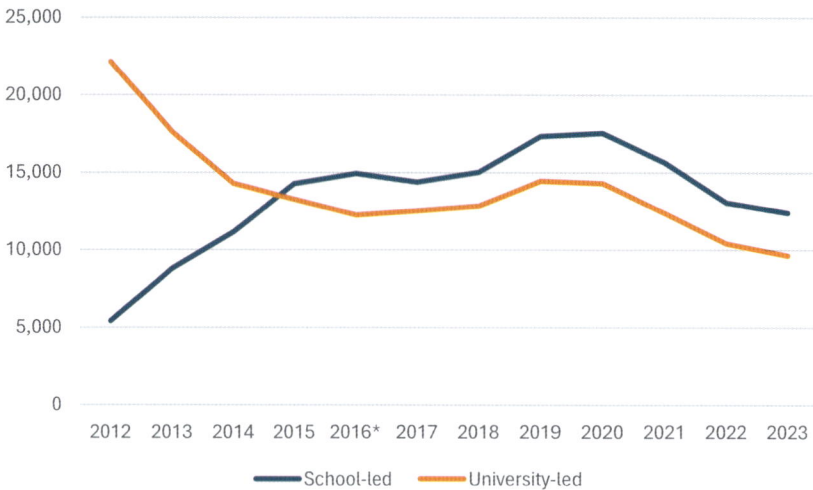

Figure 11.1 Numbers of postgraduate trainees on school-led and university-led training routes 2012 to 2023.

trainees on school-led routes—made up of SCITTs, School Direct, and Teach First (see Chapter 8)—rose to 14,231, compared to 13,191 on university-led routes, and up from 5,371 in 2012. Postgraduate trainees on school-led routes have outnumbered those on university-led routes every year since (see Figure 11.1).[16]

What was true of schools was also true of teacher training. We wanted to see existing institutions, with their ossified progressivist ideology, challenged by new entrants to the market. What is more, we believed that new entrants would encourage existing institutions to improve their practice. By the end of the first Parliament in 2015, such a process was clearly underway. The grassroots evidence revolution that was taking place amongst teachers and in schools was filtering through to school-based teacher training courses.

However, there is a problem with this diversified market for teacher training: confusion. For anyone wanting to become a teacher, it became increasingly difficult to understand the different routes they could take. Had there been one advantage of the old model, where most trainees undertook a university-based PGCE, it was its simplicity. In contrast, by 2014, teachers could train through SCITTs, School Direct, School Direct salaried, Teach First, and a host of smaller schemes such as Troops to Teachers and Researchers in Schools. To help us bring some sense to the teacher training market, Michael Gove asked Sir Andrew Carter to chair a review of Initial Teacher Training (ITT) in May 2014. Andrew was the successful and well-respected headteacher of South Farnham School, a large primary school which had established a multi-academy trust in 2011, and took over the running of the Surrey local authority's SCITT in 2013. Carter published his report in 2015, setting the agenda for the next stage of our reforms.[17]

The Carter Review contained many eminently sensible recommendations, but of particular interest to me was a section on the content taught during teacher training. It pointed to the variation between different teacher training providers and the gaps many trainees felt existed in their training in areas such as behaviour management, subject knowledge development, and special educational needs. So, we asked a new expert group to create a framework of core content for ITT, which they delivered in July 2016. The group was chaired by Stephen Munday, the CEO of an academy trust in Cambridgeshire, and I paid close attention to its workings. As usual, I ensured those with long and trusted experience were present in the expert group, such as John McIntosh, and Tom Bennett, along with Rachael Hare, the head of ITT at the Harris Federation's very successful SCITT. Munday's new ITT Core Content Framework was a step in the right direction. For the first time, it put into writing the expectation that ITT providers teach many of the concepts that the evidence revolution in education had popularised: systematic synthetic phonics, cognitive load theory, repeated practice, times tables, and the ability to teach a 'knowledge-rich' curriculum all gained a mention.[18] However, there is a world of difference between such concepts existing on a piece of paper (or, more accurately, a PDF hosted on the government website) and actually being taught on a teacher training course.

In theory, the ITT Core Content Framework should have been the teacher training equivalent of the national curriculum. In reality, it was impossible to ensure it was being followed. Unlike the school curriculum, which is accompanied by national assessments, the only means of enforcing the new Framework was by asking Ofsted to use it as a basis for their ITT inspections. However, it felt unlikely that Ofsted would fail an ITT provider for their lack of adherence to the Framework. I gained worrying feedback about how it was playing out on the ground through one former employee from Read Write Inc who was training to be a primary teacher with a university in the West Midlands. When she attended her now compulsory session on systematic synthetic phonics, it was not a practical session on how to deliver phonics in the classroom but a diatribe about how such an approach would ruin a child's love of reading. That was the stage we had arrived at in 2016. We had the right ideas and the right documentation in place, but we had no mechanisms to ensure they were being followed in teacher training institutions across the country.

The Golden Thread

Two arrivals at the Department for Education would help me change this situation. The first was Justine Greening, the new Secretary of State for Education from July 2016. A natural coalition builder, she won early support in the sector by pledging to make the improvement of the trainee and newly qualified teacher experience one of her cornerstone policies. The second was my new policy adviser, Rory Gribbell, a Maths teacher who had trained through Teach First in Southampton. Like many bright young teachers at the time, Rory wrote and published a blog. It first came to my attention when he posted about the absurd content of his own teacher training (not through Teach First, I should add, but through the university with whom they were partnered). During one seminar, Rory was given a hand-out from a 1991 book on the philosophy of mathematics education. The handout, which he duly posted online, offered a tabular overview of 'Five Educational Ideologies'. A 'progressive educator' ideology of maths teaching, it claimed, believed in a 'child-centred teaching' approach based on 'activity, play, exploration', and should be equated with a 'liberal' worldview of 'caring, empathy, human values'. In contrast, the 'Industrial trainer' ideology of maths teaching, which believed in 'hard work effort, practice, rote . . . drill . . . chalk and talk', should be equated with the 'radical right', and a 'crypto-racist, monoculturalist' worldview.[19] Rory, a thoughtful 20-something maths teacher with an interest in evidence-led teaching methods, was understandably perplexed to hear it suggested that this made him, in essence, a fascist.

Such blog posts were always helpful fodder for my own meetings with officials, helping me to make my case. Intrigued to meet Rory, I invited him to the Department and found him to be a passionate and insightful teacher who had drunk deep at the well of Christodoulou, Willingham, and Hirsch. When Robert Peal returned to the West London Free School in September 2016, Rory became my new policy adviser.

In February 2017, Justine Greening spoke of her ambition to create a 'golden thread' of high-quality professional development through every stage of a teacher's career. She was motivated by a concern that too many teachers were dropping out of the profession in their first few years of teaching.[20] At the time, around 13 percent were leaving within a year of qualifying, and 30 percent were leaving within five years.[21] Her great insight was that, looked through the other end of the telescope, the recruitment challenge is actually a retention challenge. If we kept more teachers in the profession, fewer would have to be recruited. So, Justine saw improved provision for newly qualified teachers as a ready area for reform and promised a revised approach would be in place by September 2019.

It was an encouraging development. I frequently heard teachers trade stories of their 'year from hell', in which after qualifying, they taught close to a full time-table, with insufficient mentoring, and—if their department was not functioning properly—no shared resources, meaning they had to stay at their computer late into each night preparing lessons from scratch. Both Justine and I were accountants and would reflect on how gradual and structured our early professional journeys had been compared to the sink-or-swim approach taken in many schools. Justine launched her consultation in December 2017, although Theresa May reshuffled her out of the Department two months later. Thankfully, her replacement, Damian Hinds, was more than capable of helping to bring the policy into harbour, no small feat considering that the summer of 2018 was the peak of the Government's Brexit negotiations.

In January 2019, we released the new Framework. Newly qualified teachers would become known as Early Career Teachers (ECTs), and their induction period would be extended from one year to two. This meant one further year during which new teachers would enjoy a timetable reduction and mentoring from a colleague, but with no reduction in pay. We also worked with a select group of ITT providers to prepare resources which provide further training to ECTs and more detailed guidance on how mentors should approach their role. This policy came with the promise of £130 million for schools to support ECTs and to offset the lost teaching hours from timetable reductions for both them and their mentors.[22]

Most importantly, the Early Career Framework included a curriculum detailing what content the training for new teachers should contain. We worked on this content over the course of 2018, and it was remarkable how different the climate of debate was compared to just four years previously. In 2014, during the Carter review, the evidence revolution was in its infancy, with debates over teaching methods still generating more heat than light. In 2018, the debate had matured significantly. When I began suggesting that we include only evidence-based practices and specifically warn against common fads for which there is no research base, I was no longer looked at with suspicion. I was pushing at an open door. As a former teacher with an interest in evidence-led approaches, my policy adviser Rory was integral to the success of this reform, as was his successor and fellow Teach First alumnus Will Bickford-Smith, who took over when Rory left the Department to work as education adviser to the Prime Minister. They helped put together a first-class expert group to produce the teacher training curriculum, including Stuart Lock, who was now CEO of the Advantage Schools MAT, and the former Head of teacher training at Ark, now Executive Director of the Ambition Institute, Marie Hamer.

I was determined that the new Framework would be evidence-led. For this reason, the advisory group worked hand-in-hand with the Education Endowment Foundation, which assessed and endorsed every comment included in the Framework. Thankfully, the impartial research experts at the EEF were ready to endorse many of the features of teacher-led, knowledge-rich teaching. And why shouldn't they? That is where the best evidence lies. When I read the first draft of the Early Career Framework, I was delighted. It might sound like a narrow corner of education policy, but reading the Framework was when I first realised that our movement had come of age. Advocates for evidence-led teaching had gone from being ignored to being insurgents to being the new establishment.

All the good stuff was in there. Standard 2 on 'How pupils learn' stipulates that new teachers should learn the importance of prior knowledge, memory, regular practice, the retrieval effect, and worked examples. Standard 3 on 'Subject and the Curriculum' stipulates the following: 'In order for pupils to think critically, they must have a secure understanding of knowledge within the subject area they are being asked to think critically about.' It also explained that pupils are likely to struggle to transfer what is learnt in one discipline to another, a key argument against cross-curricular or thematic learning. Standard 4 on Classroom Practice explained many of the tenets of effective, teacher-led practice, such as modelling, scaffolding, and questioning. There was a lively discussion within the expert group as to whether we should warn against popular but unevidenced fads, but—as the research is so clear—the EEF gave their assent. Standard 5 warns against the 'common misconception' that pupils have different learning styles and the practice of 'artificially creating distinct tasks for different groups', in other words, differentiation.

The more strident advocates for teacher-led instruction in the advisory group did not win every argument. 'Group activities', Standard 4 states, 'can increase pupil success', though this is followed by the caveat that 'to work together effectively pupils need guidance, support and practice'. Likewise, teaching pupils 'metacognitive strategies' was an approach which caused me instinctive concern, but the evidence for its success does—apparently—exist, so in it went. However, the Early Career Framework is undoubtedly a document born of the reform movement in English schools, as the extensive bibliography attests. It includes a now familiar roll call from the academic case for knowledge-rich, teacher-led instruction: Christodoulou, Willingham, Sweller, Kirschner, Roediger, Rosenshine, and so on.[23]

When we published the Framework in January 2019, I was delighted and relieved by how readily it was welcomed by the profession. This was no doubt in part because it was delivered in combination with a generous pledge to improve the experience, and therefore retention, of early career teachers, accompanied by £130 million of annual funding, winning support from the unions, teacher training providers, and headteacher groups. However, the Framework's ready acceptance also reflected how far the debate had evolved. Just five years previously, such a document would have been seen as controversial and even hostile. In 2019, its contents were welcomed as self-evident. The Early Career Framework is one of the most successful policies I helped deliver whilst in government, and its reception won us a mandate to extend its provisions from early career teachers to Initial Teacher Training. Sam Twiselton of Sheffield Hallam University chaired a new group, which adapted the Early Careers Framework into an ITT Core Content Framework, published in November 2019.[24] The same principles in five core areas—behaviour management, pedagogy, curriculum, assessment, and professional behaviours—would now feature consistently through a teacher's first three years in the profession: one year as a trainee and two years as an Early Career Teacher.

Of course, placing content on a government document and seeing it faithfully delivered in universities and SCITTs across the country are two very different things—as we discovered with our first attempt at such a teacher training curriculum in 2016. To borrow language from debates surrounding the national curriculum, there is no reason to assume the 'intended curriculum' produced by the Department, and the 'enacted curriculum' delivered by providers will be the same. Thankfully, to ensure that the gap between the intended and enacted curriculum in teacher training was not a gulf, we had Amanda Spielman as Her Majesty's Chief Inspector at Ofsted. As well as inspecting schools, Ofsted inspect teacher training providers, of which there were 240 in 2019, made up of 70 Universities and 170 SCITTs.[25] Amanda was a true believer in the new ITT Core Content Framework, so under her leadership, Ofsted inspectors did not just pay lip service to its content. Instead, they were rigorous in questioning whether ITT providers were adopting its evidence-led principles and, as they found during 2020–21, not all of them were. Many had their Ofsted ratings downgraded, including—controversially—a major university provider in England's northwest, which trained more than 1,000 teachers each year.[26]

These Ofsted inspections revealed that many teacher training institutions were unable, or unwilling, to apply the new Core Content Framework. So, we appointed the brilliant Ian Bauckham to lead a review of the ITT market. Ian had been headteacher of the Bennett Memorial Diocesan School, a comprehensive secondary school in Tunbridge Wells, from which base he built an academy trust across Kent and Sussex and a popular SCITT. An enthusiast for evidence-led teaching, and the author of a good-sense review of MFL pedagogy for the Teaching Schools Council, which I commissioned in 2016 (see Chapter 9). Helpfully, as a former President of England's main headteachers' union ASCL he was well respected within the profession. Surprisingly for such an establishment figure, Ian brought to the ITT market review a radicalism—driven by a genuine passion for high-quality, evidence-based teacher training—that felt reminiscent of the early Michael Gove years. Thus, when his review of the ITT market was published in July 2021, it contained a bold suggestion: every provider should be made to reapply for their accreditation to award teacher qualifications. The success of their reapplication would depend—in part—on their readiness to incorporate the ITT Core Content Framework in full.[27]

For once, I found myself being persuaded by a member of the sector to push for radical reform, and not vice-versa. Asking universities to reapply for their accreditation and—presumably—removing that accreditation for those who were not successful carried a clear risk. A year after the Covid pandemic and in the midst of a period of high inflation and increased costs of living, we were struggling to recruit enough teachers. This policy could have made a difficult situation worse by reducing the number of teacher training providers. However, I was convinced to press ahead with Ian's recommendation on two counts. Firstly, successful providers that achieve reaccreditation would soak up the training places of those that did not. Provided that sufficient geographic spread of teacher training institutions around the country was maintained, I was reassured that trainee teachers would not be too wedded to one provider over another. Secondly, we had the momentum to achieve an unprecedented level of alignment behind evidence-led approaches in English teacher training, something I would never have thought possible only a few years previously. So, on we pressed.

Over the course of 2022, we ran two rounds of reaccreditation for ITT providers. This involved reviewing a selection of providers' trainee curriculum materials to check alignment with the Core Content Framework and assessing how ready they were to deliver other aspects of ITT, such as mentoring, training, and school partnerships. We entered the process with 240 training providers, and in the first round, we approved just 80 applications. Following the second round, we approved a further 99 applications. This brought the total number of accredited ITT providers to 179, representing 59 universities and 104 SCITTs (down from 70 and 170, respectively, in 2020).[28] There were roughly 4,000 places on the programmes that did not reopen, which we were able to reallocate to accredited providers. I am confident this policy will have brought about a step change in the quality of teacher training in England, with no loss of market capacity.

NPQs

The final element of the Golden Thread is the suite of National Professional Qualifications, or NPQs as they're known that certify continuing professional development for teachers. NPQs already existed, but we wanted to improve the quality to ensure they genuinely equipped teachers to take on new responsibilities within their schools or elsewhere. We also wanted to make sure that what was being taught was in line with the evidence. The enormous task of reforming and rewriting the NPQs was led by Matt Hood (who later played an integral role in creating the Oak National Academy—see Chapter 12) and Ian Bauckham. Expert advice was offered by people such as John Blake, then working for the ARK multi-academy trust, Richard Gill, who chaired the Teaching Schools Council, Marie Hamer of the Ambition Institute, Emma Lennard of the Knowledge Schools Trust (the multi-academy trust that included the West London Free School), Reuben Moore of Teach First and Professor Sam Twistleton of Sheffield Hallam University. All the content was overseen and signed off by the Education Endowment Foundation to ensure each and every element had a sound evidence base.

By October 2020, we had published new comprehensive frameworks for NPQs in Leading Behaviour Culture, Leading Teaching, Senior Leadership, Headship, and Executive Leadership. The next stage was to procure high-quality providers to teach the courses with the Institute of Education and the Ambition Institute as well as private sector organisations which met the criteria for delivery, such as Education Development Trust. In October 2021, NPQs in Leading Literacy and Early Years were added and, in 2023, NPQs in Leading Primary Maths and Special Needs were published. We took steps to ensure that the content of courses for both the NPQs and the Early Career Framework were of high quality and in accordance with the details set out in the framework documents.

Enough Good Teachers

Teacher recruitment has been a significant challenge since 2020. Increases in the cost of living made teacher salaries less competitive, schools cannot compete with the growing practice of flexible working, and recovery from the Covid pandemic has been challenging, particularly in areas such as pupil behaviour and absenteeism.

What is more, secondary recruitment is more challenging than primary, and a child-population bulge is currently moving from primary to secondary schools, which will mean 29,000 more secondary pupils in 2028 compared to 2024.[29] As with headteachers across the country, teacher recruitment gave me many sleepless nights whilst in post. It was simultaneously one of the areas for which I was most responsible but over which I had the least control.

In the short term, a government minister's record on teacher recruitment is at the mercy of the wider job market, inflation, global pandemics, and pay settlements driven mainly by the Treasury. There are some quick fixes that you can make if finances allow, such as increased bursaries for shortage subjects or new training routes aimed at attracting niche groups within the population to teaching. From 2019, I pressed hard for a £30,000 starting salary for teachers, as it was clear teachers were falling behind starting salaries in similar postgraduate professions. The Treasury finally allowed us to implement this in September 2023, with a 7.1 percent pay rise.[30] However, in the long term, there is only one factor that will make a significant improvement to teacher recruitment and retention: that is the quality of our schools. Teachers thrive in schools with effective management, good pupil behaviour, and policies which ensure that workload remains manageable. In schools where those things don't exist, able teachers are worn down to the point of quitting every year. Each of those individual decisions to leave the profession is a tragedy.

The only long-term solution to England's teacher recruitment struggles is—quite simply—the same solution that I would propose for most of the hardest questions in education policy: improve the quality of our schools. On this, I am an optimist. As the final chapter will explain, I genuinely believe that we have built a school system which has the potential to be continuously self-improving. Though significant challenges will always remain, I am convinced that English schools are now on the path towards sustained, transformative change.

Notes

1 M. Gove speech on academies at Haberdashers' Aske's Hatcham College, 11 January 2012.

2 This description of 'School A' is pieced together from F. Abrams, '"We're not hippies, we're punks." School that has projects, not subjects, on the timetable', *The Guardian*, 31 June 2017; and R. Sylvester, 'Is XP the school of the future?', *The Times*, 6 October 2021.

3 M. Benn, '"Drill and kill" for England's state schools while private sector goes progressive', *The Guardian*, 18 August 2020.

4 S. Weale, 'Sheffield school criticised for saying job applicants must be "wedded" to role', *The Guardian*, 20 February 2023.

5 D. Thomson, 'What does English as an additional language really mean when it comes to Progress 8?', *FFT Education Datalab*, 13 February 2020.

6 A. Old, 'Year zero', *'Scenes From The Battleground' blog*, 22 June 2019.

7 Old, 'Year zero', 22 June 2019.

8 A. Spielman, Speech to the Wellington College Festival of Education, 23 June 2017.

9 Ofsted, *Education Inspection Framework*, 2019.

10 An excellent summary of the history and state of teacher training by 2008 can be found in S. Freedman, B. Lipson, and D. Hargreaves, *More Good Teachers*, London: Policy Exchange, 2008.

11 Department for Education and Skills, *Becoming a Teacher: Student Teachers' Experiences of Initial Teacher Training in England*, Nottingham: University of Nottingham, 2006, p. 19.

12 House of Commons, *Children, Schools and Families Committee—Fourth Report Training of Teachers*, 2010, Section 1.15.

13 R. Peal, *Progressively Worse: The Burden of Bad Ideas in British Schools*, London: Civitas, 2024.

14 National Audit Office, *Training New Teachers*, 10 February 2016, p. 38.

15 A. Smithers and M. Bungey, *The Good Teacher Training Guide 2017*, Centre for Education and Employment Research, University of Buckingham.

16 Figures compiled from Department for Education statistical releases, 'Initial Teacher Training Census'.

17 Department for Education, *Carter Review of Initial Teacher Training (ITT)*, January 2015.

18 Department for Education, *A Framework of Core Content for Initial Teacher Training (ITT)*, July 2016.

19 The handout in question was from P. Ernest, *The Philosophy of Mathematics Education*, London: Routledge Falmer, 1991, p. 153.

20 J. Greening, 'Teachers—the experts driving social mobility', *Speech to the Inaugural Conference of the Chartered College of Teaching*, 17 February 2017.

21 S. Weale, 'Almost a third of teachers quit state sector within five years of qualifying', *The Guardian*, 24 October 2016.

22 Department for Education, 'Press release: New framework to support trainee and early career teachers', 30 January 2019.

23 Department for Education, *Early Career Framework*, January 2019.

24 Department for Education, *ITT Core Content Framework*, 2019.

25 Department for Education, *Initial Teacher Training (ITT) Market Review Report*, July 2021, p. 54.

26 J. Carr, 'Teacher training provider to shut after "inadequate" Ofsted rating', *Schools Week*, 21 July 2021.

27 Department for Education, *Initial Teacher Training (ITT) Market Review Report*, July 2021, p. 14.

28 F. Whittaker, 'ITT review: 5k places at risk as third of SCITTs left out', *Schools Week*, 29 September 2022.

29 Department for Education, 'National pupil projections', 18 July 2024.

30 Department for Education Blog, 'Everything you need to know about the teacher pay offer', 28 March 2023.

12 Self-improving School System

Schools have undergone a seismic shift over the last 20 years. There has genuinely never been a better time to be a pupil than now. Schools are more vibrant and dynamic than ever before.

> Sir Hamid Patel, CEO of Star Academies, interviewed
> in *TES Magazine*, 8 March 2023

A turning point in our school reforms occurred in 2019, during which year we passed multiple important milestones. In August, Michaela proved their critics wrong with their astonishing first set of GCSE results; in November, we made training in evidence-led practices an entitlement for all new teachers in the Early Career Framework; and in December, the OECD released the PISA results from 2018. Back in 2010, we had asked for these to be the scorecard by which our reforms were measured, and nine years later, our scores were moving in the right direction. In reading, England achieved a slight improvement, its score increasing from 500 in 2015 to 505 in 2018. In mathematics, the improvement was significant, with England's score increasing from 493 in 2015 to 504 in 2018, helping the UK move up the international rankings for mathematics from 27th to 18th amongst 76 participating countries.*

As the battles which we had fought early on in office started to abate, I looked forward to entering the remaining years of my ministerial career, hoping to enjoy the mellow fruitfulness of successful reform and focus on new areas of school reform, such as the teaching of sport and music. This was not to be. Firstly, our positive PISA story was overshadowed by a general election held one week later, in which Boris Johnson won a majority for the Conservative Party. Rather more significantly, the new year brought Covid-19 to our shores, and the first national lockdown began in March 2020. It is not my intention to relegislate in this book the debates from those sad and difficult years. There will be a time and a place for considering anew the wisdom of our two periods of school closure, or assessing

---

* These figures vary slightly from those included in the introduction, where only those nations involved in five consecutive surveys from 2009 to 2022 were included in the rankings.

DOI: 10.4324/9781003533474-13

how well we coped with the challenge of mass testing children, zoning schools, and cancelling national exams. However, this is not it. First and foremost, this is a book about education reform.

However, I did fear during the Covid-19 pandemic that the two prolonged periods of school closure might undo much of the positive work our reforms had delivered. In both 2020 and 2021, we cancelled national examinations, which meant the only possible means of delivering GCSE and A-Level grades to those years' cohorts was through grades assigned via teacher judgement. After a misjudged attempt to statistically moderate those grades in 2020 using a now infamous 'algorithm', teacher-assigned grades were honoured across the board. In one summer, nine years of work to combat grade inflation was lost. At GCSE, the average grade rose from 4.76 in 2019 to 5.21 in 2020, rising again to 5.28 in 2021. At A-Level, where pupils' university places depended on the grades their teachers assigned, the increase was even more pronounced. The proportion of student entries awarded an A or A* grades rose from 25.2 percent in 2019 to 38.1 percent in 2020 and up again to 44.3 percent in 2021—almost doubling in the space of two years.

There should be little surprise that pupils did better when their teachers were asked to choose their grades. What was more of a surprise was how little teachers around the country enjoyed the process. The Covid pandemic gave what the anti-exams lobby in England has long desired—a system of assessment based not on terminal examinations but on the holistic judgement of pupils' classroom teachers. In September 2020, a newly formed campaign group named 'Rethinking Assessment' wrote to the *Sunday Times*, arguing that this experiment in mass teacher assessment must act as a catalyst for finally replacing GCSE examinations with a more humane alternative, suggesting 'Portfolios', 'electronic badging' of pupils, and 'teacher judgment' as alternatives. 'All of this is achievable,' they wrote, 'and post Covid there is a growing appetite for change.' The best-known signatories were school leaders from the independent sector (such as Eton College, St Paul's Girls' School, and Bedales School), whilst those from the state sector were mostly from the progressivist fringes, such as XP and School 21.[1] Four years on, the appetite for change to which they referred does not seem to have materialised, particularly amongst teachers from the state sector.

There appears to be an acceptance amongst most teachers that terminal exams, unloved as they are, remain the least worst means of assessing pupil attainment. As teachers discovered during the pandemic, assessing your own students for high-stakes exams is not an easy or pleasant experience. Teachers had constantly to check themselves against the personal preferences for particular students they might be displaying, and—where students had underperformed—had the unenviable responsibility of assigning them lower grades in the knowledge that they might not meet the entry requirements for their desired next stage of study. What is more, the process of gathering evidence of pupil work for both internal and—as in 2021—external moderation proved hugely time-consuming. When exams returned in 2022, the sector breathed a collective sigh of relief.

More troubling, evidence suggests that teachers at independent schools were more generous in teacher assessment than their state school counterparts. The proportion of independent school pupils achieving a GCSE grade 7 or above rose from 46.6 percent in 2019 (the last year of pre-Covid GCSE exams) to 61.2 percent in 2021 (the second year of teacher-assessed grades). In state grammar schools, where pupils have a comparable spread of attainment, the proportion rose from 57.9 percent in 2019 to 68.4 percent in 2021. This meant an increase of 9.5 percentage points in state grammar schools, compared to a 14.6 percentage points increase in independent schools. Studying these figures, Natasha Plaister at the Education DataLab concluded, 'This analysis does seem to suggest that during the pandemic, under both centre-assessed grades (CAGs) and teacher-assessed grades (TAGs), independent schools gave out more generous grades than might be expected.'[2] One cannot help but conclude that it was even harder for teachers to assess their own students' attainment fairly when their parents were paying their salaries. The cancellation of terminal exams during the Covid pandemic in 2020 and 2021 provided further proof—should we need it—of what should be a guiding rule of education policy: compared to any conceivable alternative, exams are the fairest and most efficient means of giving all pupils the grades they deserve.

The pandemic also provided us with a new appreciation of the importance of face-to-face teaching. The techno-evangelist wing of education thinking has long predicted the demise of classroom teaching in favour of personalised learning in front of computers. That change came sooner than any could have expected in March 2020. However, despite the best efforts of schools and teachers around the country, it became clear that online teaching is a pale imitation of what can be achieved in the classroom. More than ever, we have come to appreciate that teaching is a human endeavour, where small interactions between the teacher and a pupil can contribute enormously to their understanding, motivation, and sense of self-worth. What is more, the school as a physical site plays a crucial role in socialising young children. As schools welcomed back their full cohorts in September 2021, few mourned the end of online learning. I doubt, after the experience of school closure during the pandemic, that advocates of computer-based teaching are calling for 'radical transformation' of the classroom with quite the same zeal as before.

After pupils returned to schools in 2021, teachers experienced a steadily growing realisation of how negatively they had been impacted by school closures. Perhaps the most unfortunate long-term legacy of the pandemic in schools has been an increase in pupil absenteeism. Prior to 2020, steadily improving attendance in England's schools had been a success story for multiple governments, with the overall absence rate decreasing from 6.5 percent in the academic year ending 2007 to 4.5 percent in 2014—a record low. Since the pandemic, however, these gains have been lost, with overall absence rates of 7.6 percent in 2022 and 7.4 percent in 2023 (see Figure 12.1). On a national scale, many pupils simply lost their previous good habit of regularly attending school. In addition, there have been many reports

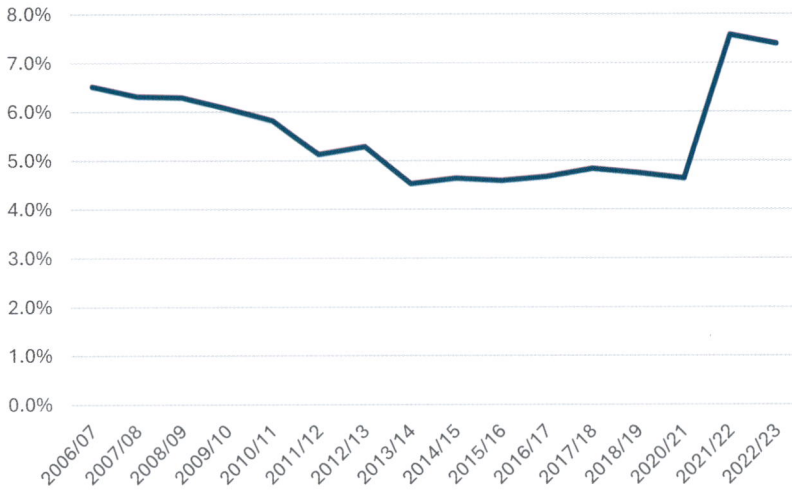

Figure 12.1 Overall absence rate in England between 2006/07 and 2022/23.[3]

of increasingly anti-social behaviour from pupils who had lost out on two forma-
tive years of interaction with their peers, though accurate data on such claims is
harder to gather.

I knew that steering schools through their acclimatisation to a post-Covid world
would be a challenge for the Department. Sadly, it was not one in which I would
immediately partake. Shortly after schools reopened in full in September 2021,
Boris Johnson reshuffled me out as Schools Minister. One year later, in September
2022, the Conservative Party dismissed Boris Johnson as Prime Minister, paving
the way for Rishi Sunak to take office in October 2023. He reappointed me as
Schools Minister, where I would remain for a further year.

Much of my work over that period was focused on safeguarding the reforms that
we had already put in place, particularly through the turmoil of seven different
Education Secretaries arriving at and leaving the Department from 2018 to 2024.
I did, on occasion, hope that I might be offered the top job, but my fate was to be
always the bridesmaid, never the bride. Instead, I sought to be a figure of continuity
and institutional memory for both ministers and civil servants. During my last year,
I failed to dissuade Rishi Sunak from his plan to replace A-Levels and T-Levels
with a new Advanced British Level—though this plan was itself stopped by the
2024 election result. However, I was more successful when he originally considered similar proposals for GCSEs, which were no doubt influenced by the people
at Rethinking Assessment and views emanating from an 'Education Commission'
published by *The Times* newspaper. I wrote him a long note cautioning against
such an idea, in which I explained a point that is so often missed by politicians:
more than half the school pupils in England do not take A-Levels, something that
those who are the product of an academic Sixth Form education can find surprising. For such students, Year 11 is the end of their formal academic schooling. They
need something to show for it, and that is what GCSE provides. GCSEs are also

hugely important in ensuring a high-quality curriculum is taught in our schools and for holding schools to account for the quality of secondary education they deliver. I received a response from Rishi Sunak, who let me know that my note had persuaded him to leave GCSEs in place.

However, it was becoming clear that whatever plans the Prime Minister and our Party put in place for the next Parliament, they were unlikely ever to be enacted. With an election due to take place in 2024 and the Conservative Party performing poorly in the polls, our policy proposals became less and less relevant. In November 2023, I stood down as Schools Minister and announced I would not be running in the next election. The following month, results from the 2022 PISA tests were published. Of course, due to the Covid pandemic, the scores gained by most participating nations fell significantly. However, England's ranking compared to other nations held up well, and it continued to improve in Maths. This added to the growing consensus around the success of our reforms following the publication earlier that year of the PIRLS survey into the reading ability of 10-year-olds, in which England now ranked 4th in the world (see Introduction).

From a personal perspective, the timing of these results was fortuitous. As the 2024 election loomed, newspaper commentary began to take a long view of the past 14 years of Conservative Government reform, and it became something of a trope that education was one of the rare examples of success. In a long article about English school reform published by the *Economist* in June 2023, it was observed, 'In a stint of government in which achievements are few, schools stand out. What went right?' The piece correctly identified that the battle of ideas was central to our reforms: ministers diagnosed progressive education as a problem and 'did not wilt' in combatting it. It also identified the statistic, which I have enjoyed retelling since, that over 13 years, during ten of which I was Schools Minister, there were 15 separate Housing Ministers.[4] In July 2024, Helen Rumbelow wrote in a piece entitled 'The one thing I am grateful to Tories for' that our reforms to the teaching of reading were: 'what governments can be brilliant at: evidence-based intervention that helps everyone, but perhaps the most disadvantaged, and impacts a generation.'[5] Five months later, Emma Duncan wrote a similar appraisal in *The Times*, observing that 'Education has been one of the few success stories of the past 14 years.'[6] Another lengthy analysis of our reforms was published in the *Economist* in July 2024, recognising that England's improving schools have been due to our insistence on following the evidence, even when it sent us into battle with the progressivist ideology.

Conservative ministers who entered government in 2010 were convinced that faddish ideologies had diverted schools from teaching in ways that evidence suggests work best. Many people believe that the reforms they wrought amount to a big step backwards. Yet lately England's schools have been climbing up international league tables. Meanwhile countries that have pressed on with more fashionable approaches have been watching their own scores fall.[7]

The Tragedy of Good Intentions

As the previously quoted *Economist* article recognised, our achievements were thrown into sharper relief when contrasted with events taking place north of the border. Over the past decades, those interested in evidence-led teaching have become conversant with the idea of a controlled trial, where participants from the same population are assigned to two or more interventions to control for other possible factors. If a controlled trial is designed properly, one intervention group outperforms the other, which can demonstrate—with a high degree of certainty—that the intervention is the cause. Just imagine if such a trial could be carried out at a national scale: two populations from the same country attend schools governed by contrasting education policies for over a decade. Then, pupil outcomes are assessed by an impartial third party to see whether any difference has emerged between the groups. Would that not be the education policy-maker's dream? Well, something not too dissimilar has occurred in the United Kingdom since 2010. At the same time we began our reforms based around high autonomy and high accountability, Scotland embarked upon a wholly different path.

Scotland has always had a separate education system from England, even before devolution restored the Scottish Parliament in 1999. In fact, until the end of the last century, high-quality state schools with rigorous academic standards were seen in Scotland as a cherished national asset. Until recently, Scots liked to boast of a national tradition they termed 'the democratic intellect', and Scottish history is generously populated with those from humble backgrounds who rose to achieve great feats through the power of schooling. Lest we forget, my comrade in England's education revolution—the Aberdonian Michael Gove—is one of them.

However, in 2004, the Scottish government began planning a new vision for schools, with the Curriculum for Excellence (CfE) at its centre. Taking six years to design through sustained collaboration with Scotland's education establishment, the CfE is—put simply—a monument to the progressivist ideology. In terms of content, knowledge is largely absent. Instead, the curriculum is built around four 'capacities', asking schools to help their pupils become successful learners, confident individuals, responsible citizens, and effective contributors.[8] From 2007 to 2010, five sets of additional guidance, known as Building the Curriculum (BTC), added further elaboration to this initial proposal. BT3 was published in 2008 and contained seven 'Principles of curriculum design' for schools, including challenge and enjoyment, personalisation and choice, and relevance.[9] The following year, BT4 contained a 'Skills Strategy' based around five 'core skills': communication, numeracy, problem-solving, information technology, and working with others.[10] In terms of teaching, the CfE favours child-centred approaches, with an emphasis placed on 'active learning'. From the early years to S6 (the Scottish equivalent of Year 13), schools are told to teach pupils through 'interdisciplinary projects and studies' as well as traditional subjects.[11] Tragically, for the home of some of the most important research into Systematic Synthetic Phonics ever conducted (see Chapter 1), the Scottish CfE makes no mention of this approach for teaching young children to read. Instead, it promotes 'mixed methods': a combination of approaches, including 'sight vocabulary', 'context clues', and some knowledge of phonics.[12]

Since 2010, the CfE—and its voluminous updates and supplementary guidance—have imposed a single teaching ideology on Scottish schools, granting them none of the free market in ideas that English schools enjoy. However, this centralisation of teaching methods has been accompanied by a relaxation in accountability measures. Between 2003 and 2017, there were no externally marked assessments for Scottish primary school pupils, and secondary exams have become increasingly modular and coursework-based. This has limited the amount of comparable data available for measuring the CfE's impact, an issue compounded by Scotland's decision to pull out of the PIRLS international literacy survey after 2006. In addition, Education Scotland—the executive agency tasked with running Scotland's schools since 2011—discontinued its annual sampling of literacy and numeracy standards at primary schools in 2017. The Scottish schools' inspectorate, HMIE, visits schools on a sample basis rather than a regular rotation, and according to data from July 2023, 43 percent of Scottish schools had not been inspected in the last ten years.[13] In contrast to what we have built in England, theirs is a low autonomy, low accountability system.

Once upon a time, Scotland was seen as something of a redoubt against the progressivist ideology, particularly compared to their woolly-minded neighbours in England. However, whilst we have fought back against these ideas since 2010, the Scottish government has endorsed them at a national level. Scotland and England, in effect, swapped places, a point made by Lindsay Paterson, a Professor at the University of Edinburgh and prominent critic of the CfE. In a piece he wrote for the *TES* in September 2012, he observed that whilst the child-centred CfE was being pursued at home, Scotland's 'old tradition' of academically rigorous, comprehensive education was being revived in England by one of their absent sons, Michael Gove. As he wrote:

> At no previous point in Scottish policy have child-centred ideas been as central as they are now. . . . Where Scottish educational philosophy used to be pre-eminently about common knowledge and common absolute standards, these values are now widely regarded here in public debate as rigid, of little help in practice, and conservative.[14]

However, few of Paterson's peers shared his concerns. At the time of its introduction, media coverage of the CfE was highly positive, as council officials, headteachers, school inspectors, and educationists weighed in to offer enthusiastic support. In 2009, a headteacher at a school in the Highlands wrote in the *TES* that the CfE 'is founded on a new collegiate and participatory culture'. He continued in the millennial tones typical of edu-speak at the time: 'the shifts in the content and nature of curriculum, and the forms and methods of learning for pupils, may then be matched by a similarly transformative change in how Scottish education reviews itself and learns about learning.'[15] Politicians from the Labour and Liberal Democrats parties, as well as the Scottish Nationalist Party (SNP), all supported the CfE. In August 2009, one year before the CfE would become mandatory for Scottish schools, the SNP Cabinet Secretary for Education Fiona Hyslop praised 'the biggest transformational development in Scottish education for decades.' She predicted:

> We are on the threshold of an exciting future for Scottish education. Our aim is to help all young people in Scotland to take their place in a modern society and economy. Curriculum for Excellence is ambitious, because it needs to be. Now is the time to charge this effort with the innovation and energy that comes with a fresh year and a new start.[16]

Fifteen years on, few in Scotland would suggest that Hyslop's optimism has been vindicated. On the contrary, the one word which now routinely appears in media coverage of Scottish schools is 'crisis'. Just consider the following recent headlines from Scotland's own print media: 'Scottish education crisis: Successive SNP ministers have just accepted the decline of our education system', *The Scotsman*, 8 December 2023; 'Slipping Scottish school standards: Who's to blame? All of us', *The Herald*, 9 December 2023; 'Once rated among the best in the world, Scottish schools are in crisis', *Edinburgh Evening News*, 1 April 2024.

Much of this concern has been driven by Scotland's falling results in the PISA international league tables, particularly when compared to England. In Maths, Scotland's 15-year-olds have gone from leading the home nations in 2009 with a ranking of 19th to being third in 2022 with a ranking of 32nd, compared to England's ranking of 11th (see Figure 0.1 in the Introduction). In reading, the results of Scottish pupils have been more stable but have slipped behind England into second place amongst the home nations since 2015 (see Figure 0.2). In Science, Scotland and England were neck and neck in 2009, but Scottish scores have been in freefall since 2012, to the point where—in 2022—England ranked 13th, whilst Scotland ranked 32nd (see Figure 0.3). It should be noted that English pupils also saw a decline in their science scores from 2006 to 2022. However, science scores have fallen across participating nations since PISA switched from a paper-based to a computer-based science assessment in 2015. Therefore, the fall in England's science score of 13 points from 2006 to 2022 can probably be attributed to changes in PISA's methodology. However, Scotland's fall of 32 points over the same period cannot.

Following the publication of the latest round of PISA results in December 2023, some Scottish politicians tried to explain away their falling scores, citing the Covid pandemic, but few were convinced. Scotland's falling scores pre-date 2020, and—whilst most participating countries saw their results fall from 2018 to 2022—Scotland's fall in both mathematics and science were all larger than the

OECD mean. Previously, the Director for Education and Skills at the OECD, Andreas Schleicher, had written positively about Scottish education reform, claiming in a 2021 OECD report commissioned by the Scottish Government:

> The current report provides one more opportunity for countries to learn from Scotland's inspiring experience. . . . The OECD team finds that CfE continues to offer a vision and a philosophy of education widely supported and worth pursuing.[17]

However, in 2023, he was reported to have observed rather more candidly, 'I think the last years have not been so great in Scotland.'[18]

Scotland's falling academic standards have been accompanied by a crisis in pupil behaviour, which many attribute to their government's promotion of permissive behaviour policies. Whilst we made it easier for English schools to exclude violent or severely disruptive pupils from 2010 onwards and have encouraged the reasonable use of sanctions, the Scottish government has limited the use of exclusions and promoted 'restorative conversations' in place of sanctions.[19] Since 2006, the Scottish government has regularly surveyed teachers about classroom behaviour. Their most recent 'Behaviour in Scottish Schools' survey from 2023 showed an extremely troubling rise in disruptive, violent, and abusive behaviour. The proportion of primary school teachers experiencing physical violence towards other pupils at least once a week increased from 32 percent in 2016 to 46 percent in 2023, whilst the proportion of secondary school teachers witnessing violent behaviour in the week before they were surveyed climbed from 15 percent in 2016 to 36 percent in 2023.[20] Over the same period, the proportion of secondary teachers 'sometimes' using detentions fell from 80 percent to less than 60 percent.[21]

As ever with severe disruption in schools, the personal stories that lie behind these figures are tragic. In July 2024, *The Scotsman* obtained 70 pages of communications from the Cabinet Secretary for Education Jenny Gilruth through a Freedom of Information Act request. It showed that during her first year in office from March 2023, Gilruth was inundated with parents, pupils, and teachers writing to her with their concerns about behaviour in schools. Some contained horrifying stories: pupils bringing knives into schools; teachers being attacked, spat at, and bitten; and children being traumatised by their classroom experiences to the point of bed-wetting. Much of this behaviour, parents and pupils alleged, was going unpunished. One correspondent even threatened a parent and pupil strike at their school, writing:

> The school my children currently attend has seen a massive increase in violent, abusive, and disruptive behaviours and if nothing is done to help it become a safer environment, I intend to organise a strike for our children. It seems this is the only way anyone will sit up and pay attention.

One pupil wrote to Gilruth about the bullying they experienced and their school's failure to deal with it. They concluded, 'If I was to say that I'm concerned for the future of Scottish education that would be an understatement.' Another correspondent, responding to what they saw as Gilruth's unwillingness to accept responsibility for the crisis, wrote, 'I am baffled, disappointed and feeling fairly hopeless about the future direction of Scottish education.'[22]

It is this sense of hopelessness evident in so much recent coverage of Scottish schools that concerns me most. It is bad enough that things are going so wrong in Scotland, but worse still that nobody appears to see a way out of it. Money is not the answer. Schools in Scotland have long been better funded than in England, and the gap has grown over the past 15 years: per pupil spending in Scotland was £8,500 in 2022–23, some £1,300 more than in England.[23] Innovation is rare, as power remains firmly in the hands of the devolved government and its 32 local authorities. Both seem stuck in the same progressivist thoughtworld, and cannot bring themselves to accept the misguided nature of the CfE or their permissive approach to pupil behaviour. I am sure there are many Scottish teachers on the ground who are desperate to try alternative approaches, but they do not have the autonomy to do so. Writing in the Scottish edition of the *Sunday Times* in October 2023, Gillian Bowditch recognised that it is teachers who make a good education system, but in Scotland, they are helpless. As she explained:

> [Teachers] have been sidelined by process, bureaucracy, self-serving unions and cynical quangos; Education Scotland and the Scottish Qualification Authority with your combined £100 million-plus budgets, I am looking at you. The regression in educational standards will have far-reaching negative consequences for current pupils and for Scotland and that is before the current industrial action bites. Education in Scotland is no longer fit for purpose.[24]

Even more precipitous a decline in the PISA tables than Scotland's has been that of Wales. Their 2022 scores saw declines from 2018 of 21 points in maths, 17 points in reading, and 15 points in science, above the average Covid-19-induced decline for most OECD nations. This decline follows on from the decision in 2015 of the Welsh government to overhaul its curriculum and introduce a new approach inspired directly by Scotland's Curriculum for Excellence. As in Scotland, the new Curriculum for Wales is almost exclusively focused around the development of general skills. It defines its four key purposes as developing children who are:

- ambitious, capable learners, ready to learn throughout their lives;
- enterprising, creative contributors, ready to play a full part in life and work;
- ethical, informed citizens of Wales and the world;
- healthy, confident individuals, ready to lead fulfilling lives as valued members of society.[25]

These are all commendable aspirations but not the basis for a rigorous and academically coherent curriculum. As Lucy Crehan, an international education consultant based in Wales, wrote in the *TES* in May 2024, such an approach leads to unequal opportunities, as schools interpret 'high-level, somewhat ambiguous statements' in very different ways. It also leads to challenges for pupils and teachers during the transition from primary school to secondary school, as there is no shared understanding of what pupils do and do not already know.[26]

Along with their new curriculum, Wales have—similarly to Scotland— abolished school league tables, made inspections less high-stakes, and allowed a large amount of coursework to take the place of exams in secondary school qualifications. What is more, they have had no reforms equivalent to England's academies policy: all schools remain under the management of local government. The level of educational failure now taking place in Wales—particularly for pupils from a disadvantaged background—is quite appalling, as laid bare in a recent Institute for Fiscal Studies (IFS) report published in 2024, 'Major challenges for education in Wales.' As the IFS showed, none of the common explanations for educational failure—poverty, high levels of immigration, government spending—can explain why children in England are doing so much better than in Wales. Disadvantaged children in England scored on average 30 points higher in the PISA tests than disadvantaged children in Wales. In fact, the performance of disadvantaged children in England is either above or similar to the average for all children in Wales.[27]

I take no pleasure in reading about the crisis in Scottish and Welsh education and the hundreds of thousands of children being let down by their schools. Nobody who designed this future for their schools during the 2000s and 2010s did so with the knowledge that it was a recipe for failure. However, when designing their respective curriculums and school systems, they did allow any appraisal of robust education research to be obscured by idealistic notions of how children learn. Beware the tragedy of good intentions.

It would be wrong of me to claim that English schools do not face many of the same challenges as those referenced previously. As in Scotland, pupil behaviour and absenteeism worsened following the Covid pandemic, particularly in disadvantaged areas. England, Scotland, and Wales are alike in worrying about teacher recruitment, industrial action, and pupils' use of smartphones. However, in England, these concerns are not discussed with the same tone of helplessness as in Scotland. Reading the coverage of the Scottish crisis, I am struck by how instinctively commentators, parents, and politicians look to the central government for the solution. It is the Cabinet Secretary for Education, the Scottish Education agency, and local authorities who are expected to come up with the answer, releasing yet another strategy, initiative, or report. And you cannot blame them—schools have no autonomy to find solutions for themselves. In many ways, the debate surrounding education in Scotland reminds me of the exasperated tone there was in England when I took on the opposition brief in 2005. However, there is one key difference: Scotland does not have their own Andrew Adonis nor an early academies policy providing some light at the end of the tunnel.

A MAT-led School System

How different the situation is in England today. Whilst central government still oversees our education system, the process of school improvement is now school-led, or perhaps more accurately, Multi-Academy Trust-led. By the time I left office in November 2023, it was at the Multi-Academy Trust (MAT) level that I could see the most potential for system-wide improvement. Much was said when we first gained power about the merits of school autonomy, and we did—to an extent—make good on those claims: the freedom enjoyed by converter academies and free schools is unprecedented in recent English history. However, it would be wrong to claim that school autonomy was spread evenly. Some academies which are part of a MAT may now have a similar level of autonomy to those of a local authority school. If the school has been failing and was forcibly converted under the sponsorship of a MAT, it probably has less autonomy than previously. However, this is a beneficial evolution of the academies policy. When the policy began, nobody quite realised how significant a component MATs would become, but they are now the main engine of school improvement in England.

Of course, the current landscape in terms of MAT size and quality is varied. At the time of writing, there are 1,180 MATs overseeing two or more academies in England. This is actually fewer than in 2019, but as the number of MATs has been falling, their average size has—through a process of consolidation—been growing, from 6.25 academies per MAT in 2019 to 8.5 today.[28] Some 324 MATs, more than a quarter of the total, have ten academies or more. As suggested in Chapter 6, it is worth remembering how novel this landscape in England is. In 2010, 99 percent of English state schools were overseen by their local authority. Today, that figure is 49 percent (the majority being primary schools), with 46 percent of schools overseen by a MAT and 5 percent existing as 'stand-alone' academies.[29] From a standing start of hardly existing 15 years ago, MATs are approaching the point where they oversee the majority of England's schools.

The best MATs have a clearly articulated and evidence-led vision for the education offered by their schools and use that vision to encourage collaboration. They identify what is working in their best-performing academies, and encourage others to adopt those approaches, be it curriculum resources, staff training, or behaviour systems. As such, they give high-performing members of staff the opportunity to paint on a much wider canvas than their own school, leading trust-wide initiatives to improve attainment. In an effective MAT, the level of school autonomy is not fixed. 'Earned autonomy' has become a popular term for the process whereby struggling schools are given clear direction on what to do differently, with the promise that if they improve, they will then gain the freedom to refine their approach. As is popularly observed, you can mandate adequacy, but excellence has to be unleashed.

Needless to say, this does not currently serve as a description of every MAT in the country. In March 2016, during the early growing pains of MATs, Michael Wilshaw wrote to Nicky Morgan following Ofsted's inspection of seven large, underperforming MATs with some typically forthright observations. 'Many of the trusts manifested the same weaknesses as the worst performing local authorities', he wrote, 'and offered the same excuses'. Wilshaw was concerned these Trusts were tolerating underperformance amongst their schools and disavowing themselves of the responsibility for their improvement.[30] However, the difference between underperforming MATs and underperforming local authorities is that the former can be shrunk or closed down, whilst the latter has their continued existence guaranteed. This means that MATs can be held accountable for their results in a way that local authorities never were, as is demonstrated by the fact that three of the seven large trusts inspected by Ofsted and referred to by Wilshaw in his 2016 letter no longer exist. This accountability of MATs for their own performance is creating a new dynamism in England's education system, directing our schools towards effective practices far more readily than ever before.

Today, I am reassured by the calibre and educational outlook of the incoming generation of MAT leaders. An increasing number of CEOs who I meet appear to be plugged into the evidence revolution in English education and keen to drive improvement within their trusts by learning from England's highest-performing schools. We must keep in perspective the pace at which such improvements will occur: if it takes years to turn around a school, it might take a decade to turn around a Trust (and a lifetime to turn around a nation's education system). However, MATs are making progress in the right direction. Previous chapters have covered the approach to school improvement taken by two pioneering early MATs, the Harris Federation and Ark Schools. Today, there is a far wider range I could cite for doing similarly impressive work. In 2016, the DfE began publishing annual league tables for MATs. By 2023, there were 19 MATs with ten or more secondary schools entering pupils for GCSEs, whom we could rank according to their average Progress 8 score. This is a challenging measure in which to do well, as large MATs have the responsibility to sponsor failing schools, each adding a downward pressure on their average score. Therefore, any large MAT with a positive Progress 8 score is—to my mind—clearly doing something right (see Table 12.1).

Fourth on the list in Table 12.1, with more secondary schools than any other MAT in England, is United Learning, where Jon Coles is Chief Executive. When I joined the DfE, Jon was our Director General for Education Standards. Having trained as a maths teacher, Jon had spent most of his civil service career at the DfE, where he was made a director in 2002. Still only 36 years old, he was given the responsibility to lead the London Challenge in 2003, doing so to great acclaim. By 2010, Jon had been promoted to Director General. However, in January 2012, Jon left the DfE to become Chief Executive of United Learning, then a growing Multi-Academy Trust of 20 schools.

Table 12.1 MATs with ten or more secondary schools and a positive average Progress 8 score in 2023[31]

MAT	# Secondary Schools	P8
1. Star Academies	18	0.63
2. Greenshaw Learning Trust	10	0.39
3. Harris Federation	26	0.32
4. United Learning	43	0.24
5. Delta Academies Trust	16	0.15
6. Ark Schools	20	0.14
7. Redhill Academy Trust	10	0.01

United Learning was an unusual Trust, tracing its existence back to 1883 when it began life as the Church Schools Company. For the following century, it ran around 12 independent schools with a Church of England ethos, including some of the most academically successful in the country. When Andrew Adonis launched the academies policy in 2000, the Church Schools Company answered his call to expand their mission to state schooling, and in 2003 took on sponsorship of the Manchester Academy. With over a century of experience running schools, the Church Schools Company had the in-house expertise to expand its academies offshoot—the United Learning Trust—with speed, becoming the largest MAT in England by the time Jon took over in 2012. That year, he merged the Church Schools Company and its academies offshoot into a single institution, United Learning. It remains England's largest MAT today, with 90 academies stretching from the south coast to Carlisle. Unlike other successful MATs, United Learning has never specialised in a particular type of school or geographical area. However, it has avoided the pitfalls characteristic of early 'empire building' MATs. Instead, it has sustained its success as it has grown, as Table 12.1 demonstrates.

Overseeing such a diverse range of schools, United Learning has not developed the same level of centralisation you might see at a trust such as Harris or Ark. In the recent 'education wars' over different teaching methods, Jon retained the studied impartiality of a civil servant, showing—perhaps wisely—no interest in identifying his Trust with any particular tribe. However, United Learning schools do take a fundamentally evidence-led approach to teaching, and there are many commonalities they share. Their primary schools all use systematic synthetic phonics schemes, whilst their secondary schools teach a subject-based curriculum with a focus on 'powerful knowledge'—one of the Trust's five guiding principles. Both primary and secondary schools use Doug Lemov's *Teach Like A Champion* and Barak Rosenshine's 'Principles of Instruction' to provide a shared language for teaching across the Trust. All schools have systems of sanctions and rewards, clear uniform expectations, and emphasise the importance of 'disruption-free classrooms'.[32]

Jon's decision to move from the DfE to a MAT and his subsequent success whilst there is an indication of where the power now lies in England's education system. Jon claims it was during a conversation with Gus O'Donnell, the head of Britain's civil service, that his mind was made up. He was told that, in keeping with the generalist ethos of the civil service, his next job should be out of education. Not wanting to give up a career serving England's schools, he decided his next job would instead be out of the civil service. He moved to United Learning to make a reality on the ground of the academy system he had helped to design on paper. 'If it goes as it ought to do,' he told me for this book, 'it should be the Burkean small platoons such as MATs which are leading change and driving improvement.'

Ark, Harris, and United Learning are all based in London. However, the single highest performing large MAT in England at the secondary level—Star Academies— is based in Lancashire, northwest England. As such, it has escaped much of the political and public attention received by London-based MATs. However, its remarkable story deserves to be told. It has its origins in the Tauheedul Islam Girls High School (TIGHS), an independent faith school run from a row of terraced houses in Blackburn. In 2000, TIGHS began the process of joining England's state sector, and—with the help of their local MP, the Labour Foreign Secretary Jack Straw—they became England's first Muslim faith school to do so in 2006. The headteacher at the time was Hamid Patel, who had previously taught in adult education. However, years of helping adults compensate for their unsuccessful school careers gave him a desire to address this problem at source, particularly for Blackburn's south-Asian community which was at risk of social isolation due to their lack of basic skills and qualifications. Under Hamid's leadership, TIGHS became one of England's highest-performing state comprehensive schools, with almost every pupil achieving 5 A* to C, including English and Maths at GCSE each year.

Hamid puts much of his success down to the fact that, as a faith school, TIGHS took its teaching approach from a different tradition from the progressivist orthodoxy that characterised mainstream English education. TIGHS had high expectations for pupil behaviour common to many other faith schools and took its inspiration for teaching approaches from high-performing countries such as China and Singapore. Though he approached it from a different intellectual tradition, Hamid reached many of the same conclusions as those involved in the evidence revolution in English schools. As he told me, 'TIGHS embraced the knowledge-rich curriculum before the concept became fashionable because of a deep-seated belief that knowledge is power. It is the lack of knowledge suffered by disadvantaged young people that limits their participation in important aspects of life.'

Early on in TIGHS's success, Hamid became Executive Headteacher of a nearby school in Blackburn with a predominantly white-working class community and helped it become the third most improved school in the country. This experience gave him a taste for spreading their recipe for success further afield, and—when we gained office in 2010—Hamid was one of the most enterprising participants in the early academies programme. In August 2010, he established the Tauheedul Education Trust and set upon his plan of expansion. Whilst it took six years for TIGHS to join the state sector in the 2000s, he told me—admiringly—that with Michael Gove at the DfE the same process could be achieved in six months. He established Tauheedul Islam Boys' High School in 2012 and their first London free school in 2013. From 2014 to 2015, he established six faith-based Muslim secondary schools in Coventry, Bolton, Birmingham, Slough, London and Preston. Then, in 2016, the Tauheedul Education Trust sponsored its first mainstream academies with no faith ethos, starting with one in Blackpool and two in Bradford. Hamid had to work hard to reassure the local communities in Blackpool and Bradford that—despite being overseen by an Academy Trust with its origins in Muslim-faith schools—their schools would remain secular. In order to reflect their expansion away from solely running faith schools, Hamid changed Tauheedul Education Trust's name to Star Academies in 2018.

Star Academies currently has 20 Muslim faith-based schools, one Christian faith school, and 15 secular schools. As such, Hamid has established an overall Trust vision which is applicable to both its Muslim and secular schools. A close follower of education debates, Hamid has incorporated much of England's evidence revolution into his Trust's operations, using Doug Lemov's teaching techniques to inform his own Trust-wide teaching vision, 'Teach like a Star'. The results being achieved by Star Academies are entirely unmatched, with five of the top ten schools in England for Progress 8 belonging to the Trust in 2023 and three of the top ten in 2024—an astonishing achievement. Hamid's most recent venture is a partnership with Eton College to address how academically high-achieving pupils from underserved areas of the country can be put on a pathway to university degrees. Calling itself a 'think and do tank', the Eton Star Partnership currently plans to open a number of academically selective sixth-form colleges in the north of England—an exciting prospect for English education.

It is sometimes suggested that faith schools hinder integration and exacerbate community division. However, whenever I have visited the schools belonging to Star Academies, this is not what I see. Instead, I see schools giving pupils from deprived backgrounds the taste of educational success and putting them on the path to successful careers and universities—one of the best guards against social isolation there is. What is more, with so many students from Star Academies' all-girls schools going to university, Hamid is a trailblazer for female education within Britain's Muslim community. In the early days of the Tauheedul Education Trust, there was some media concern about what was being taught at their schools. However, multiple Ofsted visits left us with no reason to doubt that their schools were teaching a broad and balanced curriculum with an ethos entirely compatible with modern British values. In 2021, Hamid Patel received a knighthood from the

Queen, the first Mufti ever to do so. The academies policy has given Hamid the opportunity to become not just an inspiring leader within Britain's education system but also within Britain's Muslim community.

I could continue to describe many, many more MATs and their leaders, which provided me with inspiration during my time as Schools Minister. Suffice it to say, it is in the growing institutional strength of MATs that I see the future of our self-improving school system. As the 'think and do tank' activity of the Eton Star Partnership shows, our large MATs now have the talent and resources to be significant drivers of change within England's education system. In all areas of school life, from curriculum design to pastoral care, the best new ideas in our education system are not coming from Quangos, the Education Department, universities, or the teaching unions. They are coming from MATs.

Amongst MATs, Ark Schools was early to this game. Its origins as part of a wider charity focused on helping children's life chances meant that—from the beginning—they took an outward-looking stance. This has translated into some 20 different ventures incubated by Ark but now used by schools across the country. Some are in obvious areas, such as Ark Curriculum Plus, which provides lesson plans and schemes of work in core curriculum areas, such as their English Mastery, Mathematics Mastery, and Science Mastery programmes. For schools looking for external help in improving their curriculum, Ark Curriculum Plus provides thoroughly road-tested resources that anyone can purchase and use. Ark Schools also helped to incubate the Ambition Institute, a teacher training provider which specialises in evidence-led, high-quality training for teachers working in schools with disadvantaged intakes. Last year, Ambition Institute worked with some 46,000 teachers and school leaders.

Other ventures from Ark have been more esoteric but no less impactful, such as Assembly, a software programme by Ark from 2016 onwards. Assembly allows a school's MIS (standing for Management Information Software, where schools store all of their pupil and workforce information) to share its data with other apps or programmes, such as online quizzing tools, grade books, curriculum platforms, or behaviour management systems. Ark correctly identified that the inability of schools to share data safely with third-party providers was a key factor inhibiting innovation in education technology. Assembly was their solution. Its creation has led to a flourishing of popular software programmes for teachers and schools to use, all of which can seamlessly integrate with their MIS.

Small and large trusts have been able to develop successful ventures. The Knowledge Schools Trust is based in West London and consists of seven primary schools and two secondary schools. At the primary level, the Trust created a knowledge-based curriculum inspired by E. D. Hirsch. Initially intended for internal use, the Primary Knowledge Curriculum was soon in high demand as a rare example of a curriculum resource for primary schools which is broken down into traditional academic subjects instead of cross-curricular 'project work'. Since becoming commercially available, it has been purchased in full by almost 400 schools looking to boost the academic challenge of their primary curriculum. The innovation provided by Academy Trusts was evident in the early days of the Covid-19 pandemic, when the Reach Foundation, a sister charity to Reach Academy Feltham, devised the Oak National Academy. Starting from scratch after the announcement of a nationwide lockdown in March 2020, Oak National Academy liaised with teachers across the country to create online lessons which would be freely available for pupils. Within two months, it had delivered 13 million lessons—an achievement which no arm of public sector bureaucracy could ever have achieved with the same agility.

One of the last major projects I was involved with whilst at the Department for Education was the development of the National Institute of Teaching, a new teacher training organisation we launched in January 2021. As covered in Chapter 11, most teachers entering the profession still want to gain a Post Graduate Certificate of Education (PGCE). The PGCE is not a requirement to be a teacher, but it does have the most market recognition of any teaching qualifications. As a post-graduate qualification, only universities can deliver PGCEs, and because it is so notoriously difficult to create new universities with degree-awarding powers, no new entrants to the market can create innovative PGCE programmes from scratch. We hoped a new National Institute of Teaching could design teacher training courses which reflected the evidence revolution happening elsewhere in English education and then work towards becoming a university with degree-awarding powers.

Different organisations were permitted to bid for the National Institute contract, and in May 2022, we announced a coalition of four leading academy trusts as the preferred bidder. They were the Harris Federation (see Chapter 8) and Hamid Patel's Star Academies, as well as two other trusts—Oasis Community Learning, a large Trust operating throughout England, and the Outwood Grange Academies Trust, which operates in the north of England and the East Midlands.[33] Together, these four trusts have pooled their expertise and geographical spread to develop the National Institute in four locations across England, and hope to have degree awarding powers by the start of the academic year 2025. These four trusts, none of which even existed 20 years ago, are now providing innovation in post-graduate teacher training—an area that had always been the exclusive preserve of universities. This shows just how far power has shifted from the old education establishment and towards schools. When in the 2010 White Paper, we wrote of creating a school system which is 'self-improving', this is what we meant.[34] We knew that our job as government was not just to find solutions for schools but to build an education system where schools can find solutions for each other.

Today, the innovation of academies and free schools, and the growing expertise of MATs, has—I hope—gone some way to making this a reality. Notwithstanding any major overhaul by a different government, this is the new reality in English education: MATs are pioneering solutions to myriad school problems, successful schools are helping struggling schools to improve, and good ideas are crowding out bad. This, I hope, will be our legacy.

Notes

1 'Rethinking Assessment: Mutant exam system is failing our children—Open Letter', *The Times*, 26 September 2020.

2 N. Plaister, 'Why were GCSE grades in independent schools so high during the pandemic?', *FFT Education Datalab*, 29 June 2022.

3 R. Long and N. Roberts, *Research Briefing: School attendance in England*, House of Commons Library, 2024, p. 8.

4 'The strange success of the Tories' schools policy', *The Economist*, 13 July 2023.

5 H. Rumbelow, 'The one thing I am grateful to Tories for', *The Times*, 1 July 2024.

6 E. Duncan, 'On schools, the Tories were a class act', *The Times*, 5 December 2024.

7 'England's school reforms are earning fans abroad', *The Economist*, 7 July 2024.

8 *A Curriculum for Excellence: Building the Curriculum 1—The Contribution of Curriculum Areas*, Scottish Executive, 2006.

9 *A Curriculum for Excellence: Building the Curriculum 3—A Framework for Learning and Teaching*, The Scottish Government, 2008.

10 *A Curriculum for Excellence: Building the Curriculum 4—Skills for Learning, Skills for Life, and Skills for Work*, The Scottish Government, 2009.

11 *A Curriculum for Excellence: Building the Curriculum 3*, p. 41.

12 Taken from the fantastic comparative report into reading instruction in the United Kingdom and Ireland: J. Buckingham, *An Investigation of Literacy Instruction and Policy in the United Kingdom and Ireland*, Churchill Fellowship, 2004.

13 R. McCurdy, 'Half of Scots state schools "not inspected in a decade"', *The Scotsman*, 9 July 2023.

14 L. Paterson, 'Gove's exams could shed light on our two traditions', *TES Magazine*, 28 September 2012.

15 N. MacKinnon, 'Two cultures of a child-centred approach', *TES Magazine*, 27 November 2009.

16 F. Hyslop, 'Take charge with a fresh, new start', *TES Magazine*, 21 August 2009.

17 OECD, *Scotland's Curriculum for Excellence: Into the Future, Implementing Education Policies*, Paris: OECD Publishing, 2001, p. 3.

18 H. Puttick, 'Scotland's failings revealed in first Pisa scores since pandemic', *The Times*, 5 December 2023.

19 *Behaviour in Scottish Schools 2023*, The Scottish Government, 2023, p. 10.

20 *Behaviour in Scottish Schools 2023*, pp. 72–75.

21 *Behaviour in Scottish Schools 2023*, p. 144.

22 'Parents' threat to take school children out on strike is a wake-up call for SNP government', *The Scotsman*, 14 July 2024.

23 L. Sibieta, *How Does School Spending per Pupil Differ Across the UK?*, Institute for Fiscal Studies, 2023, p. 13.

24 G. Bowditch, 'Our education system is bottom of the class', *The Sunday Times*, 29 October 2023.

25 Welsh Government, *Curriculum for Wales*, 2019.

26 L. Crehan, 'The new curriculum challenges shared by Scotland and Wales', *TES Magazine*, 14 May 2024.

27 L. Sibieta, *Major Challenges for Education in Wales*, Institute for Fiscal Studies, 2024.

28 N. Plaister, 'The current state of play for MATs', *FFT Education Datalab*, 10 July 2024.

29 Figure compiled from Department for Education statistical release.

30 M. Wilshaw letter to Secretary of State N. Morgan, 'Focused inspections of academies in multi-academy trusts', 10 March 2016.

31 Figure compiled from Department for Education statistical release.

32 See online documents entitled 'The United Learning Way' for primary, secondary, and independent schools in the Trust.

33 Department for Education, 'Press release: Teacher training to ensure excellent teachers in every classroom', 26 May 2022.

34 *White Paper: The Importance of Teaching*, p. 13.

Conclusion

When my co-author, Robert Peal, came to work at the Department for Education as my policy adviser in August 2015, I said to him that our objective was to change the whole education philosophy driving practice and curriculum in our schools—to change permanently the zeitgeist. As I uttered these words, I thought it was a fanciful ambition, so entrenched was the progressivist ideology in the UK's education system. Nevertheless, it remained our objective and continued to drive policy.

Ten years on from that conversation, there is a strong case to be made that the educational zeitgeist in England has changed from one dominated by progressivist, child-centred orthodoxies to one led by evidence. Across the English school system, the term 'knowledge-rich' is embedded in the lexicon of curriculum development; interactive, teacher-led teaching is the dominant approach to instruction, 'warm-strict' behaviour policies are recognised as beneficial, and systematic synthetic phonics is the prevailing method of teaching children to read in primary school.

In multi-academy trusts such as ARK, Advantage Schools, Astrea Academy Trust, Dixons Academies Trust, Delta Academies Trust, Future Academies, Harris Federation, Knowledge Schools Trust, Lift Schools, Northern Education Trust, Outwood Grange Academies Trust, Reach Schools, Star Academies, Twyford CofE Academies Trust, United Learning and—I am sure—many others about which I am not as aware, these are the ideas that are driving their most successful schools.

Ten years ago, absurd notions such as 'learning styles', 'multiple intelligences', and 'brain gym' infuriated well-meaning professionals. Today, they seem like a distant memory from another age. In their place, evidence-based practice has become commonplace.

In order to endure, new intellectual currents have to be buttressed by institutions and practices. When I first took an interest in knowledge-based teaching, it was almost impossible to demonstrate what this meant in practice. There were few exemplar schools to visit or current teachers to see. In terms of resources, I had to purchase long-out-of-print textbooks, those published specifically for the independent sector, or curriculum resources from abroad, such as Hirsch's Core

DOI: 10.4324/9781003533474-14

Knowledge series, to imagine how knowledge-based teaching might appear in English state schools. Today, the situation could not be more different. I can no longer keep up with the volume of newly available knowledge-based teaching resources being designed for pupils in subjects across the curriculum and key stages. These range from innovative online platforms to textbook series which blend a content-rich approach to knowledge with cutting-edge thinking on curriculum design.

Today, we know so much more about how children learn and about how the brain functions when performing higher-order activities. From E. D. Hirsch to John Sweller to Daniel Willingham, our understanding of cognitive load theory allows us to dismiss with confidence the notion that important skills such as critical thinking and problem-solving can be taught as subjects in their own right rather than as the products of rich, domain-specific knowledge.

These new ideas have only been able to embed themselves within English schools due to the structural reforms that we pursued from 2010 onwards. School autonomy has allowed debates over curriculum and teaching methods to move from the abstract theorising of academics and into teachers' classrooms. The consequence? The further schools have moved away from the progressivist orthodoxy, the better their pupils have attained. The very fact that today, there is a state comprehensive school with a socially deprived intake in north-west London, where roughly the same proportion of pupils gain top grades at GCSE as at Eton College, becomes no less remarkable each time you read it.*

However, as I argue in Chapter 3, the transformational power of the academy movement is not autonomy (which is crucial), but emulation. The bold visions that institutions such as Mossbourne Academy, King Solomon Academy, and Michaela Community School were able to pioneer are now being emulated by hundreds, if not thousands, of schools across the country. Research papers, conference speeches, and academic debates can only take a movement so far. However, nobody can ignore the existence of outstanding schools where pupils from deprived backgrounds perform as well as their peers at the most exclusive schools in the country.

Our reforms—sustained, protected, and built upon over nearly 15 years—made this possible, but it was teachers who seized the new freedoms and revolutionised our understanding of what makes good teaching. It is teachers who have now grasped the intellectual mantle and are developing their ideas and turning them into effective practice in their classrooms. First on blogs, then on Twitter, and now in podcasts and an ever-growing number of books and teaching resources, the evidence revolution in English education shows no signs of stopping. In fact, watching it develop was one of the most enjoyable and satisfying experiences of my time as a minister.

Revealingly, university education faculties have been—with one or two exceptions—notable only by their absence from such debates. In their place, conferences of teachers

---

* The school is, of course, Michaela Community School, where 52 percent of their pupils' entries at GCSE achieved a Grade 9 in 2024, compared to 53 percent of GCSE entries at Eton College.

such as researchEd have proliferated. From its first event held in South London in 2013, researchEd has gone global, with conferences now having been held across six continents, most recently in Sweden, Australia, the USA, Chile, South Africa, and Dubai.

Internationally, interest in England's reforms continues to rise. This is no doubt due to our improving performance in the PISA and PIRLS league tables, but also due to the novel nature of our reforms. Since standing down as a government minister in November 2023, I have started to attend conferences around the world talking about our reforms. And, while it frustrates me that the mood music at some of these events is still the comforting, child-centred platitudes of the progressivist ideology, England's experience is being recognised, and delegates, including ministers, are keen to hear the gospel of a knowledge-based curriculum.

The same debates that took place in England ten years ago are now underway in Australia, New Zealand, and various American States, as well as in European countries such as Sweden, the Netherlands, and Belgium and increasingly in Asia and the Middle East.

The signs so far are promising. In 2019, South Australia introduced a phonics screening check modelled on ours, and a number of other States have since followed suit. In New Zealand, Education Secretary Erica Stanford is replacing her country's 2007 competence-based curriculum with a knowledge-rich curriculum, having sought inspiration from our own 2010 curriculum review. She is also introducing a phonics screening check.

In the USA, Emily Hanford's devastating podcast series, 'Sold a Story', has led to numerous States barring whole language strategies in the teaching of reading; in their place, they are emphasising the need for systematic synthetic phonics. I have recently had the fortune to attend conferences in Sweden and Belgium where their government ministers have been in attendance, and the prevailing progressivist ideology has been challenged. I have also been working in India and across the Middle East, where an increased focus on knowledge-rich curricula is challenging long-held assumptions about how children learn.

While there is room for much optimism that the tide is beginning to turn on the progressivist educational ideology around the world, in England, the political drive for reform has stalled. The Labour government elected in July 2024 shows little understanding of the reasons for England's rise in the international league tables. There has to date been no attempt to ensure that the worst performing schools adopt the practices and curriculum content that we know bring success. Curriculum and teaching methods are vital to this, but behaviour remains the *sine qua non* of any school turnaround. As every single one of the top-performing state schools in England demonstrates, pupils thrive when the culture is underpinned by clear and consistently enforced rules.

The drive to embed these reforms remains crucial. The academies programme must be allowed to continue its evolution into a multi-academy trust-led system, where groups of academies work together to deliver ever higher standards. In such a system, best practices will spread as trusts, competing to grow in both size and esteem and learning from each other. If the Labour Government wishes to continue the steady improvement in England's schools, it must encourage that development and resist the blandishments of teacher unions determined to halt progress in its tracks.

Tony Blair has spoken of the importance of consistency in policy between administrations of differing political hues as one reason for the success of his administration from 1997 to 2007. We need that consistency in education policy today. There will be many who argue either that our reforms have not led to an improved education system or that our focus on academic attainment has been damaging. Others will make the case that the challenging of education orthodoxies in England would have occurred in any case and have little to do with the reforms introduced from 2010. I hope that the explanations of policy-making set out in this book do something to counter such arguments.

I have no doubt that more needs to be done. The reform process is not complete. There are still challenges over teacher recruitment, particularly when the labour market demand for the best graduates is so strong, and there are challenges of increasing mental health problems amongst young people, in part driven by the pressures on them from social media and smartphone addiction. The quality of education for children with special educational needs and disabilities is still in need of reform, and there are post-Covid attendance and behaviour issues to tackle. What is more, an enormous outlay of money will be needed to maintain the fabric of England's 24,000 state schools at a time when funding will be very difficult to find.

Nevertheless, as I look back on the 20 years since I joined the House of Commons Education Select Committee, I do believe that England's schools have fundamentally changed for the better. This is due to the reform programme that Michael Gove and I led. Michael is a once-in-a-generation politician; working with him for three years in opposition and for two years as a minister was an honour and an experience. During that time, we learned a huge amount from planning for office and, once elected, driving through an extensive programme of reform. From these years and beyond, I have distilled ten key lessons about how to implement a successful reform programme, that I hope can be applied more broadly. These are, as the book's title promises, my reforming lessons.

1. Immerse yourself in the sector over a period of years to learn about its institutions, its challenges, and its strengths.

Ministers (or, better still, Shadow Ministers) need to immerse themselves in their sector, meeting practitioners and leading thinkers, in particular those who challenge received wisdom. If approached with an open mind, this immersion will reveal both the deep-seated problems confronting the sector and the seeds of their possible resolution.

We were lucky. I had five years as a Shadow Schools Minister, and Michael Gove had three as Shadow Education Secretary. When we came into government in 2010,

Prime Minister David Cameron was fully committed to the reform agenda that Michael and I had developed, and he shared our determination to drive through change. In other departments, either where the hard work of developing policy solutions had not been done or where the Prime Minister was less interested, Ministers were changed every few years, giving them little time—even if they were so inclined—to get to the heart of the problems they faced.

2. Question received wisdom and gain a deep understanding of the problems you are trying to solve.

It is important to invest time to understand the problems you are trying to solve rather than waste time responding to politically driven issues of the day. In education, the problem was falling academic standards, as evidenced by precipitous drops in our position in international league tables. The key issues were not school funding or inequality, or too much or too little sex or financial education, or the need for more or less discussion about climate change or the cost of school uniforms. The overwhelming issue was the progressivist ideology, particularly when it came to the content of the curriculum and the approach to teaching.

3. Identify the ideology underlying the problems you face and build the intellectual case to slay those sacred cows.

From 45 years of active political engagement, I have come to believe that ideology is at the root of most problems in public service delivery. By ideology, I do not just mean grand intellectual philosophies such as 'socialism'. Instead, I mean guiding principles which become orthodoxies within a sector and about which it becomes unthinkable to ask questions or challenge. This is true of almost all government departments, from the Treasury to Transport, Housing to Health. Such ideologies never defer to evidence, which is why they inevitably drive failure. Conservatives, by their nature, eschew ideology in favour of the practical. However, this can make them wary of challenging ideological positions in order to avoid appearing to be ideological themselves.

In education, Michael and I had spent our time before gaining office reading, speaking to teachers, and visiting schools. Coupled with the fact that Michael is a rare Conservative with a deep understanding of political philosophy, we gained confidence in our diagnosis that a Rousseauian ideology of progressive education was the fundamental problem in English schools. From the teaching of reading and maths, to the content of the wider curriculum, to pedagogy in the classroom, not to mention classroom configuration and behaviour policy, ideological progressivism was driving practice. And it was failing.

4. Only devise policy prescriptions once you have achieved a coherent analysis of the existing problems and ideology within a sector.

Only once a minister has a genuine understanding of the problems in a sector should they turn their minds to the potential solutions, lest the focus is diverted to important but less fundamental prescriptions. In education, our understanding that falling academic standards was the key issue drove a research-led move to understand why.

5. Test and test again the emerging policy proposals. Prepare the ground.

It is obviously important that policy prescriptions succeed in remedying the identified problems. Consultation with trusted experts and round table discussions with a wider range of opinion will help the emerging policy succeed and reveal the level of controversy it is likely to generate. You can then begin to make the case for the policy to key stakeholders or interest groups so that it will not come as a surprise in the sector when it is announced.

6. Identify those within the sector who share your understanding of its failings and involve them in implementing your solutions.

Finding allies within the sector is crucial for any reforming minister. They may not be your political friends (they may even vote for your political opponents), but if they share your analysis and passion, they will become your allies. Being overly partisan as a minister can deter potential allies from supporting your policies. In any case, the public is no longer as responsive to party political argy-bargy as it once was.

7. Do not assume others will carry out the painstaking work of policy implementation as effectively as is needed.

Policy can easily go off the rails if the details of implementation are not right. On even the smallest changes, ministers have to get into the weeds. Attention to detail is crucial. In Chapter 9, I wrote about the lengths to which I would go to ensure that the documentation for key policies was correct. Never underestimate the importance of getting the drafting right. It is not unheard of for civil servants to use ambiguous language in a deliberate attempt to nudge a policy with which they disagree, off course.

As a minister in the British government, you are given a Red Box of policy submissions to read each evening and over weekends. Reading everything in the Red Box is hugely important, as is challenging anything you don't understand. If there was something I did not understand, this was likely to be where problems lurked or where attempts to redirect a policy were hidden: subversion obscured by clumsy drafting. On the policies that mattered most, I had to challenge everything.

8. The battle of ideas is never won, so never stop making the case for what you believe.

As well as preparing the ground for a policy's announcement, it is essential to keep making the case for its rationale. As a Minister, you should never assume that once you have explained something on the prestigious 8.10am slot on BBC Radio 4's Today Programme, everyone will have heard about your policy and understood the reasons for its implementation. As Cecil Parkinson, a member of Margaret Thatcher's Cabinet, former Party Chairman, and my mentor and friend taught me long ago, one of the frustrations of being a politician is that after you have become sick of repeating the same arguments time and time again, the public will only just be beginning to hear it. If you ever think you are being boring by repeating the same message, you are wrong.

9. Keep the focus on your own reforming agenda by stopping bad policy from being introduced.

If you have developed a proper understanding of the problems you are trying to solve and have devised a full programme of policy prescriptions, it is important to be wary of policy proposals which will push your agenda off course. These will emanate from other ministers, including the Prime Minister and the Chancellor of the Exchequer, the civil service, the sector, lobbyists, and vested interests, and will be considerable in volume. In office, it often felt that we spent more time resisting well-meaning proposals that ran counter to our agenda rather than pursuing policies of our own.

10. Compromise when necessary, but do so judiciously.

I hated compromising. If you believe you have the right answers to, say, closing the educational attainment gap between disadvantaged children and their peers, why would you dilute that policy so that it is less effective? However, democracy inevitably requires compromise, and you have to take at least part of the sector with you if a policy is going to succeed. One of our key advisers, Chris Paterson (see Chapter 6), used to talk of achieving 7 out of 10 as a great outcome for some of our more controversial policies. As painful as I would find it, I learnt to accept 7 out of 10 if the alternative was a thumping zero.

But, I still believe that keeping compromise to a minimum is important to ensure the overall effectiveness of your programme. It can be tempting to compromise for political convenience rather than political necessity: anything for a quiet life. However, the risks are high, as every compromise comes at the price of chipping away at the effectiveness of your overall agenda.

* *

I began this journey in 2003 as a newly appointed member of the House of Commons Education Select Committee. During the 20 years that followed, I have been part of a reform programme that has achieved more than I could possibly have imagined. On the structural side, we have overhauled the management of schools in England through mass academisation and made schools—not universities—the predominant focal point for the training of new teachers. On the standards side, we have restored faith in the exam and assessment system and transformed school accountability. Most importantly, in doing so, we have incubated an evidence revolution in teaching methods and curriculum design within the profession. I was incredibly fortunate to have the opportunity to serve in government for such an extended period of time and to shape and oversee these changes.

As a result of our reforms, there is now an education ecosystem in England from which—if left alone—improvements will continue to emerge without the same need for ministerial direction. In 2010, we had an education system where 5 percent of secondary schools were academies. Today, that figure is 83 percent, and 43 percent of primary schools. In 2011, there were 66 multi-academy trusts (MATs) running schools in England; today, that figure is 1,180. It is within these organisations that the agency for further school improvement now lies.

Undoubtedly, the current government has the power either to enhance or frustrate such improvements. However, I do not believe they have the will or the political capital to undo the ecosystem we have created. This system of high autonomy and high accountability for schools now has its own momentum to move away from the progressivist ideology and towards practices with a proven track record of school success. However, even in the best-case scenario, the pace of such a movement will be slow. School improvement through challenging an orthodoxy is pegged to the pace at which teachers change their minds and the pace at which such teachers then attain positions of leadership in schools. There are decades left to go before this process might be complete nationwide. However, we are—at least—travelling in the right direction. My greatest hope is that there will be no turning back.

On that point, I am optimistic. Teachers and school leaders who have been freed from the dogma of the progressivist ideology are not readily going to return to its strictures, particularly when their new approaches are reaping such rich rewards for students. Meanwhile, the weight of evidence that schools succeed when they embrace the golden trio of evidence-based practice—knowledge-based curriculum, teacher-led lessons, and warm-strict behaviour policies—grows with every year.

English schools are already gaining international attention for their remarkable turnaround, and my abiding hope is that this is only the start of the revolution. It will be hard fought, but I believe it is possible. The legacy of such an achievement will be immense. Generations of future adults may look back on their school days not as a source of frustration and regret but with gratitude for the brilliant institutions and inspiring teachers who gave them the best possible start in life. There are few more precious gifts a country can give to its people.

Index

Note: Page numbers in *italic* indicate a figure and page numbers in **bold** indicate a table on the corresponding page.